“ The best g[illegible] motorway services in France . . .”

The Times

2nd Edition

LE GUIDE

SELECTED AUTOROUTES IN FRANCE

by

Karol Libura

LE GUIDE Publications

First published in May 1986 as
The Motorway to the Sun Guide

Autoroutes to the Sun Guide June 1987
Le Guide for the Independent Motorway Traveller
in France March 1989
Reprinted with minor amendments April 1990,
Reprinted with minor amendments April 1991.
Le Guide Selected Autoroutes in France March 2003
This edition published in March 2011

ISBN 978 0-9511254-5-8

Printed and bound in Great britain by
Duncan Print Group, Welwyn Garden City, Herts

CONTENTS

Conversion tables and factors

Preface

As a matter of an accidental diversion from my engineering profession main subjects I published, single-handedly, my first guidebook to motorway services in France, with which, I seem to have created a wonderful publishing venture of a new breed of travel guidebooks, unique in its form and contents of no comparable publication on the book market.

Its useful simplicity, according to the supporting comments from the very users of the routes covered by the book, was well appreciated.

It wasn't an easy beginning, especially, as I had no experience of any kind, in the publishing business. But, since, I had my objectives to achieve, clearly defined, it motivated me even more, to persevere in my endeavour to reach a successful conclusion and this edition is the result to that effect.

The contents of the publication covers material of relevance to long distance travel and most of it doesn't require updating. For example, "fatigue", once defined for certain conditions will remain valid for ever.

My first guide, produced, literary on the kitchen table, was called: "The Motorway to the Sun Guide", covering the autoroutes from Calais to the French Riviera, all the way to Menton, "the Pearl of France", according to the sign-board-information at the motorway's exit-slip road which welcomes you to that splendid place, at the close proximity of the Italian border.

With the arrival of the 'Computer Age', the Desktop Publishing Era began to invade publishing industry and my kitchen table was made redundant.

It was like entering into a new World of *Extraordinaire*. The creation of pages with text, pictures, graphics etc, has become an easy task when compared with the early times of my publishing venture.

Bonne Route
et
Bonne Chance

British Embassy and Consulates in France

Paris - British Embassy Telephone: +33 (0)1-4451-3100

British Consulates General

Bordeaux	-	33 (0)5	2722-2110
Lille	-	3	2012-8272
Lyon	-	4	7277-8170
Marseilles	-	4	9115-7210
Paris	-		

Honorary Consulate

Amiens	-	(0)3	2272-0848
Boulogne-sur-Mer	-	3	2187-1680
Calais	-	3	2196-3376
Cherbourg	-	2	3388-6560
Clermont-Ferrand	-	4	7334-2429
Dunkirk	-	3	2866-1198
Le Havre	-	3	3519-7888
Lorient	-	2	9787-3620
Nantes	-	2	5172-7260
Montpellier	-	4	6715-5207
Nice	-	4	9362-1356
Toulouse	-	5	6130-3791
Tours	-	2	4743-5058

Honorary Consul

St Malo	-	(0)2	2318-3030

Consular Agent

Saumur	-	(0)2	4152-9054

You are likely to experience courtesy of others by being courteous

We are getting there

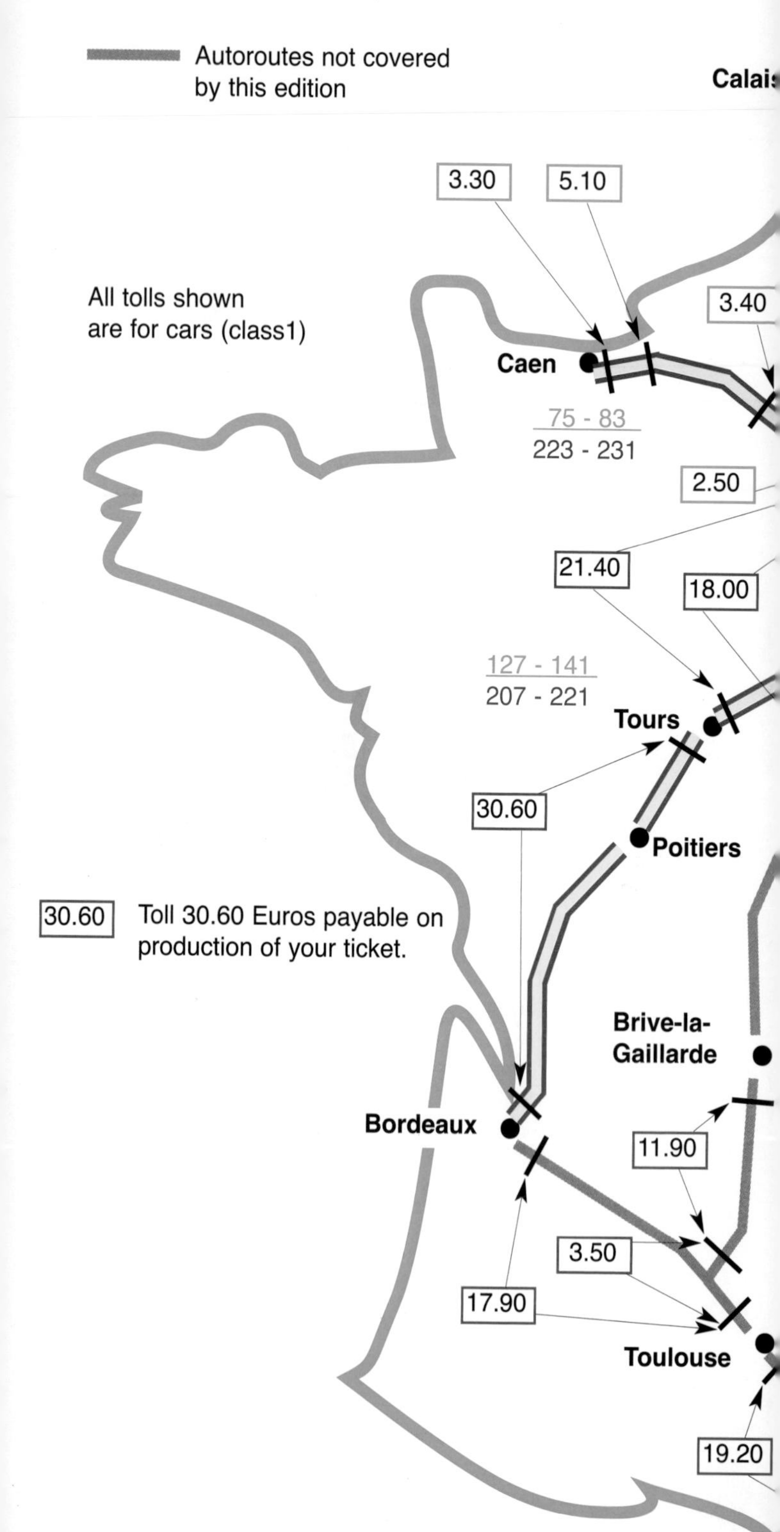

2.80 Toll 2.80 Euros payable at the automatic service barrière de péage, have your coins ready. Use separate, marked lane if change is required.

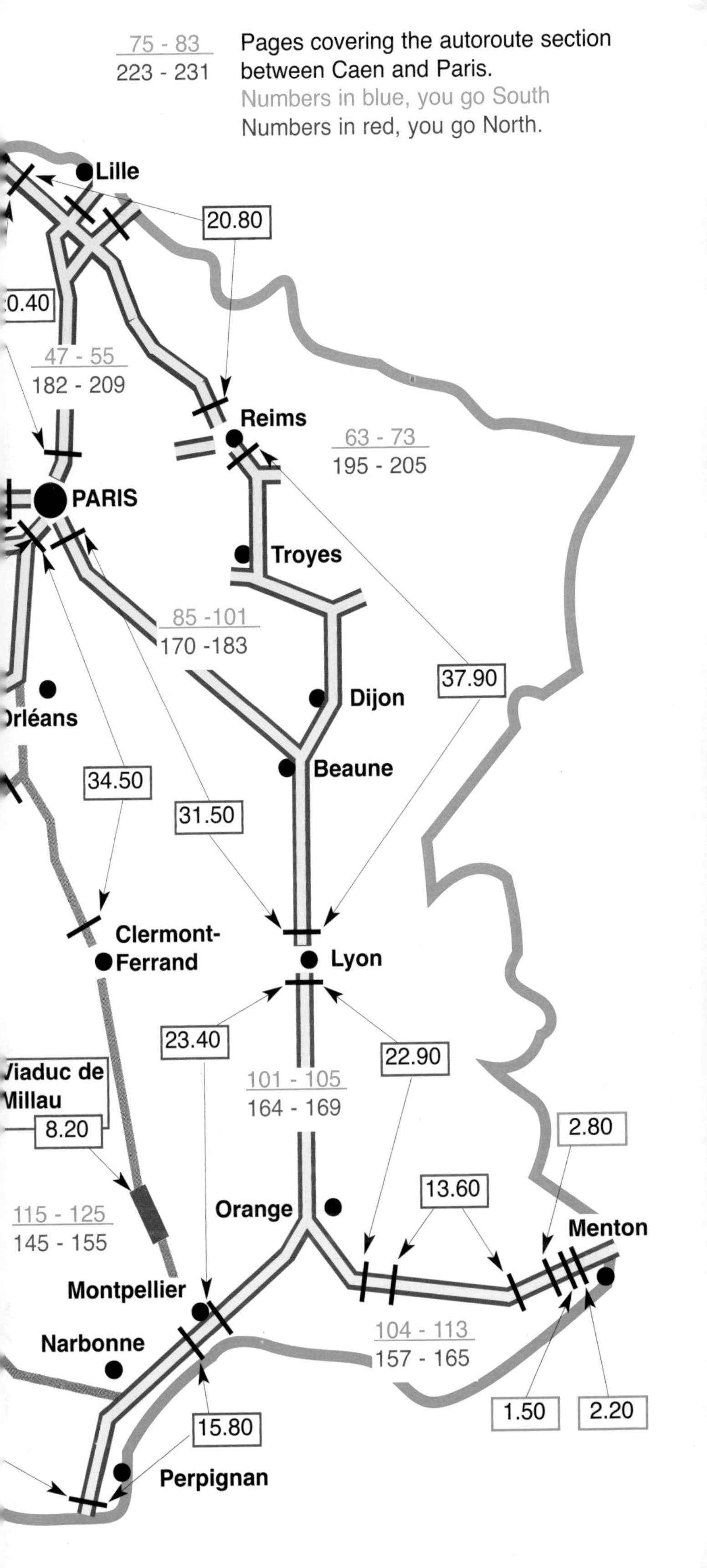
75 - 83
223 - 231
Pages covering the autoroute section between Caen and Paris.
Numbers in blue, you go South
Numbers in red, you go North.
Lille
20.80
0.40
47 - 55
182 - 209
Reims
63 - 73
195 - 205
PARIS
Troyes
85 -101
170 -183
37.90
Dijon
rléans
Beaune
34.50
31.50
Clermont-
Ferrand
Lyon
23.40
22.90
iaduc de
Millau
8.20
101 - 105
164 - 169
2.80
13.60
115 - 125
145 - 155
Orange
Menton
Montpellier
Narbonne
104 - 113
157 - 165
1.50
2.20
15.80
Perpignan

INTRODUCTION

Travelling by car along the system of motorways ***(autoroutes)*** in France could certainly be considered, as the best alternative, despite the tolls ***(péages)*** which would be to a certain extent, offset by the steady saving on petrol consumption. Besides, it offers the freedom of travel in all aspects of its connotation and also, it is considered to be a safer way to use motorways when compared with other roads.

However, it cannot be overemphasised that you understand faigue, and also, the influence of motorway driving on driving behaviour. At this point I urge you to read the learned paragraphs on the subjects which are contained in this guide.

LE GUIDE presents its contents in a self-explanatory manner as you progress along the motorways covered by the pages of this guidebook
The core of the guide are the motorways diagrammatically shown with all the information of facilities obtainable, accordingly

The rest areas on the motorways in France are generally well looked after and vary in the scope of facilities being of interest to travellers. They are marked by small green rectangles.

Petrol stations, hotels and restaurants are marked by the side of the rest areas at which the services are offered. The petrol stations are marked by a symbolic petrol pump, and similarly, the hotels and place of eating are indicated by a symbolic bed, and a knife with fork, respectively.

A small number in black, between the rest areas, shows the distance between them (km).
The distance between petrol stations, usually offering a wide range of services, is shown by a black number in a circle.

The number in red by the rectangular “greens” indicates the cumulative distance from the beginning of a section of travel, for example: Paris-Bordeaux.
A red number in a red circle, at the top or bottom of the page depending on the direction of travel, shows each page’s total distance covered.

At the top of each set of facing pages there is a small map of France with the relevant motorways shown on it, together with a red dot and an arrow.

The red dot shows your location on the particular motorway, which also, represents the content of the particular set of facing pages. The arrow indicates the direction of travel.

Parallel to the diagrammatically shown motorways, there are one-side-open rectangles on the opposite, facing page which contains the names of the rest areas, symbols of services offered there, and a brief description relevant to the particular area.

LE GUIDE provides you with sufficient information to start you up, allowing for an efficient planning of your journey.

You will find translation of most of the French phrases appearing by the side of the motorways or elsewhere that you would almost certainly like to understand. There are some tips that you may find useful, and much more.

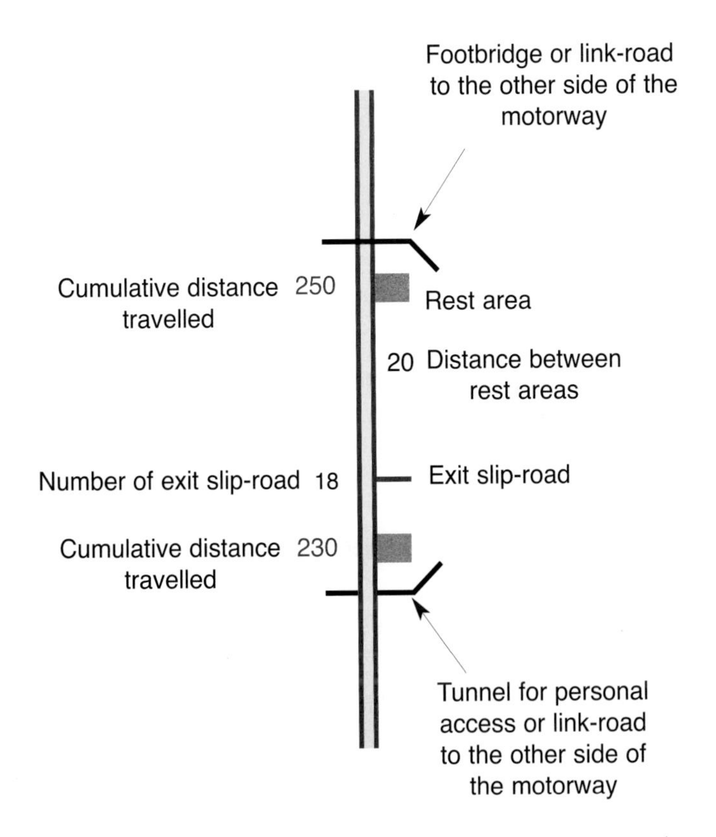

SYMBOLS

- WC, basic provision

- WC with full range facilities

- Card operated telephone

- Handicapped facilities

- Restaurant, cafeteria

- Coffee bar, snack-bar

- currency exchange

- Shop, boutique

- hotel

- nursery

- fax sending facilities

- petrol service station

- information

- letter posting service

- shower, also refreshing mist on the rest areas

- Play area for children

- caravan site

SOS - roadside emergency telephone

GEND - gendarmerie

TRANSLATIONS OF MOTORWAY INSTRUCTIONS

Accôtement non stabilisé	-	soft, hard shoulder
Allumez vos feux	-	switch on your lights
Attention, sortie de camions	-	careful, lorries turning
Auberge de jeunesse	-	Youth Hostel
Barrière de péage	-	toll barrier
Bruit	-	noise
Cédez le passage	-	give way
Centre Ville	-	town centre
Cette cabine peut être appelée à ce numero . . .	-	this cabine may be tele - phoned under this no. . . .
Changeur de monnaie	-	money exchange
Chaussée dèformée	-	uneven, bad surface
Chaussée glissante	-	slippery surface
Chute de pierres	-	falling rocks
Danger vent	-	dengerous wind
Défense d'entrèe	-	entrance forbidden
Déviation	-	diversion
Douane	-	customs
Eau potable	-	drinking water
Eteignez vos feux	-	switch off your lights
Fin d'allumage de feux	-	switch off your lights
Gravillons	-	loose chippings, gravel
Hôtel de Ville	-	Town Hall
Halte à péage	-	stop at the toll barrier
Jeux, mis a la disposition des enfants aux risque et perils de utilisateurs	-	utilisation of the apparatus should be under supervision of parents
Ni vitesse, ni bruit	-	no speed, no noise
Nids de poules	-	potholes
Parcours sportif adultes	-	exercise track for adults
Par la passerelle	-	by the footbridge
Passage protégé	-	right of way
Péage	-	toll
Pique-nique, jeux d'enfants	-	picnic area, suitable for parties with young children
Pièce acceptée	-	coins accepted (usually at barrière de péage
Pluie	-	slippery (after raining)
Poids lourds	-	heavy vehicles (normally associated with a road sign showing a route to be followed
Police de Route, Garde Mobile	-	Traffic Police Patrol
Prèparez votre monnaie	-	have your coins ready
Priorité à droite	-	priority of the traffic coming out of the right hand side

Propriété privèe	- private property
Rainnuarage	- road longitudinally grooved (special notice to be taken by motorcyclists)
Rappel	- reminding the last warning
Regardez votre distance de sécurité	- keep safe distance to the vehicle in front
Ralentir	- slow
Risque de verglas	- black ice, icy patches
Roulez au pas	- dead slow
Salle à lange	- nursery facilities
sans monnaie	- for those without coins (change)
Sans plomb	- unleaded petrol
Sauf riverains	- no entry except for access of inhabitants
Serrez à droite	- keep to the right
Sarrez à gauche	- keep to the left
Syndicat d'Iniatiative	- Tourist Information Office
Sortie (sortie de voiture)	- exit
Sortie prochaine	- next exit
Stationnement interdit	- parking prohibited
Un train peut en cacher un autre	- one train hides another one (on level crossing)
Toutes directions	- all traffic
Vehicules lents, restez à votre droite	- slow vehicles, keep to the right
Verglas	- black ice, patholes of ice
Verifiez votre monnaie	- check your change (coins)
Vers	- towards (vers Lyon)
Virages sur 3 km	- bends for 3 kilometres
Vitesse	- speed
Voir à droite	- look to the right
Vous n'avez pas la prorité	- you have no right of way

THE TOLL

The toll is charged on the French system of autoroutes, covered by this guidebook, except on sections of the immediate vicinity of towns.
The Association des Sociétés Françaises d'Autoroutes (ASFA) - Département Information Communication, supplies LE GUIDE with the information on toll charges accordingly.

At the entry to the charged sections of the motorways (Barrière de péage) a ticket is normally obtainable from an automatic dispenser where by stopping at the red light having just past the ticket slot, a ticket appears automatically in that slot.

You must collect that ticket to change the red light to green and the barrier opens for you to go. The toll is charged depending on the category of the vehicle and the distance travelled.
LE GUIDE shows the amounts to be paid, in Euros, for sections of motorways, at the appropriate toll barriers, "Barrière de péage", but not at the exit slip-roads.

At the exit "Barrière de Péage", the toll charge is normally paid to an assistant. There are alternative ways of paying, which is, for example, by throwing into a "basket" the required amount in the right coins.

The prices shown throughout LE GUIDE are for passenger cars and caravans. They may be revised slightly during the year. Higher prices are payable for other types of vehicles.

In order to obtain a receipt for payment at the exit "Barrière de péage", you ask for a "Certificate de passage" or, you press a button to get one, when using the automatic service lane.

THE TELEPHONING

It is commonly known that a unification has taken place in the "Euroland", the European Union, where by dialling "00" you obtain international entry to telephone a foreign country.

What you need to know is the particular Country Code that would follow next.

To telephone the UK from France, you dial:

- 00,
- the country code,
- the telephone area code (STD), minus the first zero,
- the telephone number.

For example, to call London from France, you dial:

00 44 20 (the telephone number)

In order to make a French telephone connection it is necessary to know the following details of the changes that have been introduced in France, and they are as follows:-

France has been divided into 5 telephone ZONES, each one has an area code, as follows;-

- Paris and Paris Area		- 01
- North West,	e.g. Nantes, Rouen	- 02
- North East,	e.g. Lille, Strasbourg	- 03
- South East,	e.g. Lyon, Marseille	- 04
- South West,	e.g. Bordeaux, Toulouse	- 05

To telephone France from the UK, you dial:

- 00,
- the Country Code 33,
- the telephone zone code, minus the first zero,
- the telephone eight digit number.

WORD OF CAUTION

Some of you may already know, there is always a rest area within a short drive that might suit your particular needs. Nevertheless, LE GUIDE may be of assistance to be right at your first choice.

But, whichever rest area you select prior to pulling-in, you may find it helpful to mark up your own detailed description of the area for future reference, as you might drive the same route again.

If, a selection of a rest area is to be made for staying overnight, make sure that safety is looked at first.

You would be considered “brave” to stay on your own, however, the other extreme could be, unwittingly joining a bunch of undesirables, unknowingly.

It happened to me personally at the end of one summer. On my own, I was cruising along the Motorway to the Sun, L’Autoroute du Soleil, I was tired, it was getting late and I felt under a compelling obligation to make a break in my journey.

The weather was naturally glorious and the tranquillity of the moment seemed to be ideal for recharging the batteries of my systems accordingly.
However, it wasn’t meant to be the case.

At random, at the first opportunity, I entered a very attractive rest area which happened to be deserted at the time.
I parked my car away from the petrol station complex, hoping perhaps for a nap on the wooden bench nearby which I soon found to be very comfortable.

After a while, a scruffy looking car pulled in, some 20 metres away and located itself distinctly towards the exit from the rest area which somehow alerted my attention.

Not before long, two human-like creatures left the car and disappeared in the shadow of trees.
My shiny car’s front door was left wide open and, at that particular time, I was doing my best impression of the “sleeping beauty”, though, I was watching the car attentively.

Soon, a shadow emerged from the scruffy car which I managed to identify, not without difficulty, to be of a female.
Visibly she seemed to be attracted by what I considered to be my territory for the moment. I began to sense trouble a foot.

An occurrence came to mind, in which, a woman attacked a man, yelling at the same time for help which was obviously available immediately.

As it happened, when the “help” arrived the man was robbed.
A carbon copy of what had been taking place, so far.

At that time I lost my interest in the further development of what might have been a good story to report.

I suddenly found that I had become an alert driver and hurriedly continued my journey.

DID YOU KNOW THAT . . .

● . . . incorrect tyres pressure and in particular those below the specified recommendation, have been attributable to many serious accidents. Pressure should be checked frequently.

Bear in mind that since the recommended tyre pressure is specified for cold tyres you would be expected to add about 3 to 4 psi (0.3 kg/cm^2) if topping-up becomes necessary when the tyre is hot.
It is important to understand that when a tyre is under-inflated, rubber fatigue is taking place which results from repeated tyre deflection. And, when you consider speed of 80 mph (about 130 km/h), the tyre deflects about 20 times in one second.

The heat which is obviously generated in the process adds to the gravity of the problem, especially, during the summer's time when the ambient temperature is high. Needless to say, the ultimate stage is bursting of the tyre.

One could go on further still: with under-inflated tyres there is an additional danger of difficult road holding, especially when negotiating bends. With correct tyres pressure you are likely to find an improvement in fuel consumption.
Avoid driving with under-inflated tyres.

● . . . according to my research exercise of many years ago it seemed to be apparent that about 55% of motorists underestimate the braking distance as a function of speed at normal conditions, 25% shows a complete ignorance, and 20% proudly boasts just about right. See page 19 showing graphs from which you will get the message at a glance.

● . . . driving at speed of 80 mph (about 130 km/h) you travel 40 yards in one second. So, when you need to bring your car to a halt the matter becomes of a complex connotation.
First of all, you would require at least 0.7 of a second to process the requirement of the moment and react by pressing the brake pedal.
By then your car will have travelled 28 yards when the actual braking process begins to be effective, obviously subject to the condition of the braking system of your car, to say the least.
And now, and in addition to the above, the braking distance would vary, depending on the road conditions.

Continued on page 32

THE GRAPH

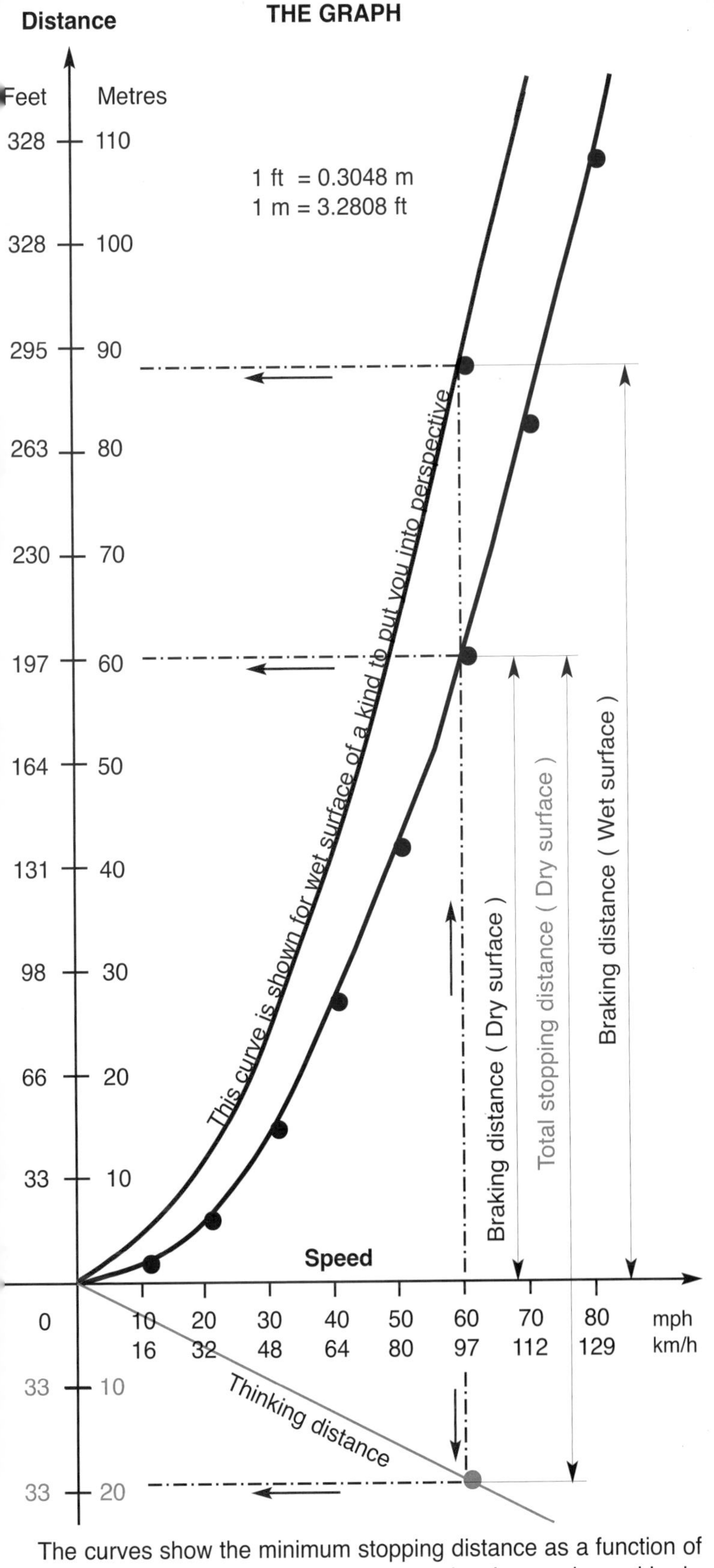

The curves show the minimum stopping distance as a function of speed at normal conditions: alert driver, level ground, good braking system of your car, good tyres.

MOTORWAY DESIGN AND USAGE AS CAUSES OF BEHAVIOURAL PROBLEMS AMONG DRIVERS

By Dr Ivan D.Brown (extracts)

Motoways have improved mobility and safety in the road transport system. However, their safety relative to other roads is often overstated: drivers are probably only 50% safer on motorways, compared with non-built-up A roads.

Most motorway accidents are attributed to “errors” in driving behaviour, such as speeding, close following, poor lane discipline and failure to adapt to adverse conditions.
Some of these problems undoubtedly result from recklessness and carelessness.

However, there is evidence suggesting that the design and normal use of motorways can be a contributory factor in accidents.
Their relatively featureless nature poses problems for the perception of speed and distance, the judgement of safety margins and, particularly, the maintenance of alertness.

Continuous high speed driving causes speed to be underestimated and in heavy traffic, contributes to speed stress effects.
All these problems are exacerbated among professional drivers working irregular hours and suffering from sleep disruption.
Behavioural problems of this kind are presented as the natural response of human brain when driving is prolonged i a motorway environment.

Motorways are necessary development in high-speed road transport, if society is to balance its increasing requirements for mobility and safety.
Mobility has certainly been enormously improved by the introduction by relatively straight and well-surfaced multi-lane roads, with hard shoulders, no opposing traffic streams,

traffic streams, no crossing traffic, no pedestrians, cyclists, or learners, and clear route information. In theory, this reduction on demand on drivers should also have improved safety, and of course it has.
The casualty rate on motorways has gone down to less then one-seventh that of the casualty rate in the road system as a whole (Dept. of Transport 1986).

However, exception must be taken to the repeated assertion (e.g. see Dept. of Transport, 1987) that motorways are " 8 times safer than other roads ".
This claim is spurious. Safety is a function of usage relative safety can therefore be expressed validity only if it involves comparisons of similar user groups.

The higher accident rate on "other roads" involves numerous road users who are not legally permitted to use motorways. Thus, vehicle occupants are not 8 times safer on motorways than they would be on "other roads" is also of little significance for transport authorities, because it contrasts parts of the systems serving quite different functions.

Using a more legitimate and meaningful comparison of alternative routes for powered vehicles, we find that motorways are only 3 times as "safe" as non-built-up A roads (Dept. of Transport, 1986, p.71). They are only twice as safe when road works are in evidence (Dept. of Transport, 1996, p.27).

An even more relevant comparison, for my present propose, is between driver safety on motorways and reasonable alternative non-motorway routes. The total number of casualties is about equal for car drivers and motor vehicle passengers (87, 302 vs 81846, Dept. of Transport, 1986, p.111).
Therefore, at a rough estimate, the 3:1 safety benefits of motorway travel compared with non-built-up A roads may actually reduce to only a 50% safety advantage for motorway drivers.

This is highly important for any consideration of behavioural problems among motorway drivers. Drivers' behaviour is determined partly by what they believe about safety. If they are told that "motorways are 8 times safer than other roads" and they believe this to mean that driving is 8 times safer, when in fact it may be only 1 & 1/2 times safer than on an alternative route, they may be encouraged to behave far more riskily than traffic situations actually demand.
Spurious claims for the benefits of motorways are thus likely to be counterproductive for road safety.

Fortunately, in this respect, driver behaviour is determined more by their own perceptions of risk and safety in traffic situations than by what they are told about objective safety.

Unfortunately, however, risk perception depends upon two unreliable factors:

1. drivers' identification and evaluation of potential hazards in traffic and,

2. their belief in their ability to deal with traffic hazards.

There is evidence that most drivers think they are safer and more skilled than the average motorist, which clearly impossible.

This overrating of their own abilities may lead drivers into taking risks they cannot handle adequately, which suggests that driver training and education have more of a role to play in road safety than we have been prepared to accept to accept so far, in this country *(Ed. Great Britain).*

More importantly, in the present context, is the evidence from laboratory and field studies showing that factors common in motorway driving can actually impair drivers' ability to identify and evaluate traffic hazards appropriately.

The aims of this paper are to outline the nature of such behavioural problems and the types of appropriate remedial measure that could reduce their contribution to accidents.

SOS Telephone - the least you need to know

They are located, in pairs, at intervals of 2 km on both sides of motorways, one opposite the other. Most often they are sited in close proximity of the rest areas.
In case you might need to use the SOS telephone you would be connected directly to the Police.

You do:
- push the button and release it,
- wait for the operator to respond,
- you talk to the built-in interactive speaker.

You tell the operator:
- your location: SOS number,
- direction of travel

In case of accident:
- location of accident,
- number of vehicles involved,
- number of people injured and the state of injuries, if any.

The Police or Gendarmerie will act accordingly.

MEDICAL MATTERS OF RELEVANCE

(Ed. Extracts from Papers of Dr IVAN D. BROWN from Medical Research Council, Applied Psychology Unit , Cambridge, permitted to appear in LE GUIDE by the copyright holders The Medical Commission Accident Prevention)

FATIGUE

What is Fatigue?

Most people would have little difficulty in unswering this question. Their answers would almost certainly imply that fatigue is what they experience after a prolonged period of work: an increasing disinclination to continue performing the task in hand, accompanied by general and localised aches and pains, the nature of which depends to some extent on what they have been doing.
Subjectively, this experience seems to be the output of a feedback mechanism which prevents the body over-exerting itself.

Pressed harder, some people might find it more difficult to explain why fatigue is sometimes experienced when they have been working for only a short time, whilst others may admit that they can feel fatigue merely thinking about work waiting to be done!
Perhaps even more surprisingly, most people readily accept that fatigue symptoms often disappear completely when the work in hand is exchanged for some novel or more enjoyable activity.

CONCLUSIONS

(Ed. The following is the result of research on Medical Aspects of Fitness to Drive)

A

Driving Fatigue is not solely determined by the length of time spent at the wheel, although most individuals will experience some fatigue symptoms if driving is prolonged about four hours.

B

Fatigue can be transferred to driving from prior manual or non-manual activity.

C

In practice, fatigue from prolonged driving interacts with behavioural changes that results from normal diurnal variations in physiological activity. These factors combine to maximise adverse effects of fatigue when driving extends into the normal sleeping hours of the individual.

D

Sleep loss and degradation in sleep quality which result from irregular driving schedules seriously exacerbate effects of driving fatigue. Persistent irregular work-schedules can lead to chronic fatigue.

E

Certain personality characteristics mediate the effects of driving fatigue. Extroversion seems to exacerbate these effects.

F

Prolonged static muscular contraction is the prime cause of physiological fatigue in driving. Psychologically, the main dangers result from boredom when driving under fairly undemanding environmental conditions and from motivational pressures to complete a journey for professional or social reason.

G

Individuals are normally sensitive to their state of fatigue. Problems arise for road safety mainly when fatigued drivers' judgements are impaired by alcohol or illness, and when commercial or social pressures persuade them to override the warning conveyed by their own fatigue symptoms.

ADVICE

A

The seating in the vehicle should be comfortable, to ensure good posture and stability with minimal static muscular contraction. Dials should be clearly visible, without glare and producing no disturbing reflections in the windscreen. A ll controls should be within easy reach. seat adjustments should be made to eliminate stretching or slumping, both of which restrict circulation. Postural changes which usually accompany aggressive driving, or attempts to maintain unrealistic time schedules, will exacerbate static muscular fatigue and should be avoided.

B

The temperature and ventilation controls of the vehicle should permit the body to be comfortably warm while allowing cool air to be directed to the face. care should be taken that engine fumes and exhaust gases do not enter the car and cause monoxide poisoning.

C

A high noise level from the engine, or continuous wind roar from open windows, is more likely to induce fatigue in the long run than an adequately ventilated car with closed windows and a quiet engine.

D

It is inadvisable to undertake a long drive immediately after exhausting muscular activity.

E

Meals taken before and during a drive should not be heavy, or the subsequent processes of digestion will induce sleepiness and difficulty in concentration.

F

Alcohol especially should be avoided before and during a long drive. Even quite small amounts can disrupt the distribution of attention among task demands and larger quantities readily lead to drowsiness, inaccuracy and impaired judgement, whilst at the same time giving a false sense of confidence.

G

Many drugs in therapeutic doses can induce fatigue especially in the early stage of treatment, patients should be warned about this.

H

Driving demands a high order of concentration, which must

be maintained for long periods of relative monotony when no particular need for attention is apparent. Regular rest periods are therefore desirable.

Breaks of at least 20 minutes seem necessary if alertness is to be restored, although the effectiveness of rest periods in permitting recovery diminishes as driving is prolonged beyond four or five hours.
Where the total driving period extends beyond about nine hours, breaks may produce negligible recovery of alertness.

I

If a driver feels physically uncomfortable **he should stop the vehicle and take a short walk** to relive the adverse effects of static muscular contraction.
Recovery from muscular fatigue is best achieved by frequent short breaks, preferably including opportunities for sleep are indicated.

J

Regular rest pauses are more important where driving conditions are relatively undemanding of attention, such as on a motorway, or at night in light traffic, because alertness can fall dangerously low **before the driver becomes aware of his impaired efficiency.**

K

Drivers should avoid taking occasional long journeys which extend into that part of the 24 hours **when they would normally be sleeping.** Diurnal changes in physiological activation can combine with effects of prolonged driving to depress alertness drastically between midnight and 06:00 hours.

L

Drivers of an extreme **extrovert personality** seem particularly susceptible to fatigue under relatively unchanging environmental conditions. They should therefore take special note of the above environmental conditions.

The older driver (i.e. over 45 years) is also more susceptible to fatigue, recovers increasingly less completely from restpauses during prolonged driving and is more adversely affected by irregular working hours.

M

No drivers can afford to ignore, for long, subjectively experienced fatigue symptoms of discomfort, drowsiness or irritability. They should certainly take a break when fatigue effects are detected in their driving performance, such as mistimed gearchanges, unanticipated events , and nearmisses.

FATIGUE AND DRIVERS OF HEAVY GOODS VEHICLES AND PUBLIC SERVICES VEHICLES

The above recommendations apply to all drivers, but the following points should be emphasised:

A

With the greater forces and more frequent control movements normally required in larger vehicles, there is a greater need to ensure a good stable posture by taking full advantage of any adjustments provided to the driving position. there is also a greater need to avoid the tense posture which usually results from working under time stress.

B

Much greater concentration an anticipation is required with larger vehicles, because of their lower manoeuvreability.
It is therefore particularly important to avoid taking alcohol and heavy meals just before or a work-spell, as these are known to impair anticipatory judgements and reduce alertness.

C

Regular and frequent short rest-pauses permit efficient recovery from muscular fatigue, but breaks of at least 20 minutes seem necessary to restore alertness.
The effectiveness with which an acceptable level of arousal is recovered declines with total time spent in driving. After about nine hours, psychophysiological recovery is minimal, even after rest-pauses of 20minutes or more.

D

Shared driving which requires the off-duty driver to travel and sleep on the vehicle produces more fatigue than that in which sharing operates on a relay system, because both the

E

Drivers should aim for as regular a work-schedule as possible, from one day to the next, with ample time (at least 6 hours) allowed for consecutive hours of sleep.

Irregular hours not only reduce the effectiveness of sleep, they can also depress alertness by disrupting the physiological changes which the body normally undergoes each 24 hours when more stable routine are worked. irregular hours may also produce a cumulative sleep debt.
Older drivers are particularly susceptible to these adverse effects arising from prolonged and irregular hours of work.

F

Legislators should aim to regulate the “duty hours” of professional drivers, rather than their “driving time” , if fatigue effects transferred from non-driving aspects of the job are to be minimised.
Regulations should tend to produce stable work-schedules, which permit adequate periods of continuous sleep at regular times each day.
Provision for mandatory breaks during the “duty time” is essential, although there is much to be said for giving the individual driver some latitude as to when, and for how long, he takes his daily allowance of rest breaks.

G

Employers should comply with the mandatory requirements on drivers’ hours of work and minimise motivational pressures on drivers to complete journeys when they are consciously aware of major fatigue symptoms.

ACCESS TO HEALTHCARE ABROAD

European Health Insurance Card (EHIC)

To qualify for a free or reduced-cost emergency medical treatment in France and other countries of the European Economic area (EEA), the possession of the European Health Insurance Card is a must.
However, since, it doesn’t cover all healthcare cost you might wish to consider travel insurance, to that effect.
To get the EHIC call **0845 606 2030** or, apply online **www.dh.gov.uk/travellers.**

THE BASICS ON FRENCH WINES

(Extracts from the work of Sally Brompton, permitted to appear in LE GUIDE, by the copyright holders, the Eveldon Press)

There is more pretentious clap-trap talked about wine than any other drink in the world.
The fact is that most of us really couldn't care less whether a wine is a little cheeky or downright insulting.
What we want to know is whether it is red or white, dry or sweet, still or sparkling, delicious or disgusting.

One point to remember when choosing French wine is that they are graded by law into four main categories.
In descending order these are:

Appellation contrôlée (AC),
Vins délimité de Qualité Supérieure (VDQS),
Vins de Pays,
Vins de table.

AC wines are the best and, generally speaking, the specific the appellation, the better the wine.
So, a named vineyard is more important than a village, followed by an area and, finally, a region.

The vintages are intended only as a guide. A good year depends on the climate but there are always a few poor wines produced in a vintage year while the occasional fine wine can slip through in an otherwise bad year.

Forget everything you have ever read about the right glass for a particular wine.
For normal drinking any glass will do for any wine - the bigger, the better, but leave your wine space to breathe by filling the glass no more than half way.

But if you are drinking wine with a meal, avoid vinegar and lemon as they tend to make the wine taste sour.

WHITE WINE

As the ideal, anytime, all-round drink, white wine takes a lot of beating. It can adapt to any situation, whether it is the kind of celebration that calls for a bottle of Champagne, or a glass of dry white in your local pub.

It goes with food or without it, is equally at home as an aperitif, or a long drink- mixed with ice and soda, to quench the fiercest summer thirst.
It can be sweet or dry, still or sparking, light or heavy and, of course, good or bad.

White wine should be chilled before drinking and the cheaper or sweeter the wine the colder it generally needs to be.
Do not stick the bottle in the freezer which can kill the flavour and - if you are forgetful - turn the wine into ice-lollies.

Unlike the red wines, white wines are normally drunk when they are young, although some of the better ones will improve with keeping - especially the sweet dessert such as Sauternes.

As far as food is concerned white wine goes with pretty well everything. It probably at its best with fish and poultry but if you want to drink it with roast beef - go right ahead.
A few of the really sweet wines are better by themselves or with a simple fresh fruit dessert. But, there again, it is all a matter of taste.
Champagne certainly does not need food with it although there are people who will drink it happily all the way through a meal.

RED WINE

Red wine is normally dry and should, ideally, be served at room temperature which means opening it an hour or two before pouring it.
It can be sipped or quaffed, drunk by itself or with food, and goes with pretty well everything except fish, which is nothing to do with etiquette but the fact that red wines tend to make the fish taste metallic.

Rose wine can be sweet or dry, still or sparkling, should always be served chilled and can be drunk at any time, But do not waste good food on it.

And, talking of food, while you cannot really go far wrong drinking your favourite wine with your favourite meal, there are a few simple rules you may want to keep in mind.

Firstly, good food deserves good wine so if you are having roast beef pick the best wine you can afford. Peasant foods such as spaghetti bolognaise or shepherd's pie call for something cheap and cheerful.

Blander foods such as chicken and ham go with lighter wines such as Beaujolais. While rich dishes like oxtail need something hearty like a Burgundy.
All cheeses go splendidly with wine but milder ones are best with heavier, more mature wines while strong flavours like Roquefort take something younger and lighter.

And do not be ashamed to order the house wine when you are out. It is often better than most of the alternatives at the lower - sometimes even the middle - part of the list.
It makes sense since the proprietor is probably getting a better deal by buying it in bulk.

Finally, remember that when it comes to the nitty-gritty, the most important thing about any wine is whether you enjoy it. The best wine in the world is worthless if you, personally, do not like it.
So don't be intimidated by the know-alls who try to impress you with their copy-book opinions of what is good and what is not. **Cheers!**

DID YOU KNOW THAT . . .continued from page 18

But if you brake to hard your car may lose "contact" with the road surface and you enter into skidding.

And when the skidding stage is reached you are in a grave danger yourself and also put others into the same "rotten boat" against their will. It would not be fair.
Be realistic, **keep your distance.**

- . . . alcohol in your blood stream is a killer number 2, following fatigue. The risk of an accident comes mainly from the false sense of confidence as a result of drinking, and therefore, the false ability to drive cannot match the real requirements of the road.

- . . . fatigue which normally follows lack of rest and monotonous driving is the main cause of accidents involving death. And, if you consider that 90% of information which is necessary to drive a motor vehicle comes through what you see, your vision, then you may become more sympathetic to the problem and fight fatigue by taking frequent breaks during your journeys (see pages 24-29).

FOOD FOR THOUGHT and USEFUL TIPS

● First of all, make sure that the braking system of your car is in order, if necessary, have it bled and fluid changed.

● **High altitude driving in hot weather may affect the efficiency of the braking system of your car.**

● Have the tyres pressure right, check frequently.

● Always have enough petrol in the tank for a reasonable distance of driving.

● Drive on **the right side of the road** which happens on the Continent to be the right hand side.

● **Be aware of the priority of traffic coming out from the right hand side.**

● Keep your own pace and safe distance from the vehicle in front of you.

● Do not drive between two heavy vehicles, do enjoy good view all round. Besides, at the extreme you will not get "sandwiched".

● On the main road be very careful. Some drivers appearing at speed from your right hand side, may give you a “bad headache”.
“Passage protegé” - right of way. **“Ignore it”**. It could prove to be disastrous. Just drive with care.

● Seat belts rule, as in the UK. On the whole of the French road network, including towns, it is obligatory to wear seat belts, otherwise, you risk a heavy fine. Children under 10 years of age must not sit in front.

● First aid basic items, useful to have, also basic tools and spare parts. A **“Warning triangle”** - a must. Display it in cases of emergency and have the hazard lights on.

● If you break down always ask for an estimate before allowing repairs. In most cases a European breakdown insurance cover, however, would take care of that.

● Always check/compare your bill or credit card slip with the petrol pump indicator to agree both before you pay or sign. Take the reading from the pump immediately after delivery.

● Free emergency **SOS** telephones are sited at about 2 km intervals along the autoroutes and almost every rest area has one located in its proximity (See page 23).
Once the emergency telephone is answered the Police will arrange road side assistance and medical service in case of an accident.

● Often, you may feel unhappy with some manners of driving if you are not used to it.
You may find that the "priorité à droite" rule is exercised with a religious conviction regardless of the situation. Be understanding if the unexpected takes place.

● No doubt, on many occasions you will become a pedestrian yourself and you may occasionally need to cross the road and opt for a "zebra crossing". **Watch out.** On the Continent the pedestrian has no "right of way" as in the UK.
Take special care if a car stops to let you go first. Because, if the road is wide enough, it is very likely that a local road user behind that "courtesy" car will go past.

● Be aware of the fact that driving at speed of 80 mph (130 km/h) you travel **40 yards in one second.**
Do not allow, therefore, your concentration to lapse and take frequent breaks at rest areas.

● There are frequent rest areas at your disposal. Use them, for eating, telephoning and so forth.
Put things into perspective:10 -15 minutes should make no difference to your long distance driving schedule.

● Do not ignore speed restrictions to the limits of unacceptability which happens to be a common occurrence and very often the only explanation to the cause of many serious accidents.

● More formal appearance is required if you consider a visit to some restaurants, theatres and casinos.

● On beaches, topless culture is the way of life and it is widely accepted.

● **Level-crossings:** always **stop** at level crossings to ensure safety, regardless of, whether they are manned or not, or automatic. You approach it, switch the hazard lights on, to show drivers behind you that you are slowing down to a halt, before you cross the level-crossing.

● Watch out for drivers who do not indicate their intentions when on the road, especially when they join the traffic from a parking position.

● You might come across instances of a special breed of beggars who would approach you for variety of reasons. They would be well dressed, speak your language and attempt to tell you a story of how they were robbed, for example, and needed your help (money).

●Also, unusual salesmen might descend upon you who would spuriously try to attract your attention and try to sell you goods. Don't enter the "salesman's" car in order to see the goods.

● At some locations be aware of a plague of motor scooters and alike,buzzing from every angle of vision, and snaking along the road with apparent lack of concern for their own safety.

● French Police may stop you at random in order to check your identity, and in case of dissatisfaction with the outcome you would have to go to the Police Station for as long as it takes to establish your identity.

● Keep adjusting your position in changing traffic conditions, especially on slippery surface (e.g. raining). Increase the distance to the vehicle in front of you. Take into consideration the manner of driving the driver behind you.
It is bad enough to underestimate your co-ordinates in traffic conditions by a fraction of an inch, let alone the 40 yards of travel in one second at speed of 80 mph which translates into metric:37 meters at 129 km/h.

● **Road rage never pays dividends**
Control your emotion, be patient, and show courtesy to fellow travellers. Whenever there is an accident there is a cause to that effect.

It is not about who is right
if you are part of a drama already

● We all know that aggressive driving is a recipe for a short cut to an accident. Besides, it creates an atmosphere of frustration for other users of the road which inevitably leads to a loss of concentration and a tiny fraction of a second might prove enough to make a difference.
There is always the innocent company present who pay the price, whenever drama occurs on the road.

● **Drink-driving?** The Police in France will take no chances. Take it into account.

● Fast driving attracts attention of the Police. If you are caught speeding at 180 km/h (110 mph, approx.), the best they can offer to you, is a fine of 135.00 Euros, plus a retention of your driving licence for 15 days.
Next, the licence would be returned to your private address and your "sins" might fall into oblivion.
Speeding, however, at 190 km/h will result in a fine of 750.00 Euros, plus a retention of your driving licence for 15 days.

Some more captions of relevance:

- Seat belts do save lives, you better believe it, before it is too late,
- A fleeing car is a ticking bomb,
- Don't speed to win death,
- Road rage never pays dividends,
- **Expect the unexpected and you will be safer still.**

● It is widely recognised by long distance motoring travellers that quality comfort accommodation allows to regenerate human systems more efficiently for the demanding day of tomorrow.

How to book a room in a hotel

I would like to book one room for two persons with double bed for tonight	- je voudrais reserver une chambre pour deux personne avec grand lit pour ce soir
my name is . . .	- Je m'appelle . . .
Rate per night	- le prix par jour
Voici la cléf	- here is the key
Bonne journée/soirée	- have a good day/evening
Breakfast	- le petit déjeuner
Lunch	- le déjeuner
Dinner	- le dîner
Bon appétit	- enjoy your meal

MISCELLANEOUS

SPEED LIMITS - maximum, unless otherwise posted

	Road surface	
	Dry (km/h)	**Wet** (km/h)
Toll motorways	130	110
Dual carriageways and motorways without tolls	110	100
Other roads	90	80
In towns	60	60

The French road network is classified by:

A - Motorways (Autoroutes),
N - National roads,
D - Regional roads (Departamentale)
V - Local roads (Chemins Vicinaux).

FRENCH NATIONAL HOLIDAYS

January 1st	Jour de L'An	New Year's Day
May 1st	Fête du Travail	Labour Day
May 8th		VE Day
July14th	Fête Nationale	Bastille Day
August 15th	Assumption	Assumption
November 1st	Toussaint	All Saints
November 11th	Anniversaire de L'Armistice	Armistice Day
December 25th	Noel	Christmas

<u>Moveable dates</u>

Lundi de Pâques	Easter Monday
Ascension	Ascension
Lundi de Pentecôte	Whit Monday

The week-ends incorporating July 14th and August 15th are the ideal days to break your travels and stay in Paris. On motorways there will be lot of traffic and the hotels on motorways are likely to be fully booked.

CORRELATIVE VOCABULARY

Days of the week

Monday - lundi
Tuesday - mardi
Wednesday - mercredi
Thursday - jeudi
Friday - vendredi
Saturday - samedi
Sunday - dimanche

Month of the Year

January - janvier
February - fevrier
March - Mars
April - avril
May - mai
June - juin
July - juillet
August - août
September - septembre
October - octobre
November - novembre
December - decembre

Numbers

1 - un (une)
2 - deux
3 - trois
4 - quatre
5 - cinq
6 - six
7 - sept
8 - huit
9 - neuf
10 - dix
11 - onze
12 - douze
13 - treize
14 - quatorze
15 - quinze
16 - seize
17 - dis-sept
18 - dix-huit
19 - dix-neuf
20 - vingt

21 - vingt et un
22 - vingt deux
23 - vingt trois etc.,
30 - trente
31 - trente et un
32 - trente deux
33 - trente trois
40 - quarante
50 - cinquante
60 - sixante
70 - soixante-dix
80 - quatre-vingt
90 - quatre-vingt-dix
100 - cent
101 - cent-un
102 - cent deux
200 - deux cents
500 - cinq cents
1000 - mille
2000 - deux mille

Some useful expressions

good morning	- bonjour
good afternoon	- bonjour
good evening	- bonsoir
good bye	- au revoir
yesterday	- hier
today	- aujourd'hui
midday	- midi
tomorrow	- domain
please	- s'il vous plait
excuse me	- excusez-moi
how are you	- comment allez vous
very well, thank you	- tres bien, merci
it is a nice day	- il fait beau
it is hot	- il fait chaud
lit is cold	- il fait froid
I do not speak French	- je ne parle pas français
I do not know	- je ne sais pas
here is the key	- voici la cléf
to do the shopping	- faire des courses
good luck	- bon courage, bonne chance
underground	- metro
careful, look out	- attention
to your health, cheers	- à votre santé
money	- l'argent
change	- monnaie (more meaning of coins)
footbridge	- la passerelle
push	- poussez
pull	- tirez
Spring	- le printemps
Summer	- l'été
Autumn	- l'automne
Winter	- l'hiver

Some parts of car and useful expressions

air filter	- le filtre à air
alternator	- l'alternateur
battery	- la batterie
the battery is dead	- la batterie est à plat
flat battery	- la batterie à vide
boot	- le coffre
tyre	- le pneu
I have flat tyre	- j'ai crevé

bonnet - le capot
brakes - le freins
brake fluid - le liquide de frein
brake pads - plaquettsde freins
car - la voiture
carburettor - le carburateur
clutch - l'embrayage
cooling system - le système de refroidissement
distributor - le distributeur d'allumage, le delco
points - jeu de contacts
door - la porte
car door - la portière
fan belt - la courroie de ventilateur
fine - la contravention
fuse - le fusible
fuse box - la boite à fusibles
gasket, seal - joint
gearbox - la boite de vitesses
grease - le lubrifiant
headlamp - le phare
horn - le klaxon
hose - le durite
ignition - l'allumage
jack - le cric
number plate - la plaque de voiture
oil - l'huile
oil filter - le filtre à huile
ignition key - la clé de contact
petrol - l'essence
radiator - le radiateur
sign (road sign) - le panneau
seat - le siège
seat belt - la ceinture de sécurité
spanner - la clé
spark plug - la bougie
traffic - la circulation
(the building-up of treaffic, backlog of traffic) - bouchon
tyre - le pneu
tyre pressure - la pression de pneu
wheel - la roue
windsreen - le pare-brise
wipers - les essuie-glace
wrench - la clé

Bouchon - the build-up of traffic

Fluide - liquid, flowing
(la circulation est fluide) - traffic flows freely

my car is broken down - ma voiture est en panne
something is wrong with: - quelque chose ne va pas:

the engine - dans le moteur
the brakes - aux freins

car logbook - carte grise
driving licence - permis de conduire

CONVERSION TABLES AND FACTORS

Lengths

1 inch (in) = 25.40 millimetres (mm)
= 2.54 centimetres (cm)

1 foot (ft) = 30.48 cm
= 0.3048 metres (m)
1 yard (yd) = 91.44 cm
= 0.9144 m
1 mile = 1.609 kilometres (km)
1 cm = 0.394 inch (in)
1 metre (m) = 1.094 yards (yd)
1 kilometre = 0.621 mile

Volume

1 pint (pt) = 0.568 litre (l)
1 UK gallon (UK gal) = 4.546 litres
1 litre (i) = 0.22 UK gallon
= 1.76 pint

Weight

1 pound (lb) = 0.454 kilogram (kg)
1 hundredweight (cwt) = 50.8 kg
1 UK ton = 1016.05 kg
= 1.016 metric tonnes

1000 kg = 1 metric tonne (t)
1 kg = 2.2 pounds (lb)
1 t = 2204.62 (lb)
= 0.984 UK ton

Pressure

1 lb/in^2 = 0.069 kg/cm^2
1 kg/cm^2 = 14.2 lb/in^2

Tyre pressure

lb/in^2	kg/cm^2	lb/in^2	kg/cm^2
1	0.07	32	2.25
5	0.35	33	2.32
10	0.70	34	2.39
15	1.05	35	2.46
16	1.12	36	2.53
17	1.20	37	2.60
18	1.27	38	2.67
19	1.34	39	2.74
20	**1.41**	**40**	**2.81**
21	1.48	41	2.88
22	1.55	42	2.95
23	1.62	43	3.02
24	1.69	44	3.09
25	**1.76**	**45**	**3.16**
26	1.83	46	3.23
27	1.90	47	3.30
28	1.97	48	3.37
29	2.04	49	3.45
30	**2.11**	**50**	**3.52**
31	2.18	51	3.59

Temperature

Conversion of degrees Centigrade into Fahrenheit

C	0	5	10	15	20	25	30	35	40
F	32	41	50	59	68	77	86	95	104

Fuel consumption

Conversion of miles/gallon into litres/100 km

miles/gallon	litres/100 km
10	28.25
15	18.84
20	14.13
25	11.30
30	9.42
35	8.07
40	7.06
45	6.28
50	5.65

1 mile per gallon = 282.54 litres per 100 kilometres

Conversion of kilometres to miles

km ←	km → or ← miles	→ miles
1.609	1	0.621
3.218	2	1.242
4.827	3	1.863
6.436	4	2.484
8.045	5	3.105
9.654	6	3.726
11.263	7	4.347
12.872	8	4.968
14.481	9	5.589
16.09	10	6.21
32.18	20	12.42
48.27	30	18.63
64.36	40	24.84
80.45	50	31.05
96.54	60	37.26
112.63	70	43.47
128.72	80	49.68
144.81	90	55.89
160.90	100	62.10

The Autoroutes Going South

Permission of SeaCo Picture Library to use granted

FROM
CALAIS
TO
PARIS

Autoroutes A26 & A1
lead to Parc Asterix

Drive on **the right side of the road** which happens on the Continent to be **the right hand side**

CALAIS PORT

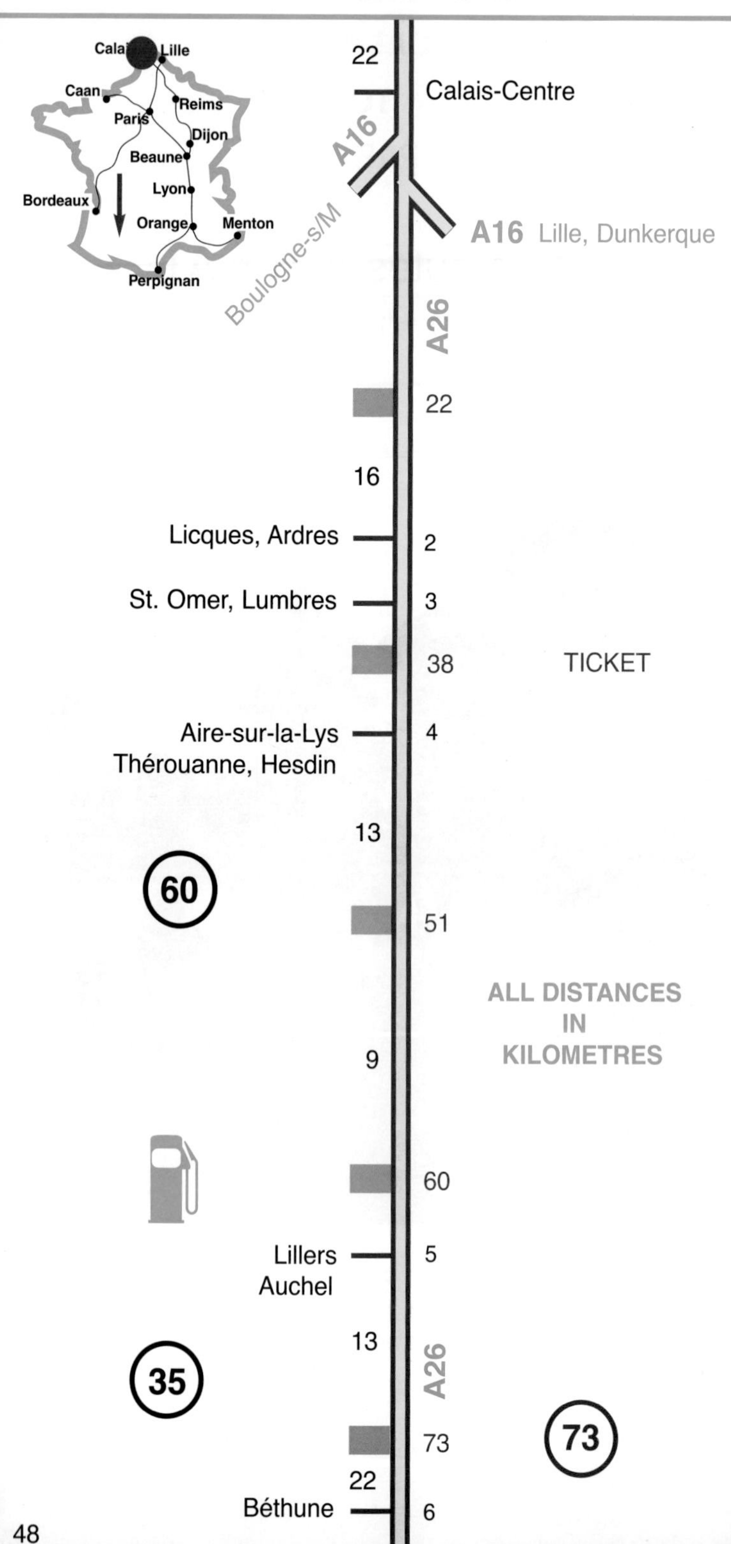

The "Mushroom" rest area, page 95

Aire de **Zutkerque**

Tables and benches, smart.
SOS - located at the side by the motorway and another one on the rest area itself.

Aire de **Barrière de péage de Setques**

Open space type of area with tables and benches, grassy.
Gendarmerie Station at the other side of the motorway.

Aire du **Grand Riez**

Grassy area with bushes and trees, various apparatus for children, tables and benches.
SOS - at the side of the rest area.

Aire de **Rely**

open space, spacious, lot of grassy spots, newly developed. Some tables and benches.
SOS - at the side of the rest area.

Aire du **Reveillon**

Arranged at two levels. The upper part of the area is a forest one. There are tables and benches.
SOS - at the side of the rest area.

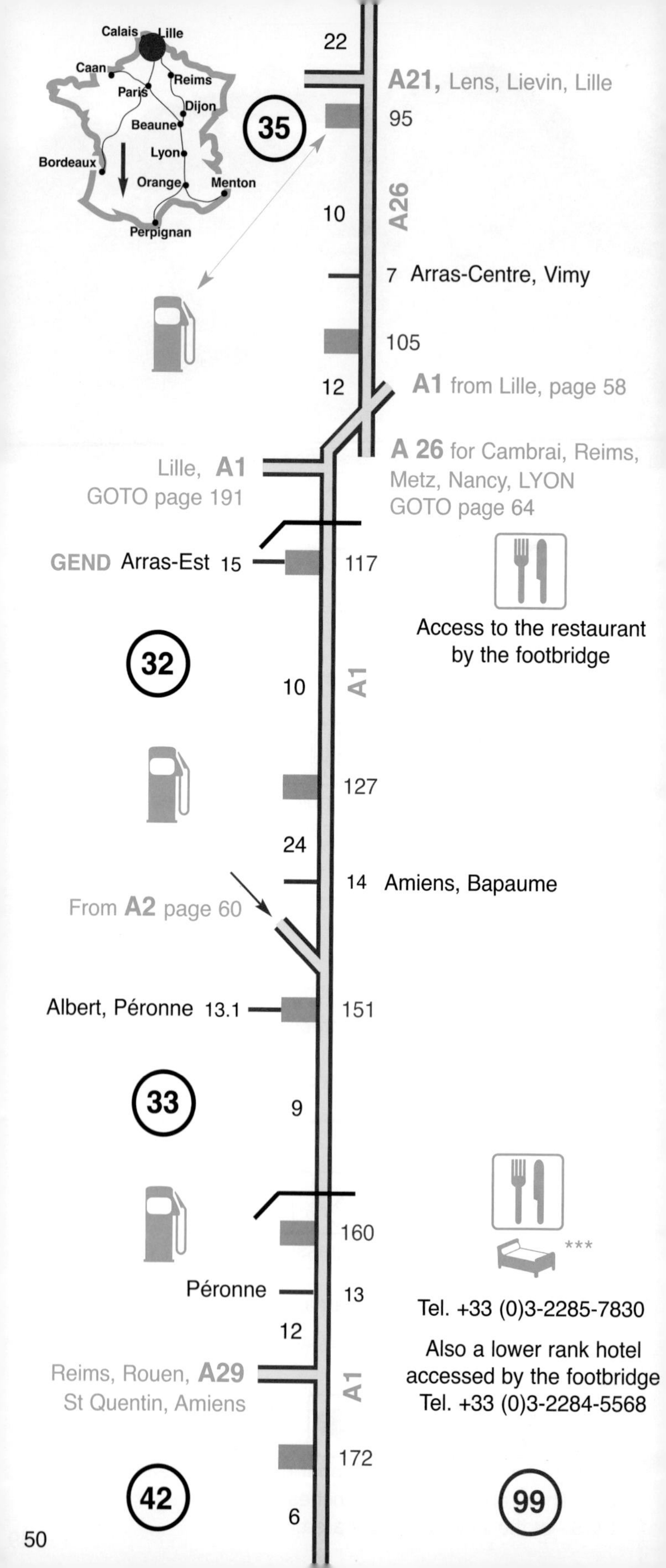
Calais
Lille
Caan
Reims
Paris
Dijon
Beaune
Lyon
Bordeaux
Orange
Menton
Perpignan
35
22
A21, Lens, Lievin, Lille
95
A26
10
7 Arras-Centre, Vimy
105
12
A1 from Lille, page 58
A 26 for Cambrai, Reims, Metz, Nancy, LYON
GOTO page 64
Lille, A1
GOTO page 191
GEND Arras-Est 15
117
Access to the restaurant by the footbridge
32
10
A1
127
24
14 Amiens, Bapaume
From A2 page 60
Albert, Péronne 13.1
151
33
9
160
***
Péronne
13
Tel. +33 (0)3-2285-7830
12
Also a lower rank hotel accessed by the footbridge
Tel. +33 (0)3-2284-5568
Reims, Rouen, A29
St Quentin, Amiens
A1
172
42
99
6

Aire de **Souchez**

Spacious rest area with tables and benches.
SOS - at the side of the rest area towards the entry slip-road.

Aire de **Trois Crêtes**

Open type with a lot of grassy area, tables and benches, spacious.
SOS - at the side towards the exit from the rest area.

Aire de **Wancourt-Ouest**

Open space with a few tables and benches. Spacious.

Aire de **St Léger**

There are tables an benches.
SOS - located close to the entry slip-road.

Aire de **Maurepas**

Small with tables and benches, grassy.
SOS - sited at side of the rest area.

Aire d'**Assevillers-Ouest**

Exceptionally spacious offering wide range of services of relevance to motoring travellers.
SOS - at the side of the rest area.

Aire d'**Hattencourt**

Open space type of area with tables and benches.
SOS - at the side of the rest area.

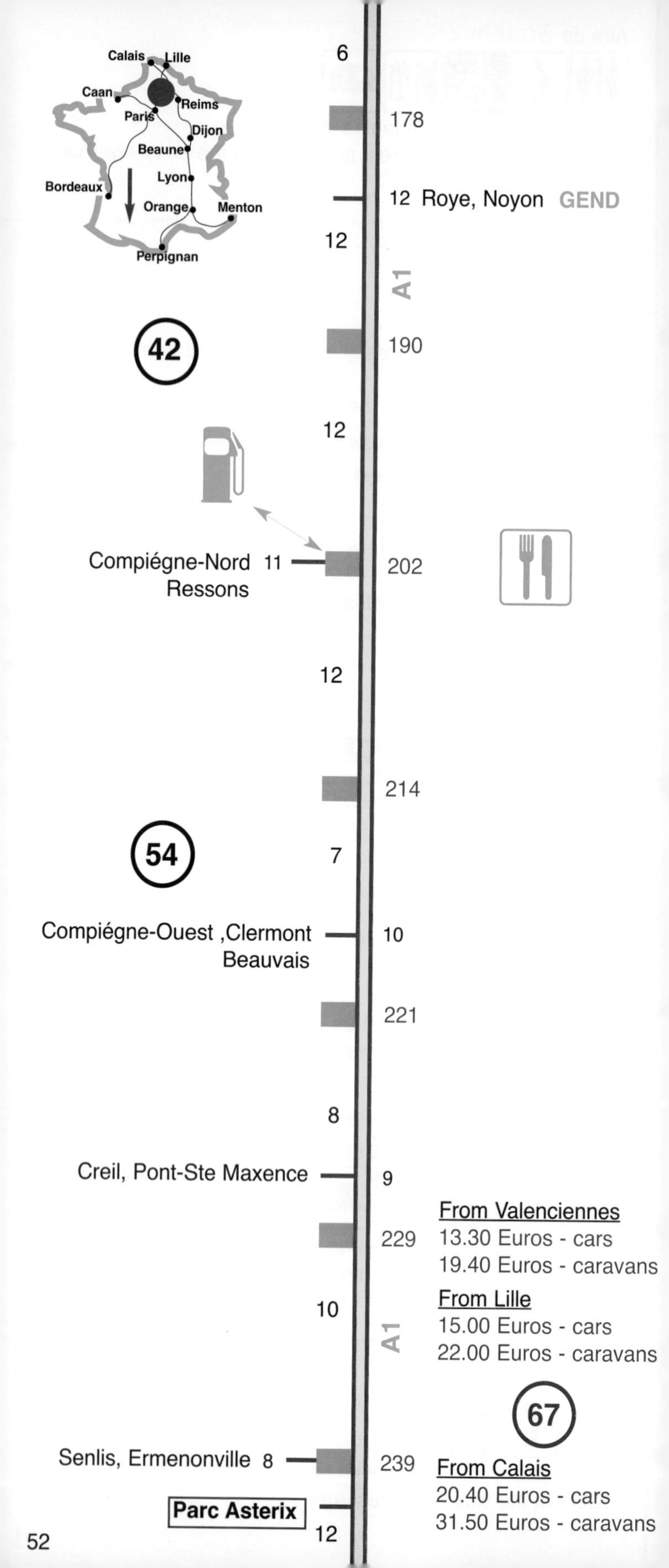

Calais
Lille
Caan
Reims
Paris
Dijon
Beaune
Lyon
Bordeaux
Orange
Menton
Perpignan
6
178
12 Roye, Noyon GEND
12
A1
42
190
12
Compiégne-Nord 11
Ressons
202
12
214
54
7
Compiégne-Ouest ,Clermont
Beauvais
10
221
8
Creil, Pont-Ste Maxence
9
From Valenciennes
229
13.30 Euros - cars
19.40 Euros - caravans
From Lille
10
15.00 Euros - cars
22.00 Euros - caravans
67
Senlis, Ermenonville 8
239
From Calais
20.40 Euros - cars
Parc Asterix
31.50 Euros - caravans
12

Aire de **Goyencourt-Ouest**

There are nests of tables and benches, some of the sets are under cover. SOS - by the motorway conveniently accessed from the rest area

Aire de **Tilloloy-Ouest**

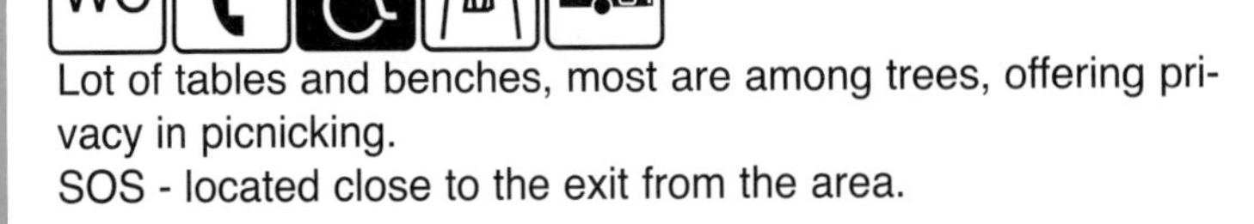

Lot of tables and benches, most are among trees, offering privacy in picnicking.
SOS - located close to the exit from the area.

Aire de **Ressons-Ouest**

Usual facilities of a petrol station complex. There are tables and benches arranged in rows in the open space.
SOS - at the side, close to the entry slip-road. .

Aire de **Bois d'Arsy**

Tables and benches among trees and in the open space, there is a site for caravanners. Spacious.
SOS - at the side, towards the exist from the area.

Aire de **Longueil-Ste Marie**

Very small, situated on a hill with tables and benches, some trees.
SOS - just past the rest area.

Aire de **Roberval-Ouest**

Tables and benches, some trees, very small but attractive.
SOS - located at the side of the rest area.

Aire de **Barrière de Péage de Chamant**

Just car parking facilities. **Gendarmerie**

SOS - at the entry to the parking area

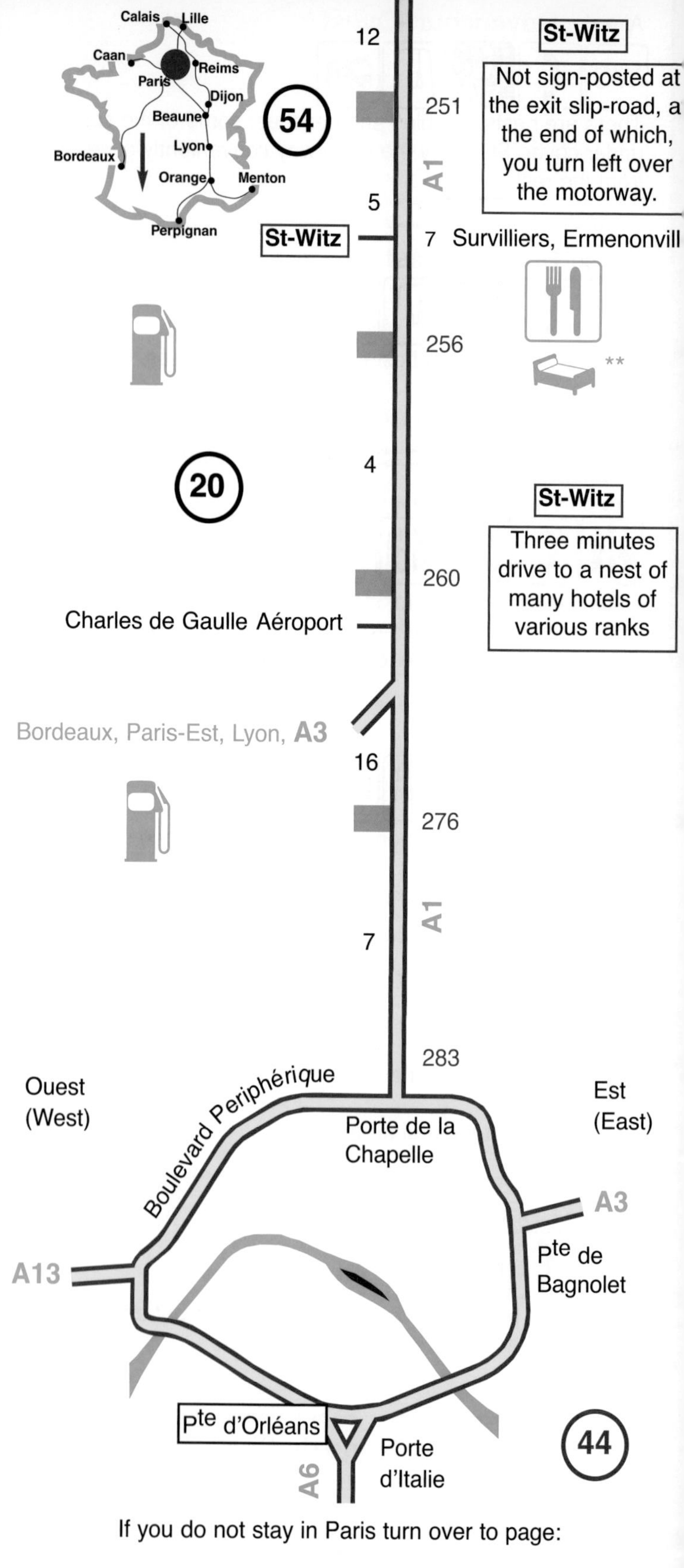

If you do not stay in Paris turn over to page:

85 - for the Riviera, Perpignan and Spain
127 - for Bordeaux

Aire de Survilliers

This rest area is meant for lorries only

SOS - actually on the rest area.

Aire de Vemars-Ouest

Mostly parking facilities. Cafeteria. In November 2010 the hotel was closed. Redevelopment of the Rest Area takes place.
SOS - by the side close to the entry slip-road.

Aire de Chennevières

There are tables and benches among trees.
SOS - at the side of the rest area

Aire de la Courneuve

Just parking facilities.
SOS - in close proximity of the entry slip-road.

And now, having passed the rest area "Aire de Chennevieres" and depending on, whether you stay in Paris or drive past you may find the following comments, as helpful:

You stay in Paris

Since there are alternatives to follow, you need to decide upon your choice, depending on your intended destination in Paris.

You may leave the motorway at the exit "Paris-Est, Lyon" and join the Boulevard Periphérique at the Pte de Bagnolet ("Pte" - short for "Porte" in this particular instance).
Or, you drive straight on, and before reaching Pte de la Chapelle, you follow the sign "Pte de Clignancourt" if you want to go Ouest (West) or, if you want to go Est (East), you follow the sign "Pte d'Aubervilliers" which is next to Pte de la Villette, the nearest to the City of Science and Industry, La Cite des Sciences et de l'Industrie at la Villette with its famous "GEODE" - a unique spherical giant structure, housing one of the biggest hemispheric screens in the world. For Paris you go straight on, following the sign "Paris".

You need to be equipped with a good map covering Paris with its great number of streets offering “one way only” traffic.

I take the opportunity to advise you to acquire the Michelin **Plan de Paris** (blue cover, 1cm = 100 metres) and you will not get lost in Paris.

You drive past Paris

Take the exit for “Paris-Est, Lyon” and at the next choice of alternatives, take the route for “Paris-Sud”, leading to the “Pte de Bagnolet”, and continue along the Boulevard Periphérique round Paris.
Keep in lane for LYON until you reach the “Pte d’Italie”, at which, it is necessary to leave the Boulevard for your destination in the South.
If you miss the above mentioned exit for “Paris-Est, Lyon”, you are still OK, joining the Boulevard at the location of the Pte de la Chapelle. Just before that Gate, you have three possibilities but must not take the Pte de la Chapelle, otherwise you will enter the City of Paris.
If it happens, that you went straight on, turn round, as soon as you realize your error, and follow the sign “Boulevard Periphérique”, and than, one of the two alternatives: “EST” - East or “OUEST” - West.
The “EST” seems to be the obvious choice (it is shorter) but either will take you to A1 - Autoroute du Soleil, if you keep in lane for LYON.

On the Boulevard Periphérique keep in lane, possibly, second from the right hand side.
The extreme right hand side lane driving might lead to some frustration, as the incoming traffic joins the Boulevard in a manner, as if, there was nobody else driving. But, the “priorité a droite” rule, the right of way, of traffic coming from the right hand side, might explain the occurrences.

If you are heading for Bordeaux, you follow the same route as for LYON until you have left the Boulevard and come across a choice for “Lyon” and “Chartres, Orleans”.

Take note:
In the immediate vicinity of Pte d’Italie you will face awkward, small radius bends entering suddenly darkened tunnel.

FROM

BELGIAN/FRENCH BORDER
LILLE AND VALENCIENNE

TO

PARIS

Autoroutes A1 & A2

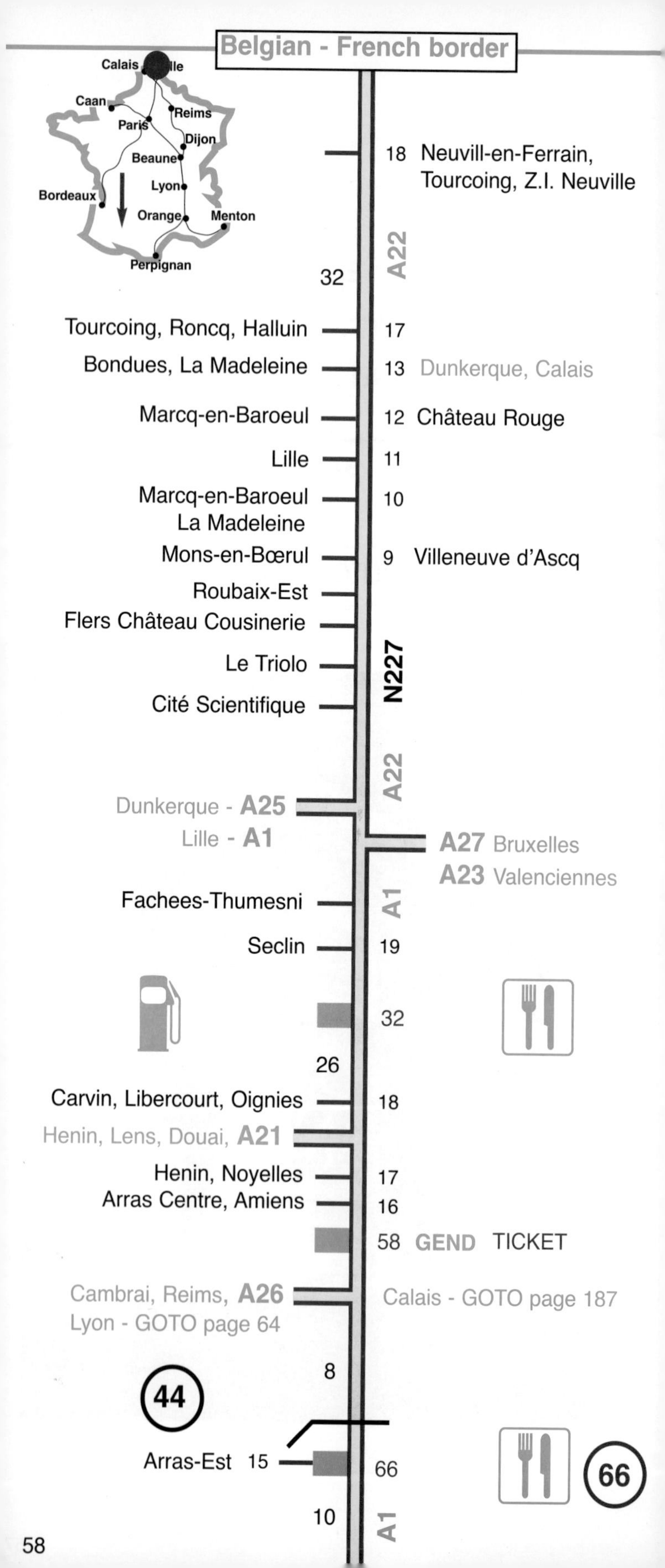

Belgian - French border
Calais
Lille
Caan
Reims
Paris
Dijon
Beaune
Lyon
Bordeaux
Orange
Menton
Perpignan
18 Neuvill-en-Ferrain, Tourcoing, Z.I. Neuville
A22
32
Tourcoing, Roncq, Halluin 17
Bondues, La Madeleine 13 Dunkerque, Calais
Marcq-en-Baroeul 12 Château Rouge
Lille 11
Marcq-en-Baroeul La Madeleine 10
Mons-en-Bœrul 9 Villeneuve d'Ascq
Roubaix-Est
Flers Château Cousinerie
N227
Le Triolo
Cité Scientifique
A22
Dunkerque - A25
Lille - A1
A27 Bruxelles
A23 Valenciennes
Fachees-Thumesni
A1
Seclin 19
32
26
Carvin, Libercourt, Oignies 18
Henin, Lens, Douai, A21
Henin, Noyelles 17
Arras Centre, Amiens 16
58 GEND TICKET
Cambrai, Reims, A26
Lyon - GOTO page 64
Calais - GOTO page 187
8
44
Arras-Est 15
66
66
10
A1

Aire de **Phalempin-Ouest**

Generally car parking spaces.There are some tables and benches offering privacy of picnicking.
SOS - at the side of the rest area.

Aire de **Barrière de péage de Fresnes**

Spacious car parking area.
SOS - actually on the parking area.

Aire de **Wancourt-Ouest** (shown here for you reference)

To continue for Paris
GOTO page 50

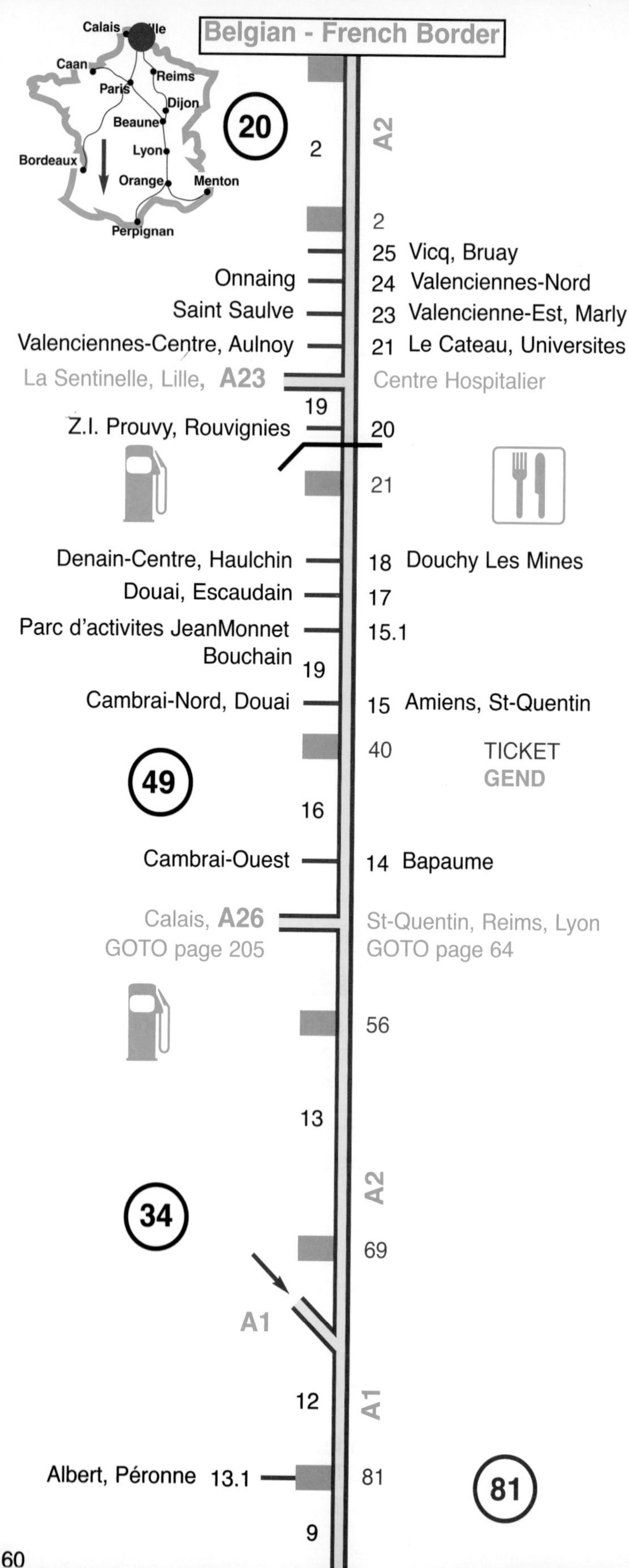
Belgian - French Border
Calais
Lille
Caan
Paris
Reims
Dijon
Beaune
Lyon
Bordeaux
Orange
Menton
Perpignan
20
A2
2
2
25 Vicq, Bruay
Onnaing
24 Valenciennes-Nord
Saint Saulve
23 Valencienne-Est, Marly
Valenciennes-Centre, Aulnoy
21 Le Cateau, Universites
La Sentinelle, Lille, A23
Centre Hospitalier
19
Z.I. Prouvy, Rouvignies
20
21
Denain-Centre, Haulchin
18 Douchy Les Mines
Douai, Escaudain
17
Parc d'activites JeanMonnet
15.1
Bouchain
19
Cambrai-Nord, Douai
15 Amiens, St-Quentin
40
TICKET
GEND
49
16
Cambrai-Ouest
14 Bapaume
Calais, A26
GOTO page 205
St-Quentin, Reims, Lyon
GOTO page 64
56
13
A2
34
69
A1
12
A1
Albert, Péronne 13.1
81
81
9

Rest area at the Belgian - French border

Limited parking facilities. Buffet, boutique, snack-bar.

Aire des Enclosis

Few tables and benches.
SOS - located at a distance of 300 m approx. from the exit slip-road.

Aire de la Sentinelle

Generally, car parking spaces.
SOS - at the side, close to the entry to the rest area, difficult to find it, as it is embedded by bushes. Another one is at the end of the exit slip-road.

Aire de Barrière de péage de Hordain

Two lane parking area, tidy, well cared for.

GENDARMERIE has its quarters at the other side of motorway.

Aire de Graincourt

There are tables and benches in the open space and under trees.
SOS - at the side, close to the entry slip-road to the rest area.

Aire de Barastre

Two lane parking facilities with quite a few tables and benches, offering privacy of pic nicking. Small .
SOS - at the side of the motorway close to the exit from the rest area. It is accessed through a recess in the tree line wall.

Aire de Maurepas (shown here for reference)

To continue for Paris
GOTO page 50.

FROM
CALAIS
TO
LYON (PARIS BY-PASS)

Autoroutes
A26, A4, A26, A5, A31 & A6

The "Mushroom" rest area, page 95

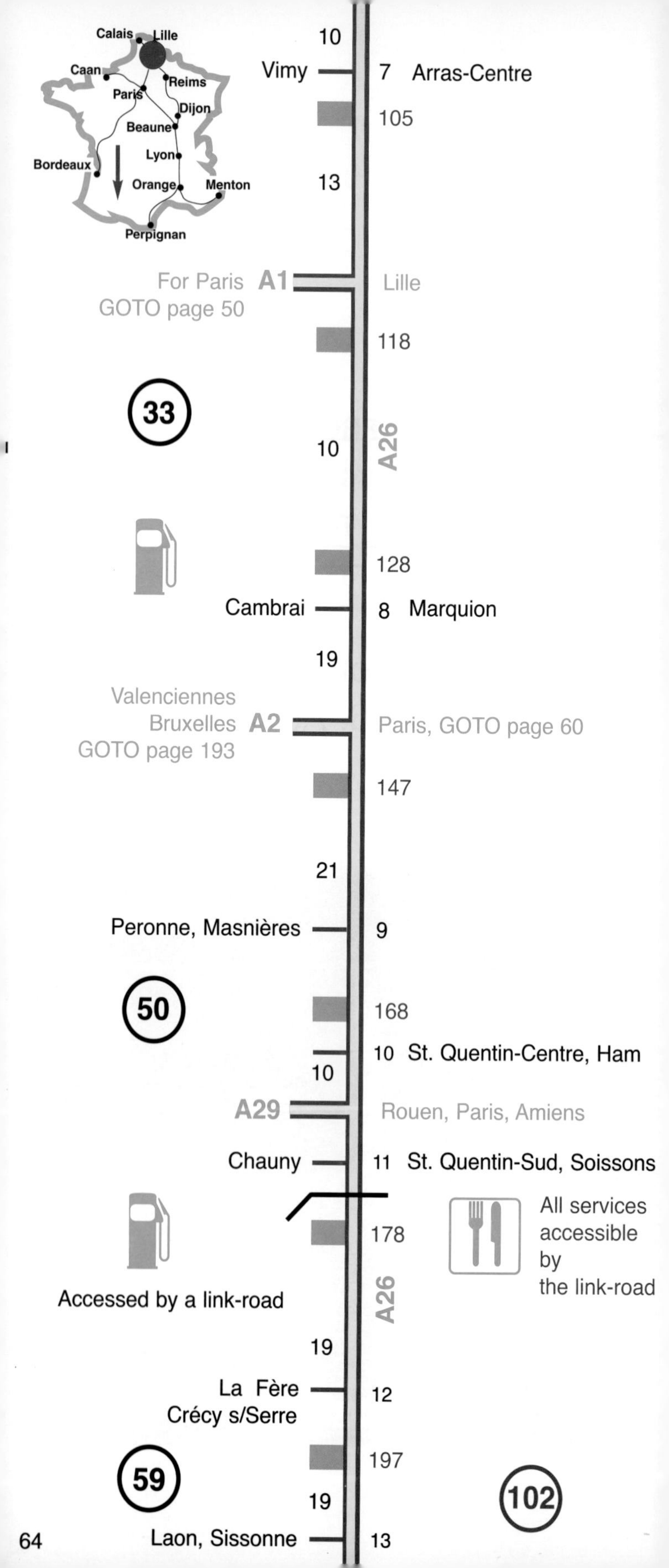
Calais
Lille
Caan
Reims
Paris
Dijon
Beaune
Lyon
Bordeaux
Orange
Menton
Perpignan
10
Vimy
7 Arras-Centre
105
13
For Paris A1
GOTO page 50
Lille
118
33
10
A26
128
Cambrai
8 Marquion
19
Valenciennes
Bruxelles A2
GOTO page 193
Paris, GOTO page 60
147
21
Peronne, Masnières
9
50
168
10 St. Quentin-Centre, Ham
10
A29
Rouen, Paris, Amiens
Chauny
11 St. Quentin-Sud, Soissons
178
All services
accessible
by
the link-road
Accessed by a link-road
A26
19
La Fère
Crécy s/Serre
12
197
59
19
102
Laon, Sissonne
13

Aire des Trois Crêtes

Continued from page 50

This area’s name is shown here for your reference only

Aide de Bois-d’Huez

Spacious, a lot of nests of tables and benches under trees.
SOS - 300 m approx. before the entry to the rest area.

Aire de Baralle

Small, few tables and benches at the end of the rest area.
SOS - sited at the entry slip-road.

Aire de Vacquerie

A lot of trees, quite a few nests of tables and benches offering privacy of picnicking.

SOS - one is located by the entry slip-road, another one on the rest area by the WC housing.

Aire de L’Omignon

Two lane parking facilities with tables and benches.
SOS - sited on the rest area, on the left hand side by the exit from the rest area.

Aire d’ Urvillers

The indicated services are obtainable on the other side of the motorway only and accessed by car.
There are quite a few nests of tables and benches.
SOS - located by the exit from the rest area.

Aire de Saint-Brice

Small, open aspect site with a few tables and benches.
SOS - one is located by the side of the rest area, another one on the rest area opposite the WC housing.

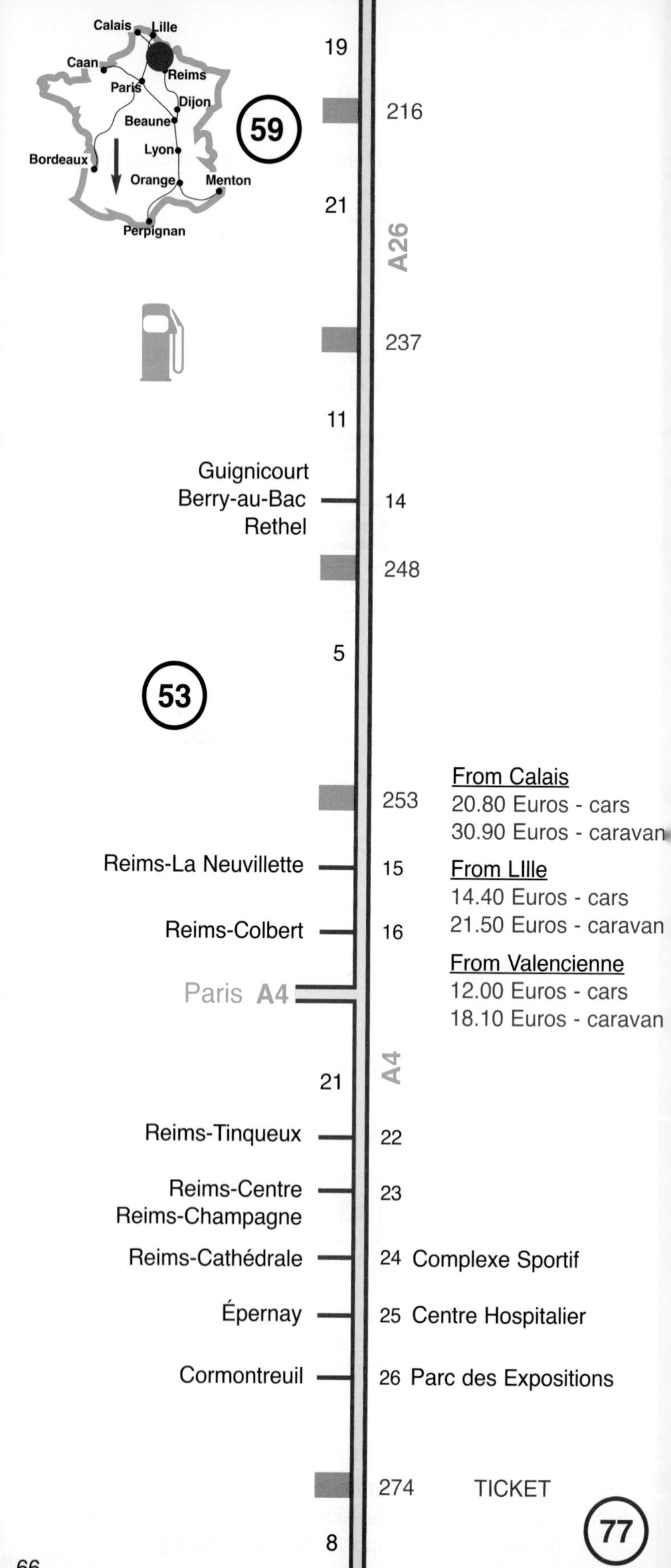

From Calais
20.80 Euros - cars
30.90 Euros - caravan

From LIlle
14.40 Euros - cars
21.50 Euros - caravan

From Valencienne
12.00 Euros - cars
18.10 Euros - caravan

Aire de la **Croisette**

Only a few tables and benches in the open space.

SOS - at the side of the rest area.

Aire de **Mont-de-Nizy**

Spacious with table and benches.
SOS - located at the very end of the rest area by the exit, not easy to spot it, as it is embedded by bushy trees.

Aire de **Cauroy les Hermonville**

Open space aspect site with a few tables and benches.
SOS - one located by the side of the rest area, another one on the rest area itself.

Aire de **Barrière de péage de Courcy**

Three lane parking facilities.

Aire de Châteauvillain Val-Marnay, page 71

Aire de **Barrière de péage de Taissy**

Small.

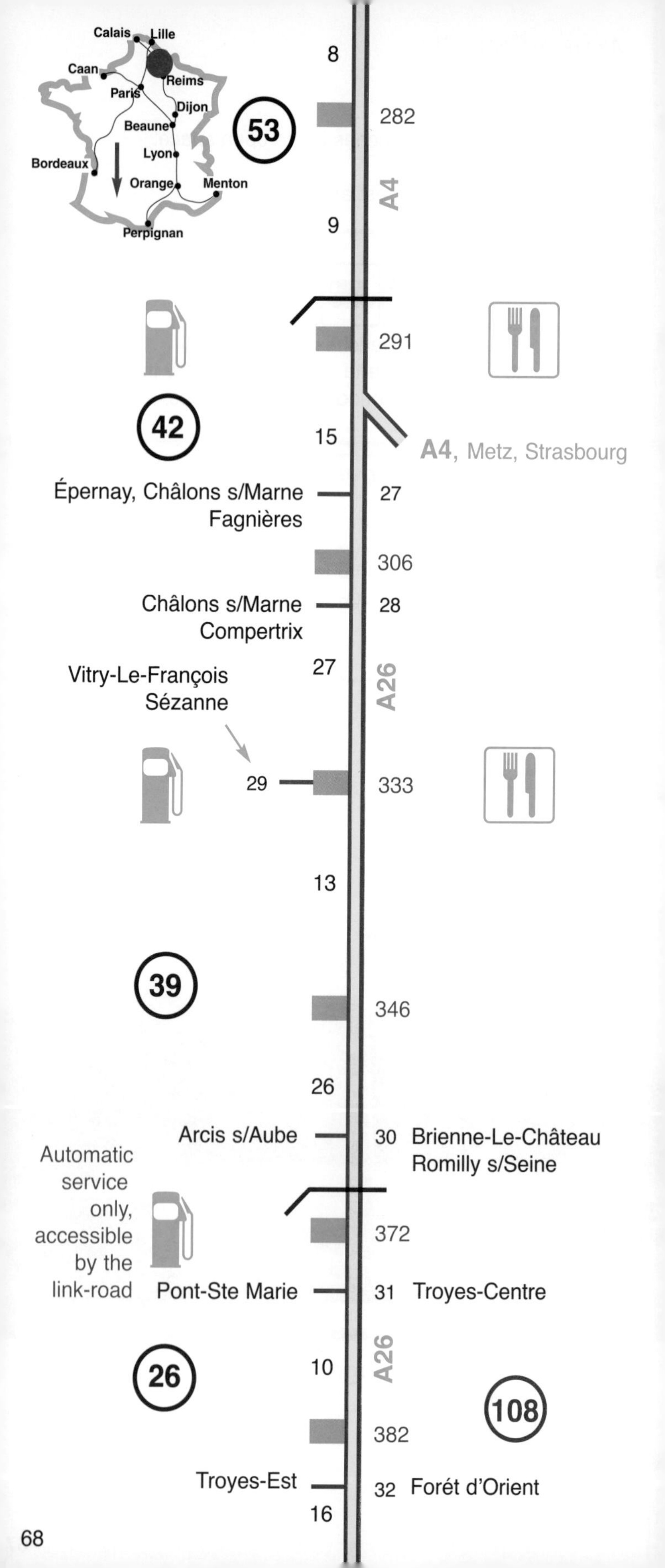

Calais
Lille
Caan
Reims
Paris
Dijon
Beaune
Lyon
Bordeaux
Orange
Menton
Perpignan
53
8
282
A4
9
291
42
15
A4, Metz, Strasbourg
Épernay, Châlons s/Marne
Fagnières
27
306
Châlons s/Marne
Compertrix
28
27
Vitry-Le-François
Sézanne
A26
29
333
13
39
346
26
Arcis s/Aube
30 Brienne-Le-Château
Romilly s/Seine
Automatic service only, accessible by the link-road
372
Pont-Ste Marie
31 Troyes-Centre
26
10
A26
108
382
Troyes-Est
32 Forét d'Orient
16

Aire de Espérance

Open space with nests of tables and benches.
SOS - located by side of m-way by the exit from the rest area.

Aire de Reims Champagne-Sud

The services are obtainable on the other side of the motoray, accessed by car. The road link is of no relevance to travellers going North. There are some tables and benches.

Aire de la Garenne

Nests of tables and benches offering a greater degree of privacy, as they are located at some distance from each other.
The area is spacious with a lot of bushes and grassy spots.
SOS - one by the side of the motorway and another one on the rest area itself.

Aire de Sommesous

The services are obtainable on the other side of the motorway. accessible by car. The exit slip-road and entry to the rest area, as one. Spacious with tables and benches. Station de gonflage.

Aire de Champ-Carreau

Some tables and benches, lot of greenery.
SOS - located on the rest area. Also, there is one sited by the side of the motorway.

Aire de Charmont

This rest area is accessed by the link-road.

Mainly car parking facilities, with a couple of tables and benches.
Petrol available from automatic distribution pumps operated by credit cards.

Aire de Villechétif

Some tables and benches, it doesn't have much to offer.
SOS - located at the side of the rest area.

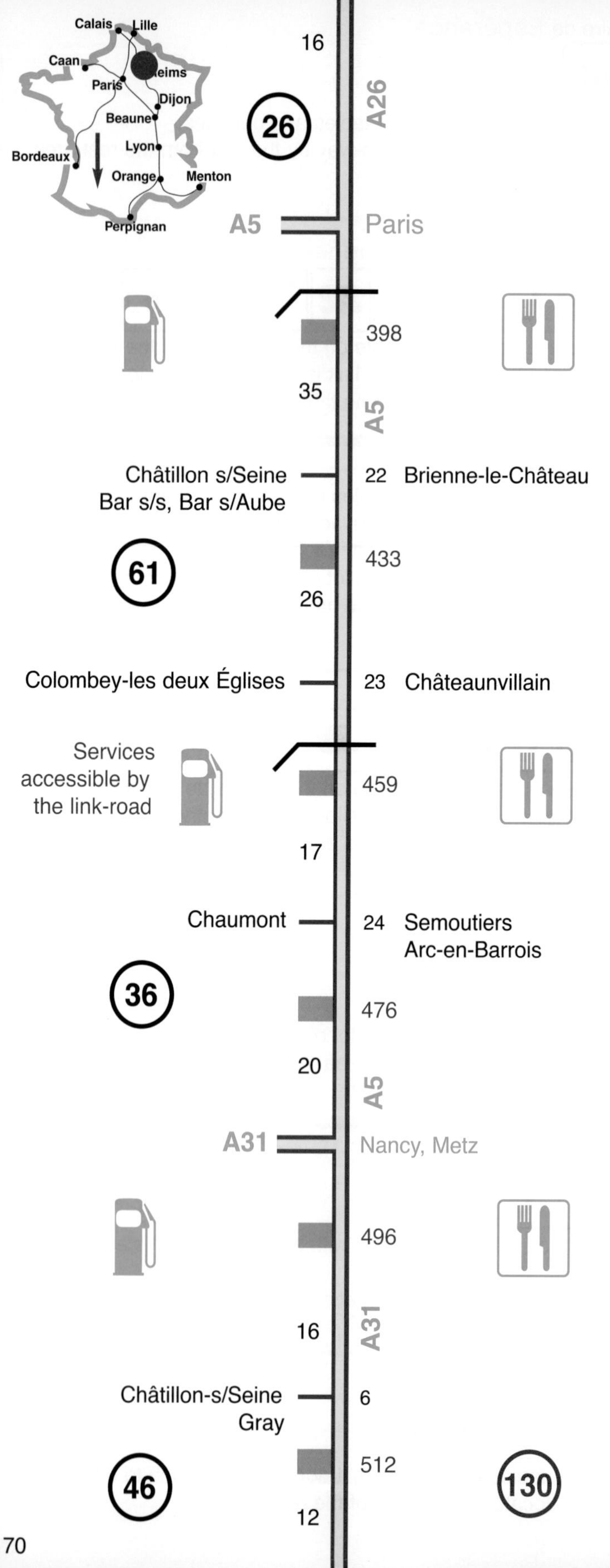

Calais
Lille
Caan
Reims
Paris
Dijon
Beaune
Bordeaux
Lyon
Orange
Menton
Perpignan
16
26
A26
A5
Paris
398
35
A5
Châtillon s/Seine
Bar s/s, Bar s/Aube
22
Brienne-le-Château
61
433
26
Colombey-les deux Églises
23
Châteaunvillain
Services
accessible by
the link-road
459
17
Chaumont
24
Semoutiers
Arc-en-Barrois
36
476
20
A5
A31
Nancy, Metz
496
16
A31
Châtillon-s/Seine
Gray
6
46
512
130
12

Aire de **Troyes-Fresnoy**

Shady spots with tables and benches among trees.
SOS - sited close to the entry slip-road to the rest area and there is another one actually on the rest area itself.

Aire de **Mondeville**

Open space, some trees, tables and stools made of concrete.

SOS- located at the side of the rest area.

Aire de **Châteauvillain Val-Marnay**

The services are available on the other side of the motorway, There are nests of tables and stools shaped as mushrooms, see page 67. SOS - one is located on the rest area itself and another one by the side of the motorway.

Aire du **Bois Moyen**

The public telephone is mounted on the wall of the WC building by the entrance. There are couple of tables and benches.
SOS - located by the side of the rest area.

Aire de **Langres-Perrogney**

There are tables and benches. Spacious.
SOS - located by the side of the motorway towards the exit from the rest area.

Aire de **Fontenelle**

Public telephone mounted on the WC housing wall by the entrance.The rest area is small with few tables and benches.

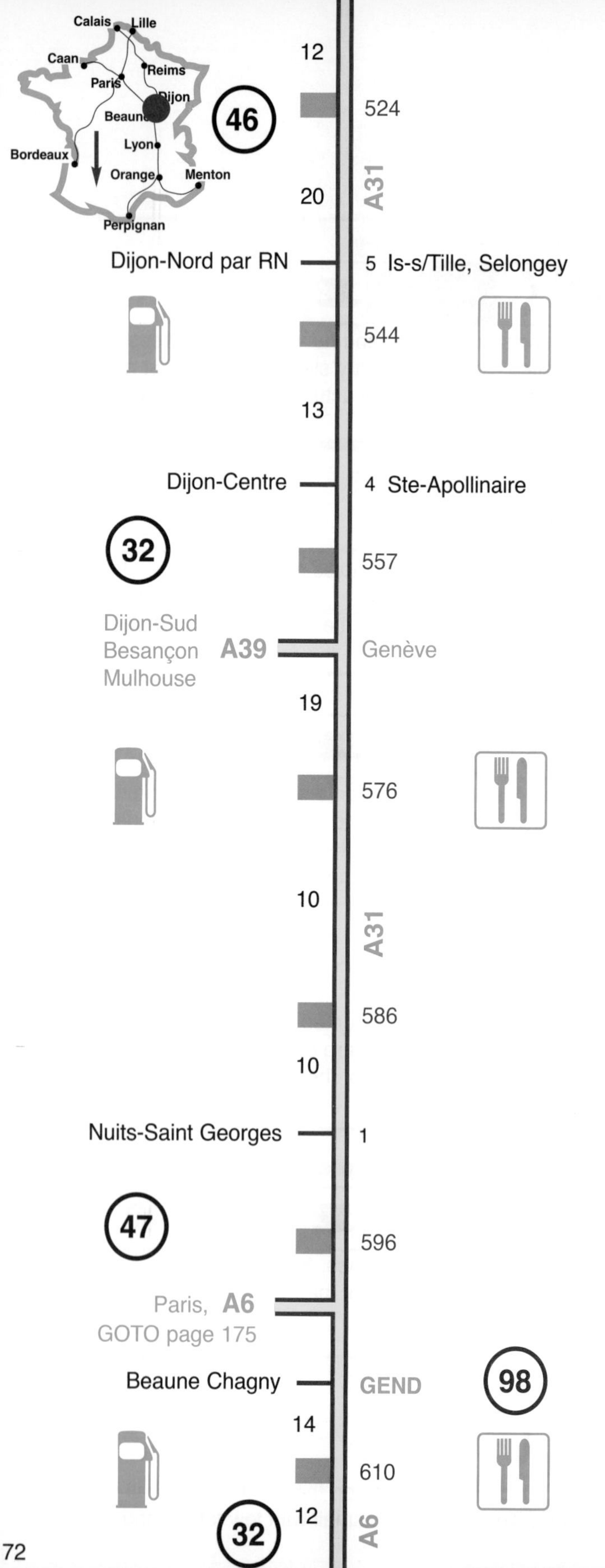
Calais
Lille
Caan
Reims
Paris
Dijon
Beaune
Bordeaux
Lyon
Orange
Menton
Perpignan
46
12
524
20
A31
Dijon-Nord par RN
5 Is-s/Tille, Selongey
544
13
Dijon-Centre
4 Ste-Apollinaire
32
557
Dijon-Sud
Besançon
Mulhouse
A39
Genève
19
576
10
A31
586
10
Nuits-Saint Georges
1
47
596
Paris, A6
GOTO page 175
Beaune Chagny
GEND
98
14
610
12
32
A6

Aire de **Ste-Gertrude**

There are tables and benches.

Aire de **Dijon-Brognon**

Quite a few nests of tables and benches under trees and in the open space, a lot of shady spots. Spacious.
SOS - located by the exit from the rest area.

Aire de la **Tille**

A lot of hedges and small trees, some tables and benches.
SOS - located close to the entry to the rest area.

Aire de **Gevrey-Chambertin**

Tables and benches among trees.

Aire de **Flagey-Echézeaux**

there are tables and benches among trees.

Aire de **Serrigny**

Forested rest area with many nests of tables and benches among trees.
SOS - located by the side of the rest area.

Aire de **Beaune-Tailly**

To continue for the South
GOTO page 95

FROM
CAEN
TO
PARIS

Autoroute A13

Drive on **the right side of the road** which happens on the Continent to be **the right hand side**

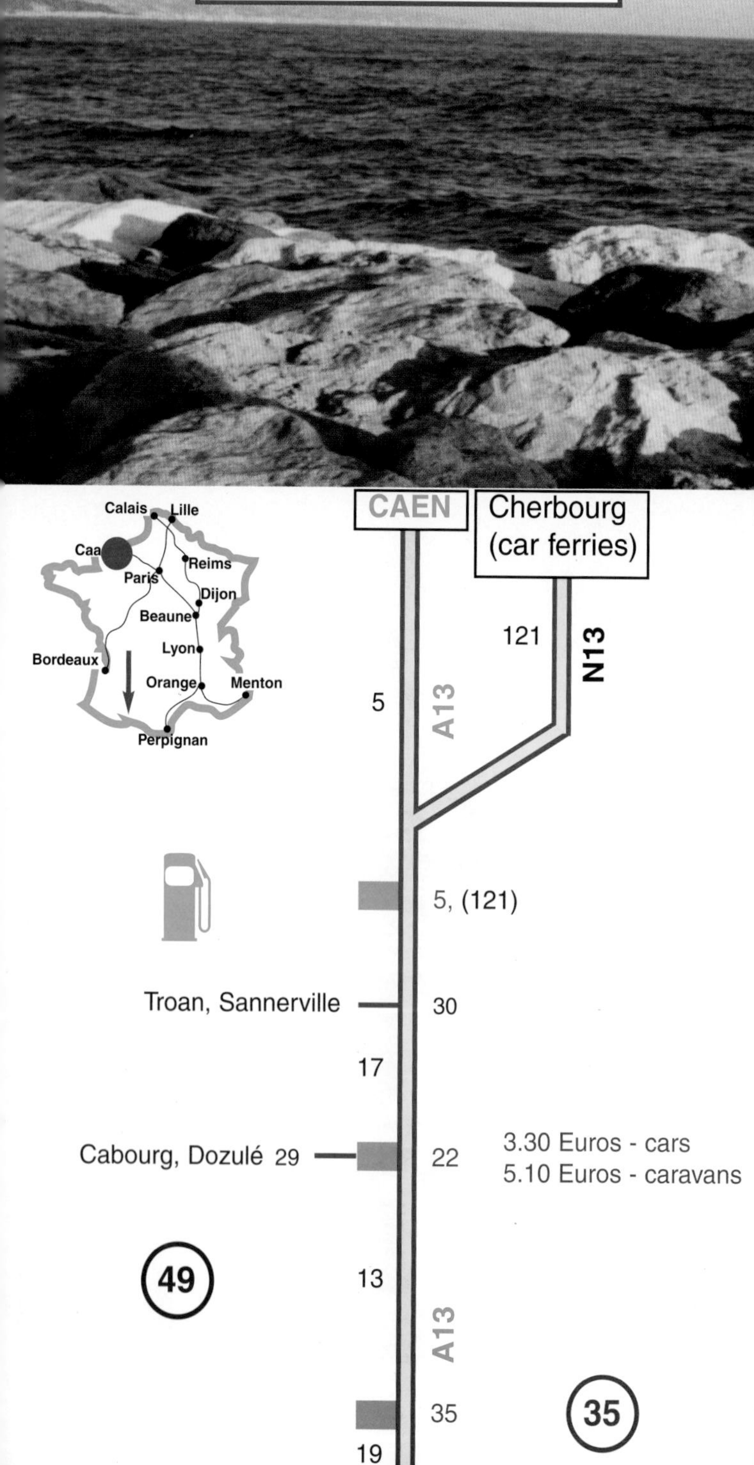

Deauville, **A132**

Trouville **GEND**

Aire Sud de **Giberville-Sud**

Open space, mostly grassy with some tables and benches.

SOS - located at the side of the rest area.

Aire de **Barrière de péage (Dozulé)**

Just car parking spaces, very small .

Gendarmerie

SOS - 200 m approx. before the entry slip-road.

Aire de **Beaumont-en-Auge**

Small, grassy with many nests of tables and benches and also apparatus for children.

SOS - located by the exit slip-road, on the right hand side.

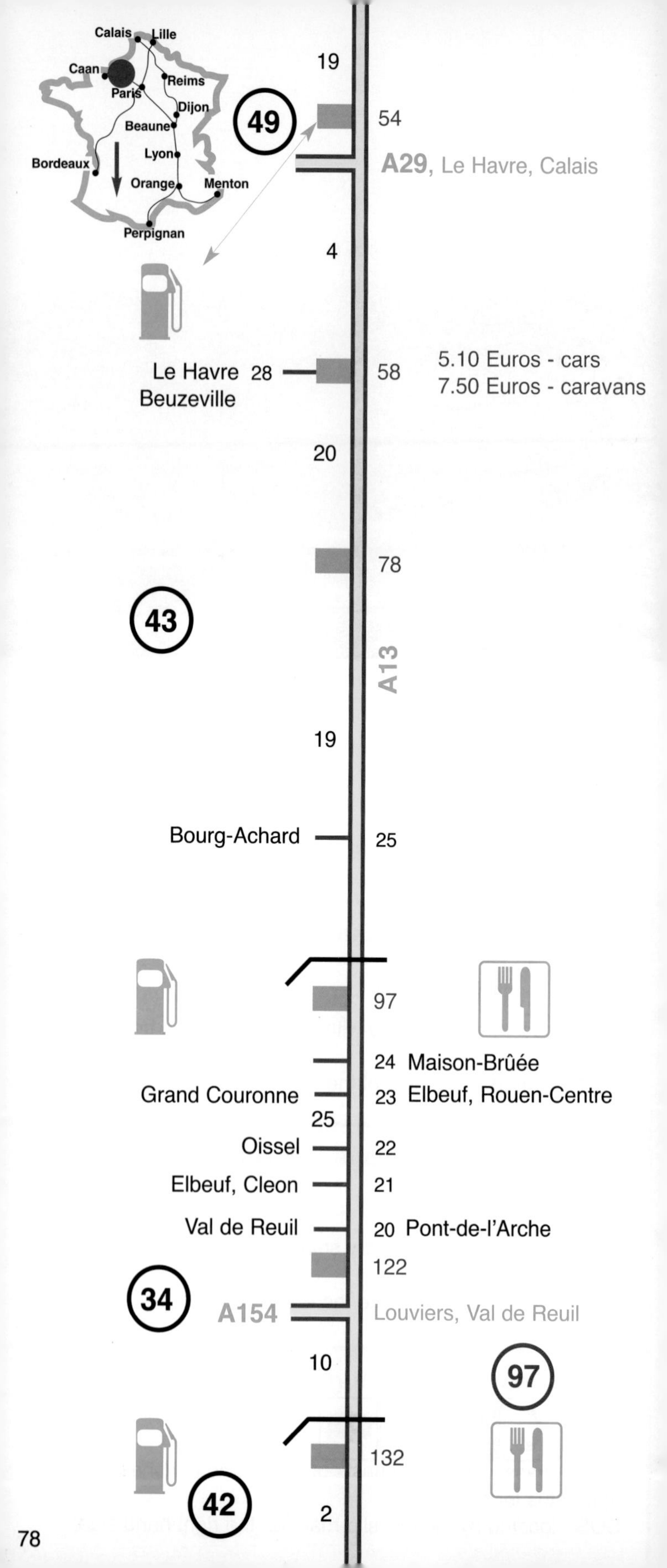
Calais
Lille
Caan
Paris
Reims
Dijon
Beaune
Lyon
Bordeaux
Orange
Menton
Perpignan
19
49
54
A29, Le Havre, Calais
4
Le Havre 28
Beuzeville
58
5.10 Euros - cars
7.50 Euros - caravans
20
78
43
A13
19
Bourg-Achard
25
97
24 Maison-Brûée
Grand Couronne
23 Elbeuf, Rouen-Centre
25
Oissel
22
Elbeuf, Cleon
21
Val de Reuil
20 Pont-de-l'Arche
122
34
A154
Louviers, Val de Reuil
10
97
132
42
2

Aire de Beuzeville-Sud

Spacious, grassy with some tables and benches, tidy, well looked after. The exit for A29 and the entry to the area as one.
SOS - located at the side, close to the exit from the rest area.

Aire de **Barrière de péage (Beuzeville)**

Small with few car parking spaces, more sort of a parking bay.
Gendarmerie

Aire du Moulin

Small with tables and benches among trees.
SOS - located just past the rest area (end of the exit slip-road).

Aire de Bosgouet-Sud

Spacious, open space with some tables and benches.
There is a snack-bar.
SOS - sited by the motorwy, just past the rest area.

Aire de Bord-Sud

There are lots of tables and benches, mostly among trees, tidy and well cared for.
SOS - located at the side of the rest area.

Aire de Vironvay-Sud

Spacious in parking facilities.
Cafeteria and restaurant accessed by the footbridge.
SOS -at the very end of the rest area by the exit slip-road.

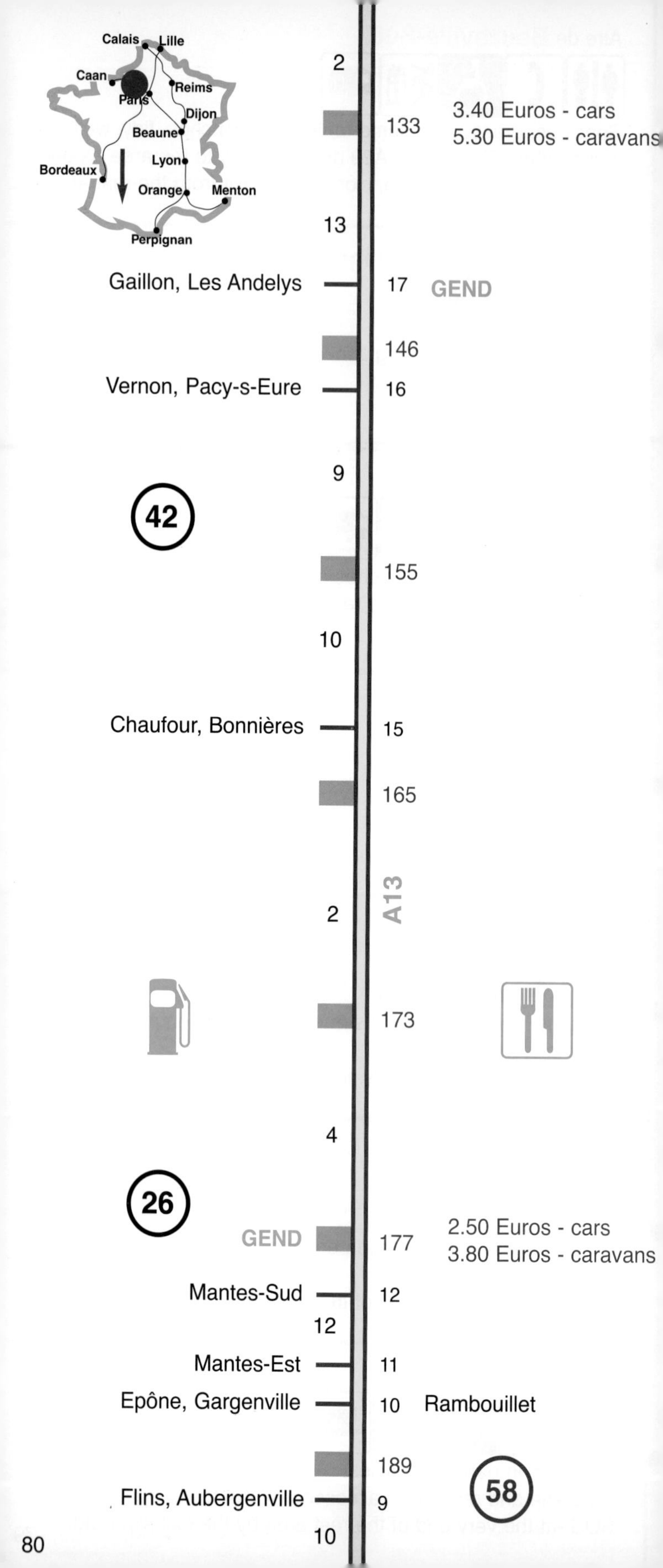
Calais
Lille
Caan
Paris
Reims
Dijon
Beaune
Bordeaux
Lyon
Orange
Menton
Perpignan
2
133
3.40 Euros - cars
5.30 Euros - caravans
13
Gaillon, Les Andelys
17
GEND
146
Vernon, Pacy-s-Eure
16
9
42
155
10
Chaufour, Bonnières
15
165
A13
2
173
4
26
GEND
177
2.50 Euros - cars
3.80 Euros - caravans
Mantes-Sud
12
12
Mantes-Est
11
Epône, Gargenville
10
Rambouillet
189
58
Flins, Aubergenville
9
10

Aire de **Barrière de péage (Heudebouville)**

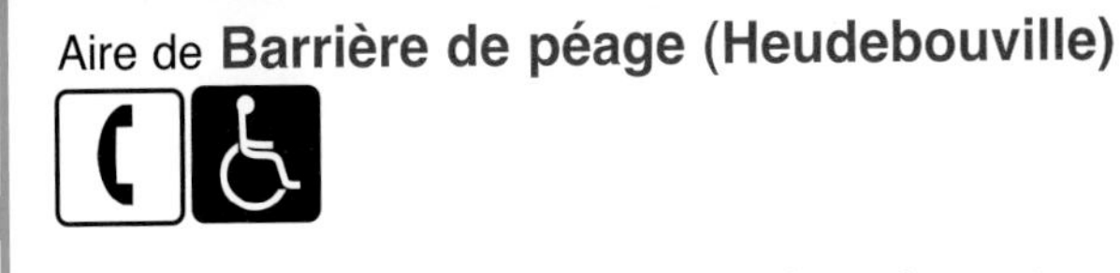

SOS - at close proximity of the exit from the rest area .

Aire de **Beauchêne-Sud**

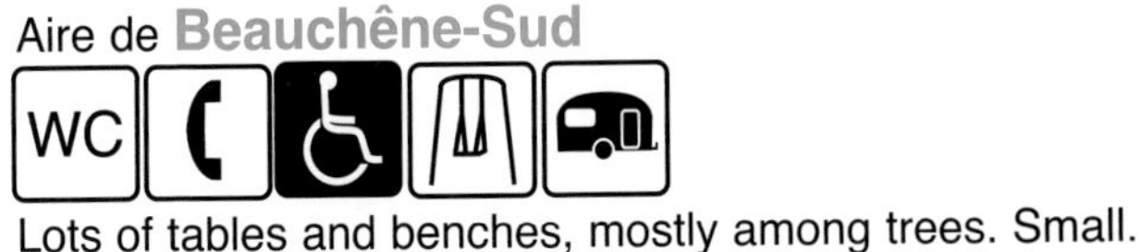

Lots of tables and benches, mostly among trees. Small.
SOS - located close to the entry slip-road to the rest area.

Aire de **Douains-Sud**

Some tables and benches in the open space, well cared for.
SOS - at the side of the rest area.

Aire de la **Villeneuve-en-Chevrie-Sud**

Small, arranged on two levels, few tables and benches among trees at the upper level.
SOS - at the side of the rest area.

Aire de **Rosny-sur-Seine**

Few tables and benches, generally parking spaces.
SOS - at the side, close to the entry to the rest area.

Aire de **Barriére de péage de Buchelay**

Just parking facilities.
Gendarmerie.

Aire de **Èpône-Sud**

WC

Small, open space. There are no tables or benches. Tidy.
SOS - Conspicuously located on the rest area, close to the WC building.

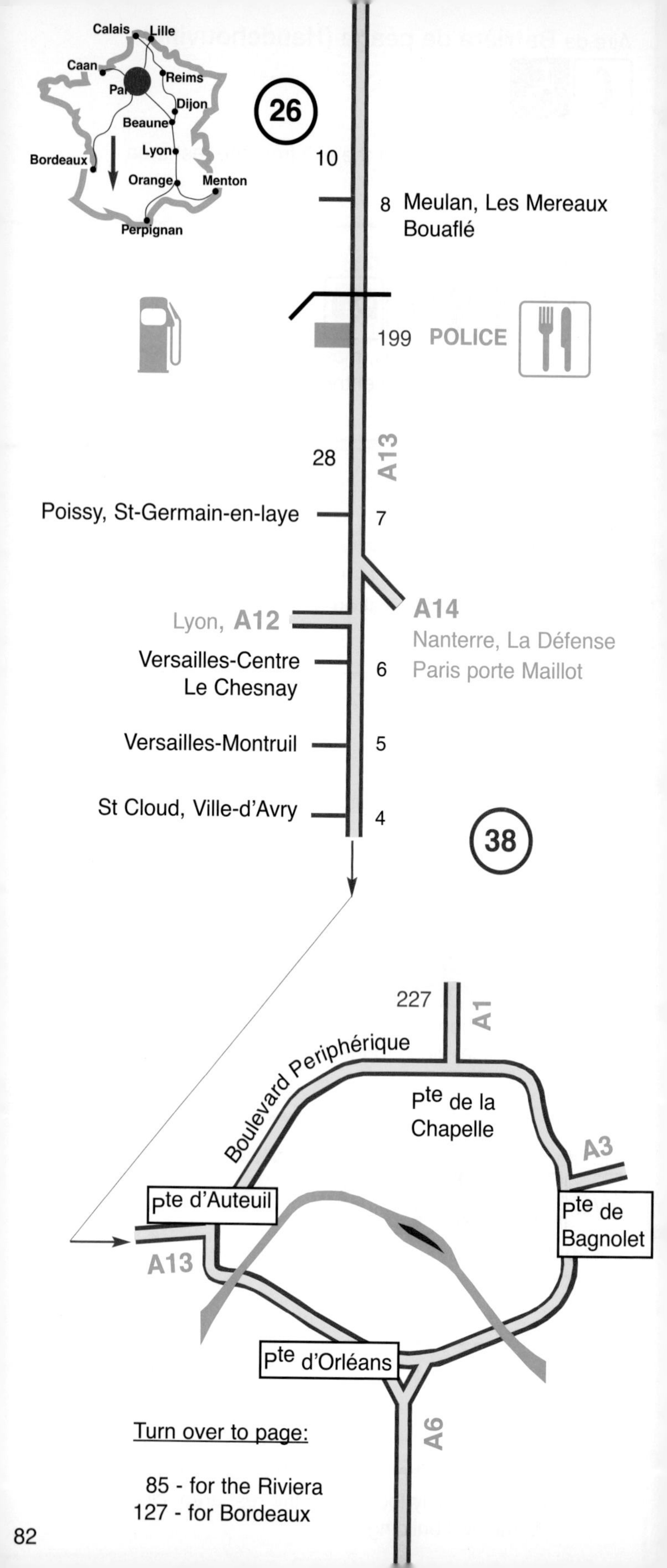

Turn over to page:

85 - for the Riviera
127 - for Bordeaux

Aire de Moraivilliers-Sud

POLICE DE L'AUTOROUTE

Ample space rest area, mostly offering parking facilities.
Restaurant accessed by the footbridge.
SOS - 400 metres before entry to the area. Another one located 300 metres approx. past the rest area.

FROM

PARIS

TO

LYON - FRENCH/ITALIAN BORDER

Autoroutes A6, A7 & A8

the "Mushroom" rest area, page 95

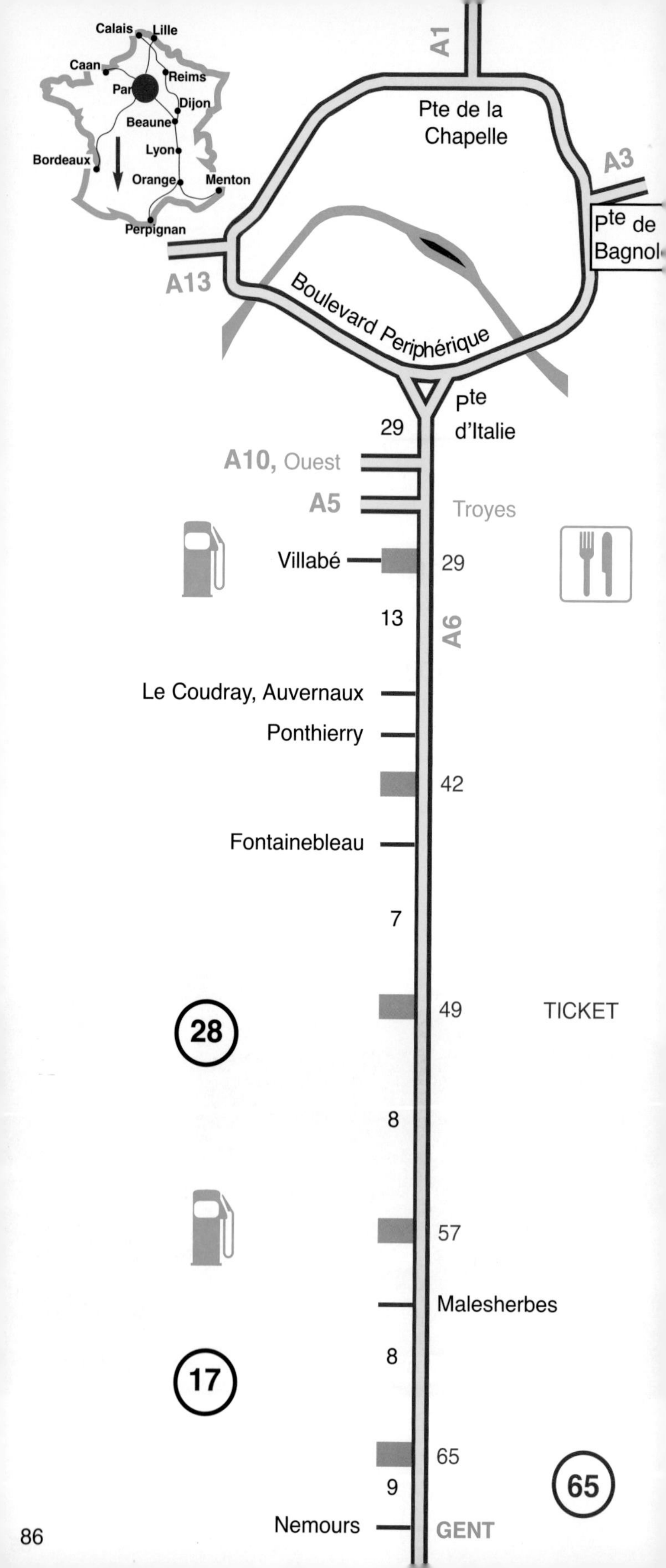
Calais
Lille
Caan
Par
Reims
Dijon
Beaune
Lyon
Bordeaux
Orange
Menton
Perpignan
A1
Pte de la
Chapelle
A3
Pte de
Bagnol
A13
Boulevard Periphérique
Pte
d'Italie
29
A10, Ouest
A5
Troyes
Villabé
29
13
A6
Le Coudray, Auvernaux
Ponthierry
42
Fontainebleau
7
49
TICKET
28
8
57
Malesherbes
8
17
65
9
65
Nemours
GENT

the “Mushroom” rest area, page 95

Aire de Lisses

Just car parking facilities.

SOS - located at the side of the rest area.

Aire de Nainville

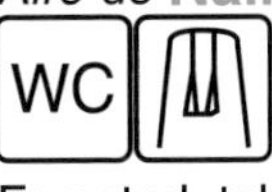

Forested, tables and benches among trees. Small but nice.
SOS - sited on the rest area itself.

Aire de Barrière de péage (Fleury)

Just parking facilities. Spacious, some tables and benches.

Aire d' Achères la Forét

There are nests of tables and benches, spacious.
SOS - at the side of the rest area.

Aire de Villiers

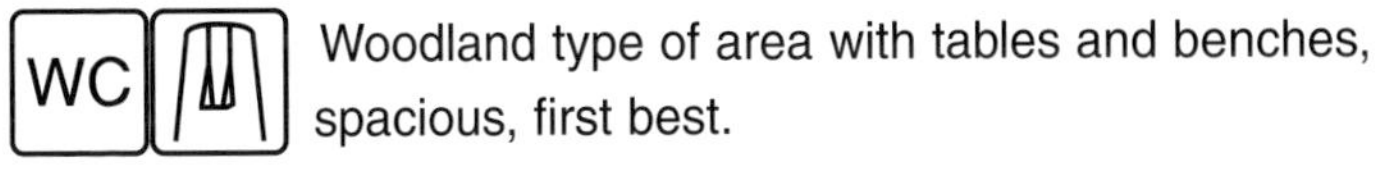

Woodland type of area with tables and benches, spacious, first best.

SOS - located on the rest area by the exit slip-road, difficult to be spotted from the motorway.

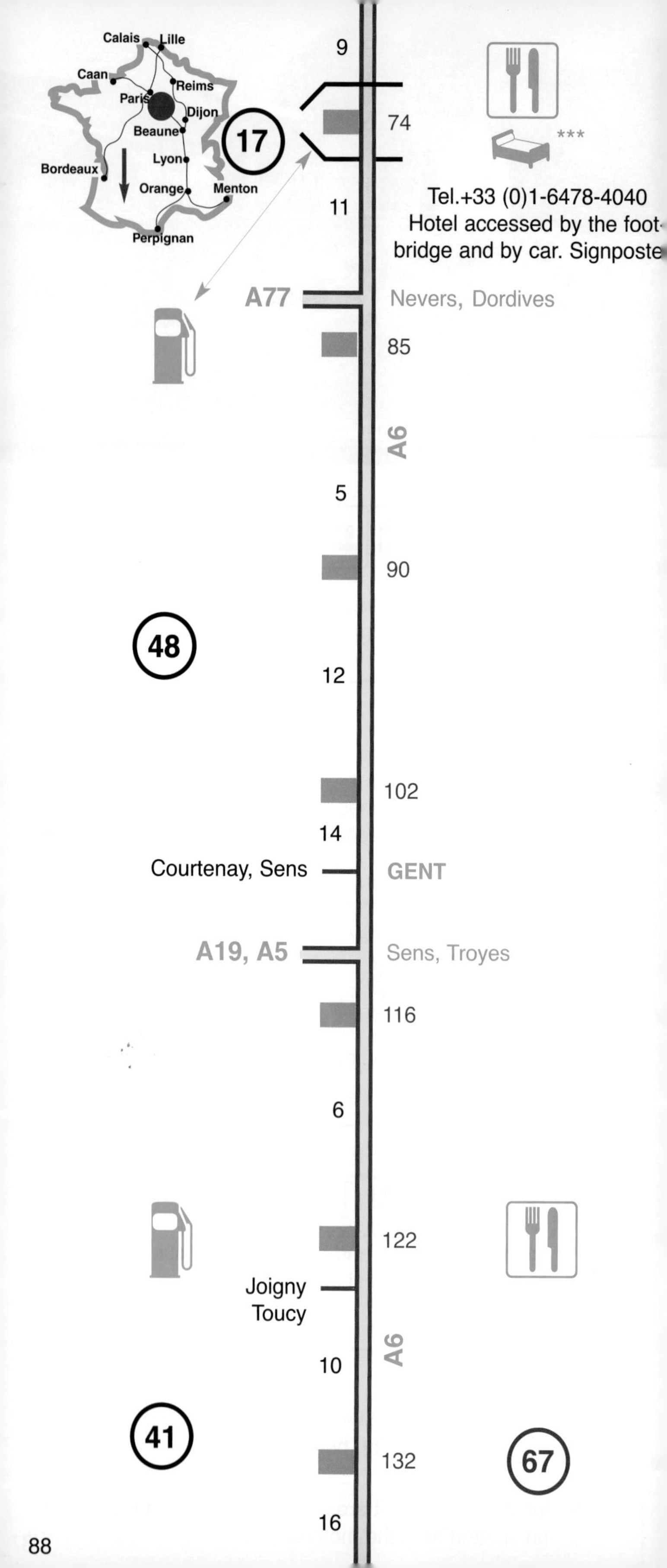

Calais
Lille
Caan
Reims
Paris
Dijon
Beaune
Lyon
Bordeaux
Orange
Menton
Perpignan
17
9
74
***
Tel.+33 (0)1-6478-4040
Hotel accessed by the foot-
bridge and by car. Signposte
11
A77
Nevers, Dordives
85
A6
5
90
48
12
102
14
Courtenay, Sens
GENT
A19, A5
Sens, Troyes
116
6
122
Joigny
Toucy
A6
10
41
132
67
16

Aire de Nemours

Extensive services provided. There are some table and benches. The hotel is accessed conveniently by a link-road.
SOS - at the side of the rest area.

Aire de Sonville

Mostly forested area with lots of tables and benches. Small but pretty.
SOS - located by the side of the rest area.

Aire du Liard

Tables and benches among trees and in the open space.
SOS - located by the side of the rest area.

Aire du Parc Thierry

It is a jungle-like type of site with plenty of tables and benches among trees.
SOS - at the side of the rest area towards the exit slip-road.

Aire des Châtaigniers

As the one above: a jungle-like site with lots of tables and benches.
SOS - at the side of the rest area.

Aire de la Réserve

Open space type of site, mainly car parking facilities.

SOS - at the side of the rest area.

Aire de la Racheuse

Forested, tables and benches, small.
SOS.

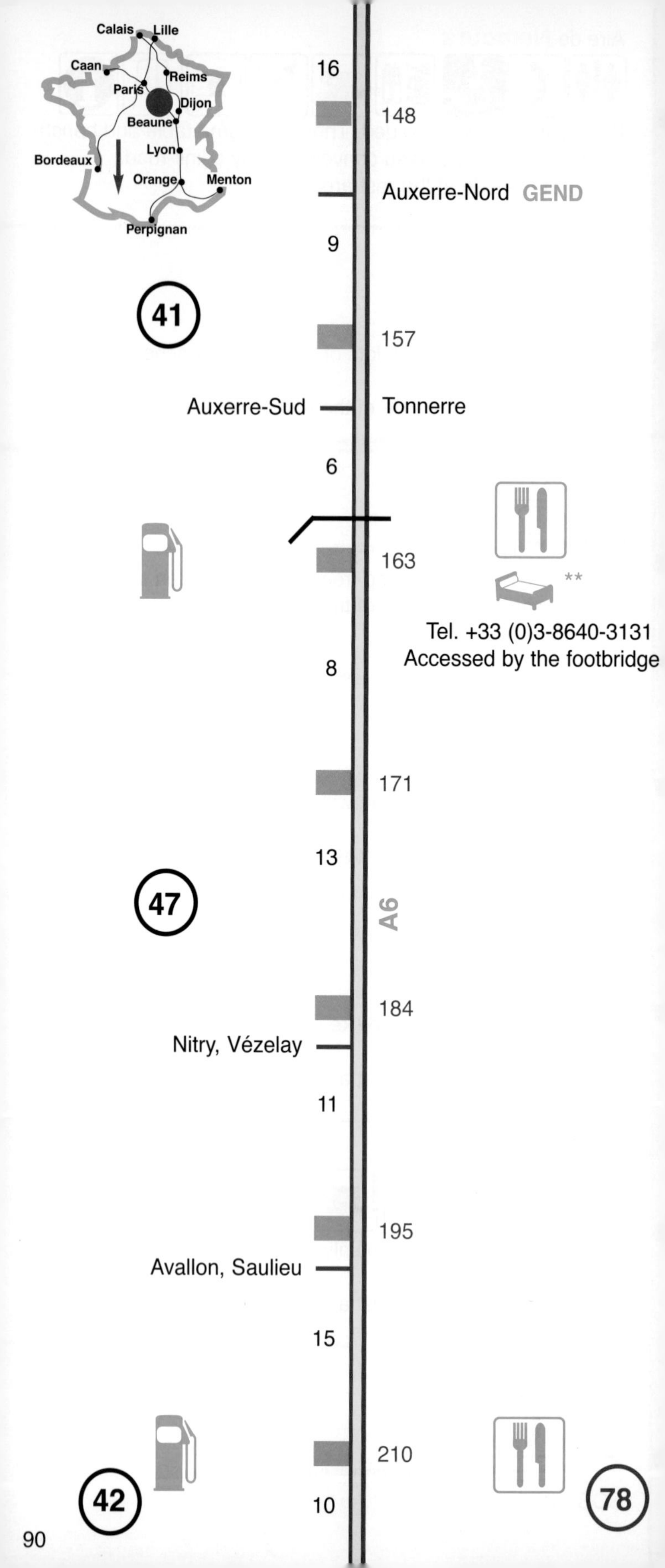
Calais
Lille
Caan
Paris
Reims
Dijon
Beaune
Lyon
Bordeaux
Orange
Menton
Perpignan
16
148
Auxerre-Nord
GEND
9
41
157
Auxerre-Sud
Tonnerre
6
163
**
Tel. +33 (0)3-8640-3131
Accessed by the footbridge
8
171
13
47
A6
184
Nitry, Vézelay
11
195
Avallon, Saulieu
15
210
42
10
78

Aire de la **Biche**

Forested area with no tables or benches provided.

SOS - located at the side of the rest area.

Aire des **Bois Imperiaux**

Small with tables and benches.

SOS - located by the exit from the area.

Aire de **Venoy-Grosse-Pierre**

Spacious, few tables and benches, bar, P.O. BOX located by the entrance to the cafeteria.

SOS - at the side towards the entry to the rest area.

Aire de la **Grosse Tour**

Small with tables and benches among trees and in the open space.

SOS - at close proximity of the exit slip-road.

Aire de la **Couée**

Small, forested with tables and benches among trees.

SOS - at close distance from the exit slip-road.

Aire de **Montmorency**

Forested with a lot of nests of tables and benches.

SOS - 400 m approx. past the rest area.

Aire de la **Chaponne**

Just parking spaces. Grill, self-service.

SOS - at the side of the rest area

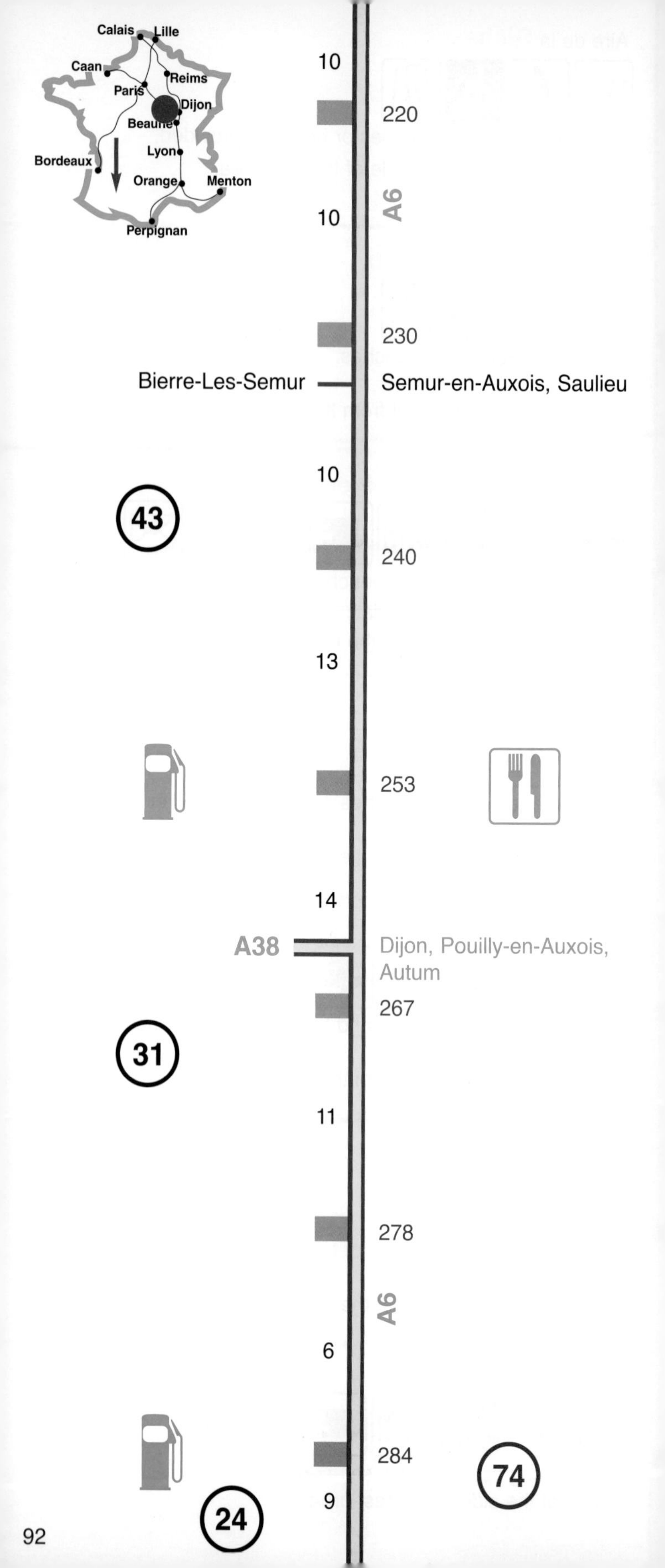
Calais
Lille
Caan
Reims
Paris
Dijon
Beaune
Bordeaux
Lyon
Orange
Menton
Perpignan
10
220
A6
10
230
Bierre-Les-Semur
Semur-en-Auxois, Saulieu
10
43
240
13
253
14
A38
Dijon, Pouilly-en-Auxois, Autum
267
31
11
278
A6
6
284
74
9
24

Aire d' Époisses

Open space type of area with tables and benches.
SOS - at the side of the rest area.

Aire de Ruffey

Open space and grassy. There were no tables or benches.
SOS - located by the entry slip-road to the rest area.

Aire de Fermont

Spacious with tables and benches among trees.
SOS - by the entry to the rest area.

Aire du Chien Blanc

Open space, spacious, interesting features in the layout, tables and benches.
SOS - at the side of the rest area.

Aire de Chaignot

Jungle-like type of site with tables and benches among trees.
SOS - at the side of the rest area.

Aire de la Garenne

Situated on the side of a hill offering panoramic views on the countryside. There are tables and benches.
SOS - at the entry slip-road to the rest area.

Aire de la Forêt

Exceptionally spacious which is not apparent at first, as it is sited beyond the petrol station complex.
SOS - at the side of the rest area.

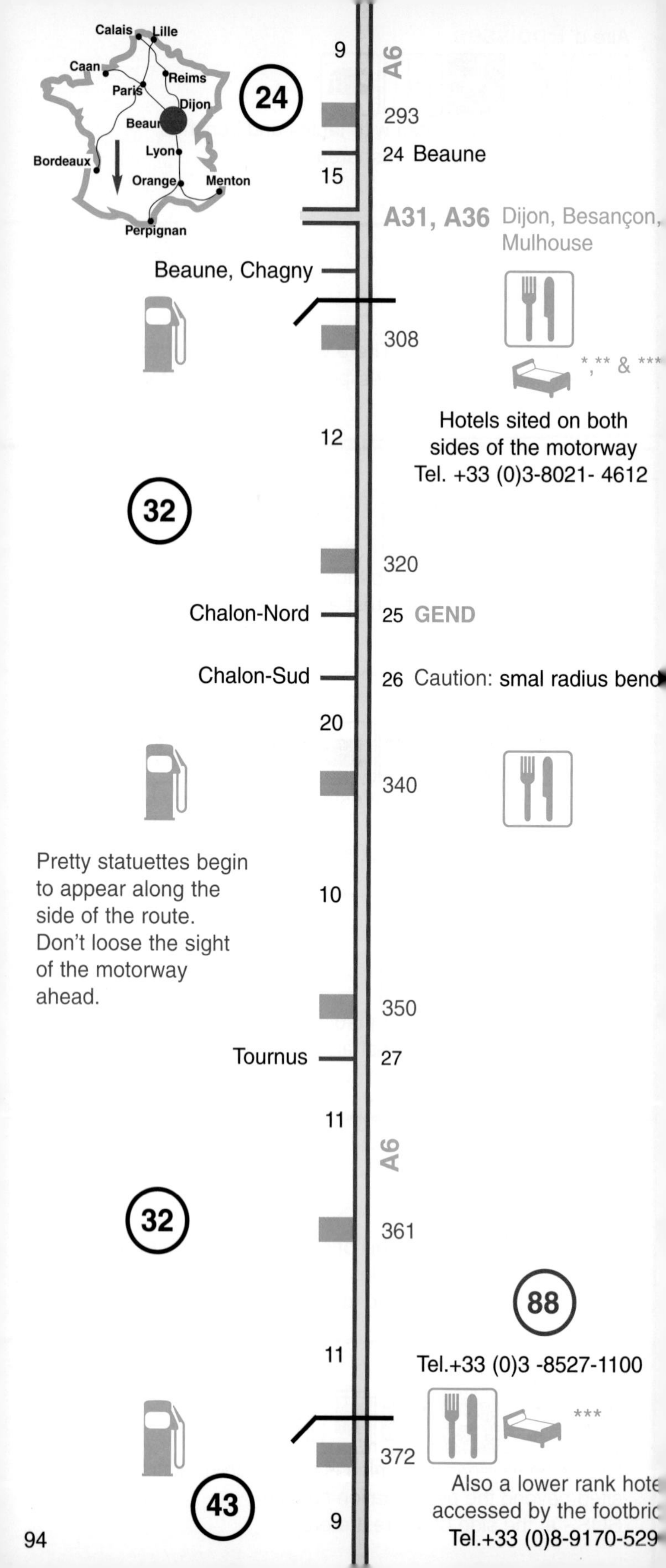
Calais
Lille
Caan
Paris
Reims
Dijon
Beau
Bordeaux
Lyon
Orange
Menton
Perpignan
24
9
A6
293
24 Beaune
15
A31, A36 Dijon, Besançon, Mulhouse
Beaune, Chagny
308
*,** & ***
12
Hotels sited on both sides of the motorway
Tel. +33 (0)3-8021- 4612
32
320
Chalon-Nord
25 GEND
Chalon-Sud
26 Caution: smal radius bend
20
340
Pretty statuettes begin to appear along the side of the route. Don't loose the sight of the motorway ahead.
10
350
Tournus
27
11
A6
32
361
88
11
Tel.+33 (0)3 -8527-1100
***
372
Also a lower rank hote
accessed by the footbric
Tel.+33 (0)8-9170-529
43
9

Aire du Rossignol

Small and pleasant, woodland type of place with tables and benches and some grassy spots.
SOS - located by the entry to the area.

Aire de Beaune-Tailly **(continued from pages 72&73)**

There is The Archeodrome, open to the public throughout the year.
SOS- at the side of the area.

Aire du Curney

There is an impressive Memorial to the victims of the "Beaune" accident of July 31st 1982. See pages 96 & 97.
The rest area is spacious, forested, with tables and benches.
SOS - conspicuously located by the exit from the rest area.

Aire de la Ferté

Just car parking spaces.
SOS - at the side of the rest area.

Aire de Jugy

"Mushroom" rest area

See sample pictures on pages 49, 63, 85, 87, 170

Pique-nique juex d'enfants. It is not enough to say all here look different. See it for yourself. Everything here is designed to look like a mushroom: slides, tables, stools, rubbish bins, toilet buildings. Make your comments.
SOS - at the side of the rest area.

Aire de Farges

Open space type of area, small.

SOS - at the side of the rest area, in close proximity of the entry slip-road.

Aire de Mâcon-St Albain

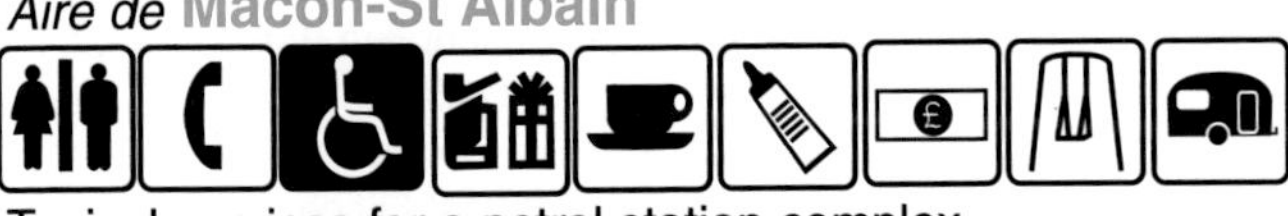

Typical services for a petrol station complex.
Spacious with some tables and benches.
SOS - by the entry to the rest area.

THE BEAUNE MEMORIAL TO

Stop here for a moment, and try to comprehend the contents of these pages. Think for a while and pay your respects to those killed and injured in road accidents

MÉMORIAL

POUR L'AVENIR

The commemorative plaque inscription translated by
Mme Pauline Hallam
Director of Public Relations
in the French Government Tourist Office in London

To do so validates the purpose of this memorial and will help us all to enjoy accident free holidays

MEMORIAL FOR THE FUTURE

Erected by the National Memorial Association for Road Victims.

"To go further than the memory of the dreadful accident near Beaune on the 31st July 1982, the many associations for victims and road safety who contributed to this memorial wish to inspire hope and stimulate the conscience of public opinion against the scourge which the traffic accidents have become."

And, if you translate the word "scourge" into the likely meaning of the word, **"barbarian conquerors"** , this would exactly mean what traffic accidents have become.
Another perception of an invisible enemy.

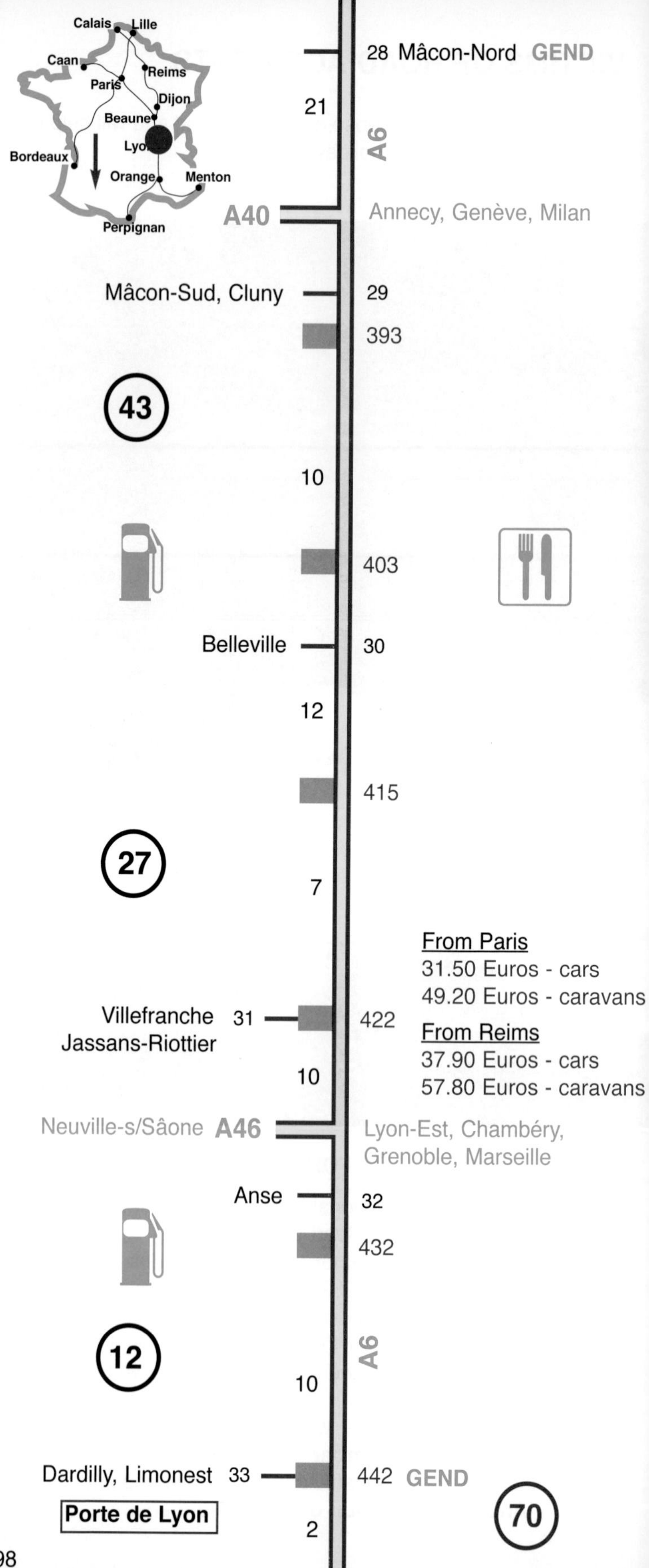
Calais
Lille
Caan
Reims
Paris
Dijon
Beaune
Lyon
Bordeaux
Orange
Menton
Perpignan
28 Mâcon-Nord GEND
21
A6
A40
Annecy, Genève, Milan
Mâcon-Sud, Cluny
29
393
43
10
403
Belleville
30
12
415
27
7
From Paris
31.50 Euros - cars
49.20 Euros - caravans
Villefranche
Jassans-Riottier
31
422
From Reims
37.90 Euros - cars
57.80 Euros - caravans
10
Neuville-s/Sâone
A46
Lyon-Est, Chambéry,
Grenoble, Marseille
Anse
32
432
12
A6
10
Dardilly, Limonest
33
442 GEND
Porte de Lyon
70
2

Aire de **Crèches**

Open space type of area with a lot of nests of tables and stools or benches neatly arranged over the area, attractive.
SOS - at the side of the rest area close to exit slip-road.

Aire de **Dracé**

Open space, tables and benches, lot of grassy area.
SOS - at the entry to the rest area on the left hand side.

Aire de **Patural**

Open space, lot of tables and benches in the open space and shady spots too, attractive.
SOS - located by the entry slip-road.

Aire de **Barrière de Péage de Villafranche-Limas**

Just car parking spaces.

Aire de **Chères**

Spacious, open type of area with tables and benches. Picnic site just past the main service complex.
SOS - at side of the rest area, closer to the entry slip-road.

Porte de Lyon, Limonest, Dardilly. (10 km to Lyon)
Small parking area with no other facilities accessed from a little roundabout off the exit slip-road. It leads to a nest of many hotels, a **CAMPING SITE** and a petrol station with a boutique. At the end of the exit slip-road you turn right.

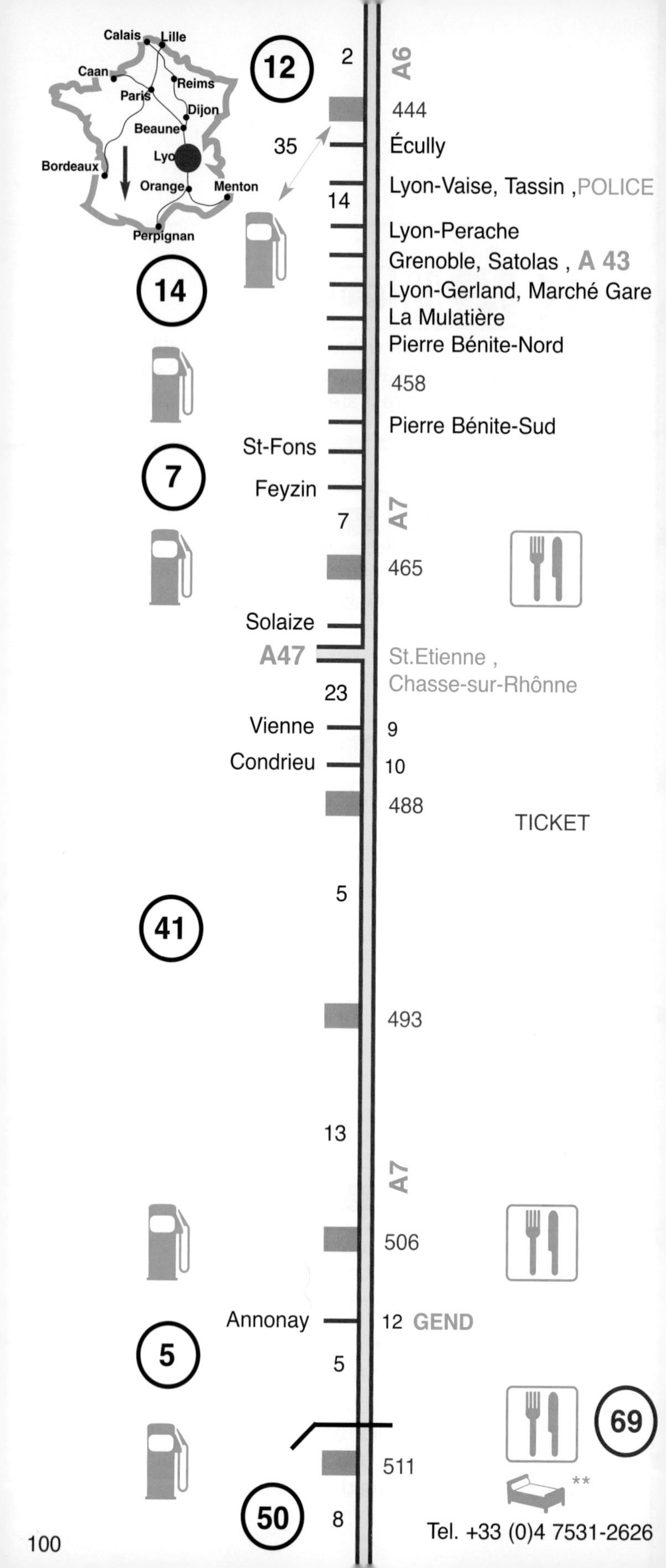

Calais
Lille
Caan
Reims
Paris
Dijon
Beaune
Lyo
Bordeaux
Orange
Menton
Perpignan
12
2
A6
444
35
Écully
Lyon-Vaise, Tassin ,POLICE
14
Lyon-Perache
Grenoble, Satolas , A 43
14
Lyon-Gerland, Marché Gare
La Mulatière
Pierre Bénite-Nord
458
Pierre Bénite-Sud
St-Fons
7
Feyzin
7
A7
465
Solaize
A47
St.Etienne ,
Chasse-sur-Rhônne
23
Vienne
9
Condrieu
10
488
TICKET
5
41
493
13
A7
506
Annonay
12 GEND
5
5
69
511
**
50
8
Tel. +33 (0)4 7531-2626

Aire de Dardilly

Just car parking facilities.
SOS - located at the side of the rest area close to the exit.

Aire de Pierre-Bénite-Nord

Just car parking facilities. The exit for Pierre Bénite and the entry to the rest area are, as one.
SOS - located just before the entry to the rest area.

Aire de Solaize

Just car parking facilities, spacious, well looked after.

Aire de **Barrière de péage de Vienne**

Just car parking facilities. There is a "Station de Gonflage" offering tyre inflating facilities free of charge.

Aire d ' Auberives

Pique-nique jeux d'enfants"- a picnic area, suitable for parties with young children.
SOS - at the side of the rest area.

Aire de Roussillon

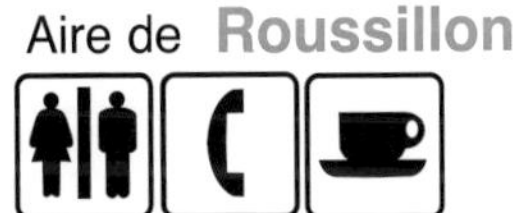

This rest area is meant for lorries onlt. It is mostly grassy with some tables and benches. Cafeteria.
SOS - at the side of the rest area.

Aire de St. Rambert-d'Albon

Incorporates a picnic area with attractive trees and nests of tables and benches.
SOS - at the side of the rest area close to the exit.

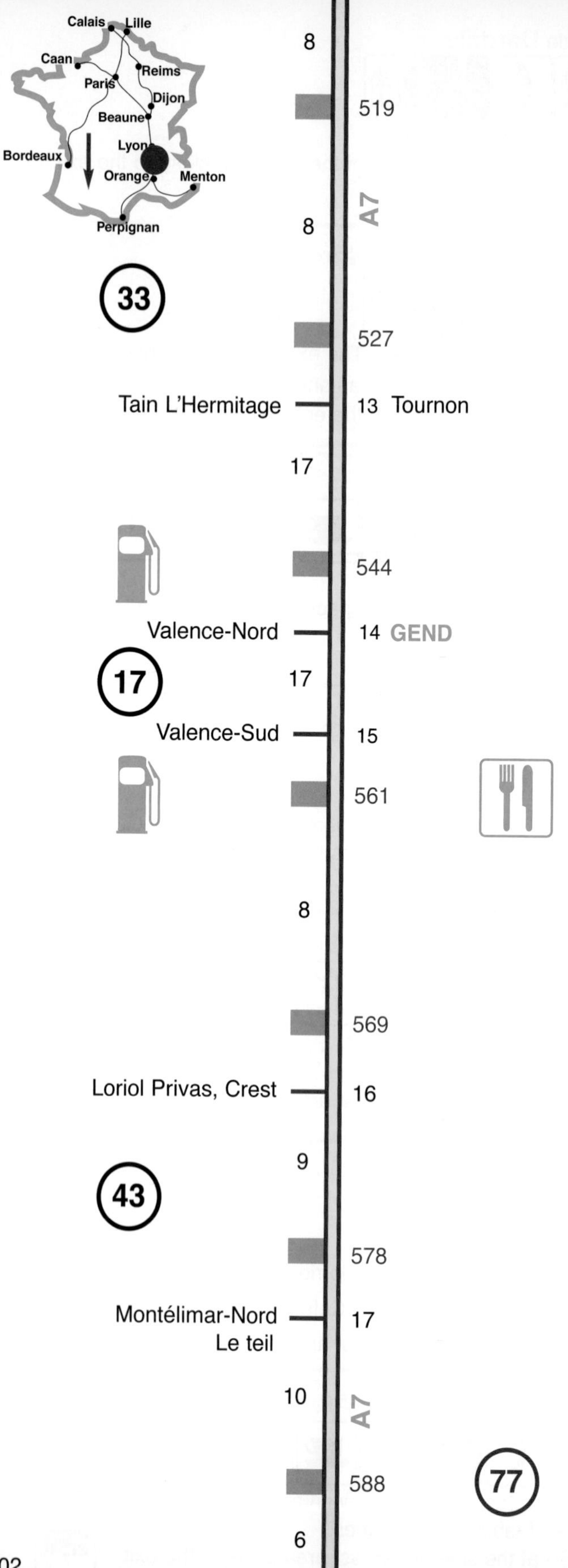
Calais
Lille
Caan
Reims
Paris
Dijon
Beaune
Lyon
Bordeaux
Orange
Menton
Perpignan
8
519
A7
8
33
527
Tain L'Hermitage
13 Tournon
17
544
Valence-Nord
14 GEND
17
17
Valence-Sud
15
561
8
569
Loriol Privas, Crest
16
9
43
578
Montélimar-Nord
Le teil
17
10
A7
588
77
6

Aire de Blacheronde

Immediately after the entry to the rest area on your right hand side there are a lot of tables and benches among trees.
SOS - at the side towards the entry slip-road to the area.

Aire de Bornaron

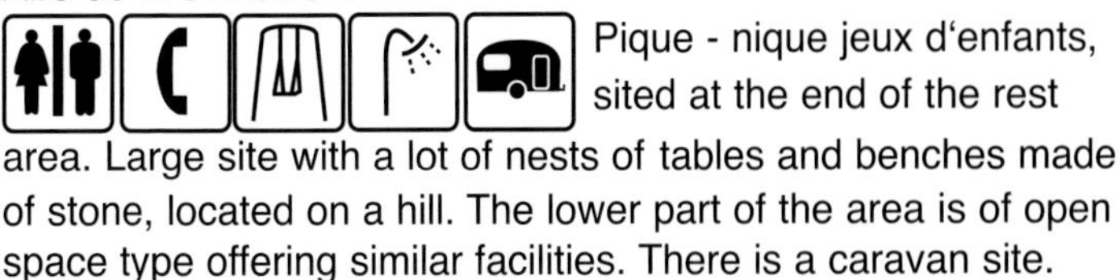

Pique - nique jeux d'enfants, sited at the end of the rest area. Large site with a lot of nests of tables and benches made of stone, located on a hill. The lower part of the area is of open space type offering similar facilities. There is a caravan site.
SOS - at the end of the rest area.

Aire de Pont de l'Isère

A lot of tables and benches arranged neatly in rows, under trees and in the open space area, offering a degree of privacy.
SOS - in close proximity of the entry slip-road.

Aire de Portes-lès-Valence

Pique - nique jeux d'enfants with tables and benches, neatly arranged among trees. Spacious.
SOS - actually on the rest area.

Aire de Bellevue

Small site with nests of tables and stools, some trees, attractive.
SOS - located by the entrance to the rest area.

Aire de Bras de Zil

Spacious with trees and grassy spots. Tables and benches in the open space and under trees.
SOS - at the side of the rest area.

Aire de la Coucourde

Pique - nique jeux d'enfants, spacious, forested, tables and benches. Also a large grassy area.
SOS - just past the rest area.

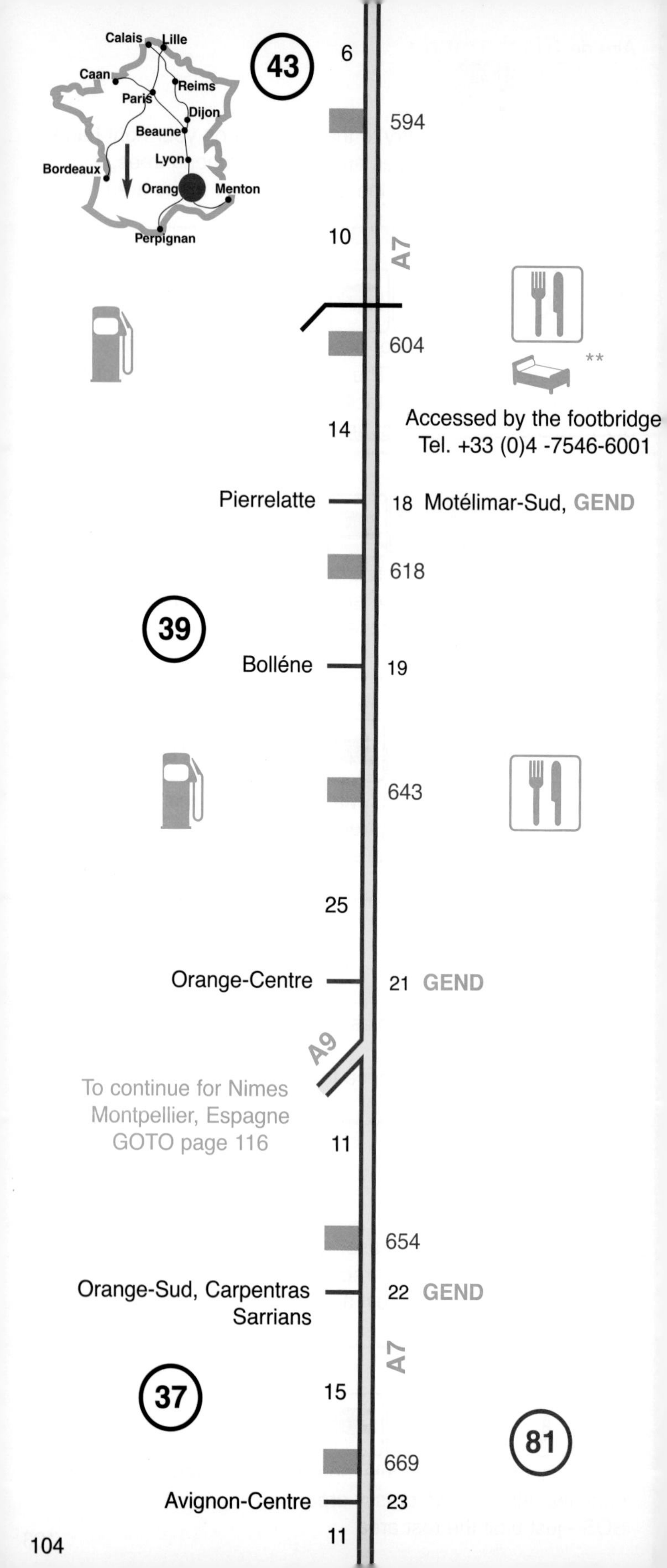

Calais
Lille
Caan
Reims
Paris
Dijon
Beaune
Lyon
Bordeaux
Orang
Menton
Perpignan
43
6
594
10
A7
604
**
Accessed by the footbridge
Tel. +33 (0)4 -7546-6001
14
Pierrelatte
18 Motélimar-Sud, GEND
618
39
Bolléne
19
643
25
Orange-Centre
21 GEND
A9
To continue for Nimes
Montpellier, Espagne
GOTO page 116
11
654
Orange-Sud, Carpentras
Sarrians
22 GEND
A7
37
15
81
669
Avignon-Centre
23
11

Aire de Savasse

Open type of area, yet, there are many shady spots with tables and benches among trees.
SOS - 200 m approx. before the entry to the area.

Aire de Montélimar

Pique-nique jeux d'enfants. It is quite a forest.
SOS - located actually on the rest area by the entry to the footbridge.

Aire de Pierrelatte

Small, open type area with some trees, tables and benches made of stone-like material, located under trees.
SOS - 400 m past the exit from the rest area

Aire de Mornas-Village

Mostly, car parking facilities, few tables and benches.
SOS - at the side by the entry slip-road to the rest area.

Aire d' Orange-Le-Grès

Pique-nique jeux d'enfants, forested, tables and benches among trees offering privacy and shady spots.
SOS - 300 m approx. before the rest area's entry slip-road.

Aire du Fournalet

Pique-nique jeux d'enfants, rather small with tables and benches arranged in a row under trees.
SOS - located on the rest area itself.

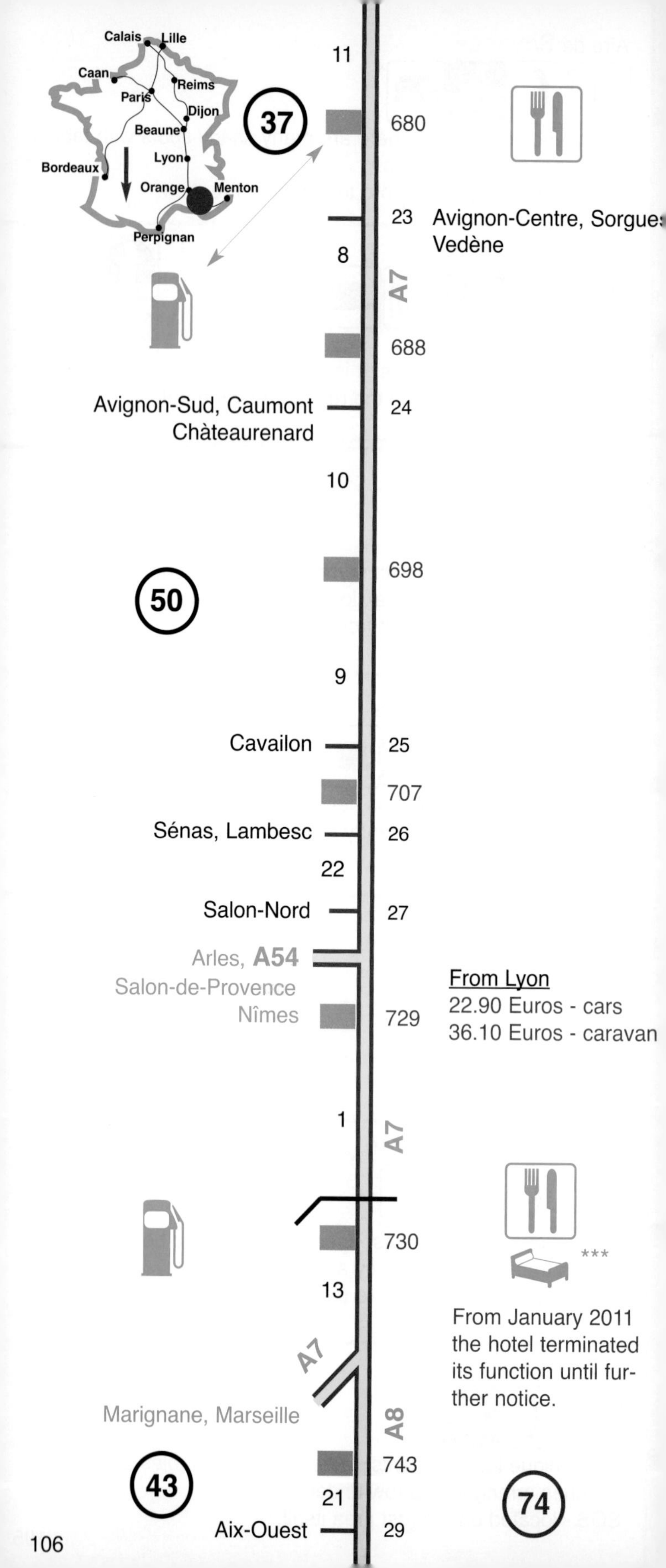

Calais
Lille
Caan
Reims
Paris
Dijon
Beaune
Lyon
Bordeaux
Orange
Menton
Perpignan
37
11
680
23 Avignon-Centre, Sorgues
Vedène
8
A7
688
Avignon-Sud, Caumont
Chàteaurenard
24
10
698
50
9
Cavailon
25
707
Sénas, Lambesc
26
22
Salon-Nord
27
Arles, A54
Salon-de-Provence
Nîmes
729
From Lyon
22.90 Euros - cars
36.10 Euros - caravan
1
A7
730
***
13
From January 2011
the hotel terminated
its function until further notice.
A7
Marignane, Marseille
A8
743
43
21
74
Aix-Ouest
29

Aire de **Morières**

Exceptionally spacious with two sites for caravenners: one offers privacy with many tables and benches among trees, the other one is of an open space site. Both are smart and well looked after. SOS - by the exit slip-road.

Aire de **Cabannes**

Very small, one lane parking, tables and benches.
SOS - 300 approx. from the exit.

Aire de **Cavaillon-Plan d'Orgon**

Two lane parking with tables and benches among trees and also in the open space of grassy area.
SOS - at the side of the rest area

Aire de **Sénas**

Small, two lane parking facilities with tables and benches.
SOS - at side of the rest area.

Aire de **Barrière de péage de Lançon de Provence**

Two lane parking facilities.

Aire de **Lançon de Provence-Ouest**

Ample car parking facilities with some tables and benches
SOS - at side of the rest area.

Aire de **Ventabren-Sud**

Pique-nique jeux d'enfants.
SOS - 400 m approx. before the entry to the rest area.

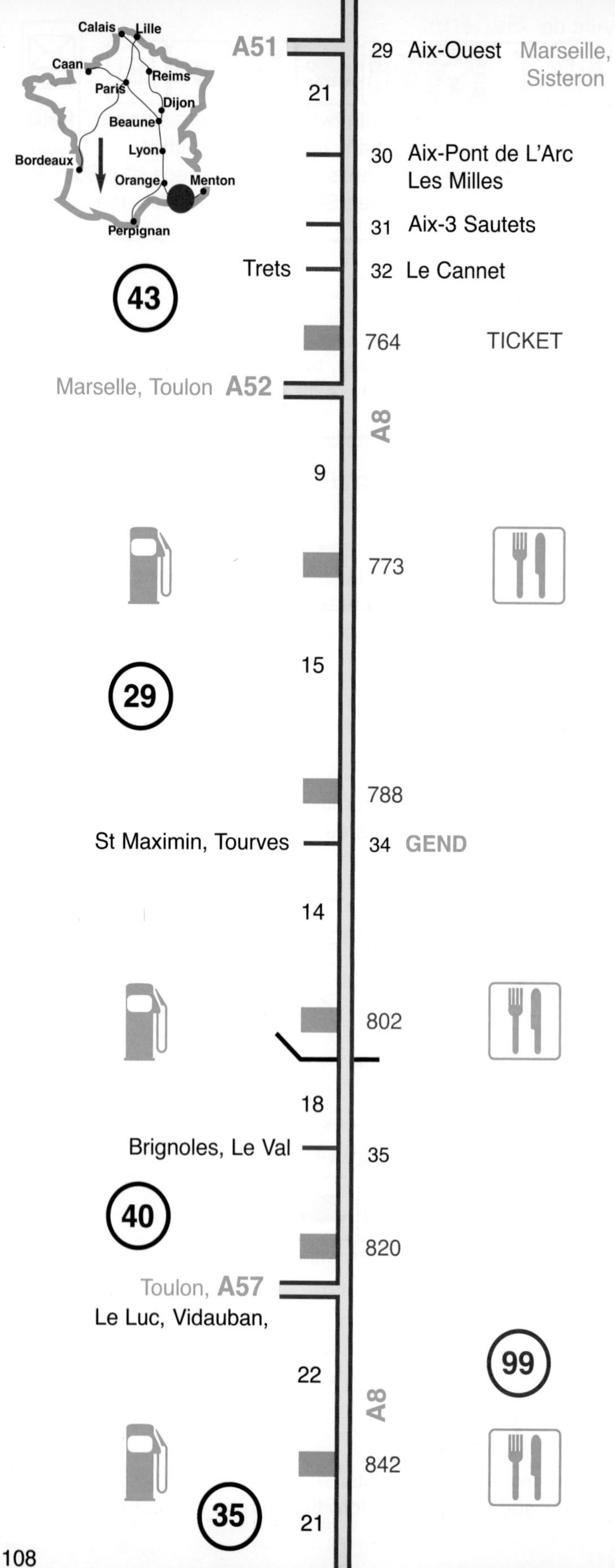
Calais
Lille
Caan
Reims
Paris
Dijon
Beaune
Bordeaux
Lyon
Orange
Menton
Perpignan
A51
29 Aix-Ouest Marseille, Sisteron
21
30 Aix-Pont de L'Arc Les Milles
31 Aix-3 Sautets
Trets
32 Le Cannet
43
764
TICKET
Marselle, Toulon A52
A8
9
773
15
29
788
St Maximin, Tourves
34 GEND
14
802
18
Brignoles, Le Val
35
40
820
Toulon, A57
Le Luc, Vidauban,
99
22
A8
842
35
21

Aire de Barrière de péage (Aix-en- Provence)

The two lane rest area is located at a distance of 100 m away from the toll barrier.

Aire de L'Arc

Mainly car parking facilities, spacious. There are tables and benches among trees.
SOS - at the side of the rest area.

Aire de Barcelone

Tables and benches, some under cover.
SOS - at the side of the rest area.

Aire de Cambarette-Sud

Just parking facilities, interconnected with the other side of the motorway rest area by a link-road.
SOS - at the side of the rest area.

Aire de Roudaï

Sited on the side of a hill, spacious, many tables and benches among trees.
SOS - located by the entry to the rest area. Another one is located at the upper level of the rest area.

Aire de Vidauban-Sud

Just parking facilities.
SOS - at the side towards the entry slip-road.

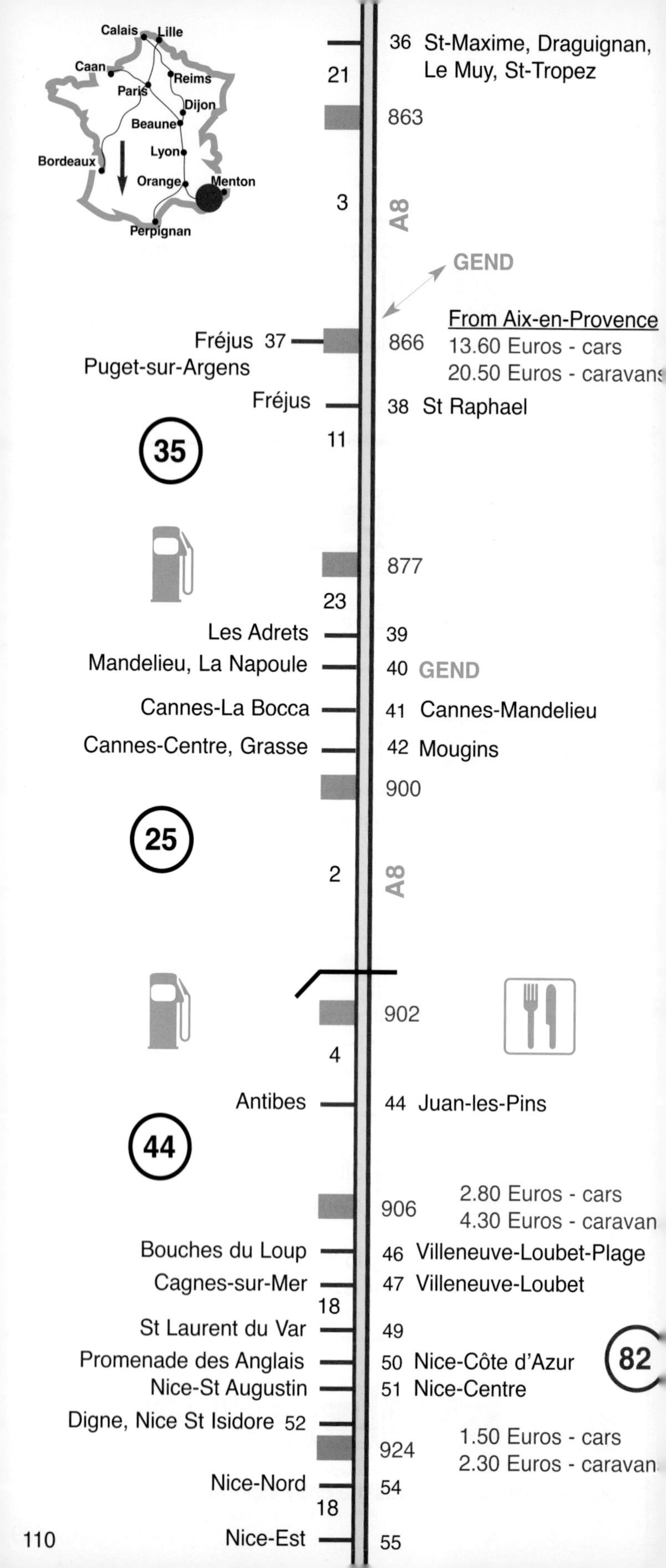
Calais
Lille
Caan
Reims
Paris
Dijon
Beaune
Bordeaux
Lyon
Orange
Menton
Perpignan
36 St-Maxime, Draguignan, Le Muy, St-Tropez
21
863
3
A8
GEND
From Aix-en-Provence
13.60 Euros - cars
20.50 Euros - caravans
Fréjus 37
Puget-sur-Argens
866
Fréjus
38 St Raphael
11
35
877
23
Les Adrets
39
Mandelieu, La Napoule
40 GEND
Cannes-La Bocca
41 Cannes-Mandelieu
Cannes-Centre, Grasse
42 Mougins
900
25
2
A8
902
4
Antibes
44 Juan-les-Pins
44
906
2.80 Euros - cars
4.30 Euros - caravan
Bouches du Loup
46 Villeneuve-Loubet-Plage
Cagnes-sur-Mer
47 Villeneuve-Loubet
18
St Laurent du Var
49
Promenade des Anglais
50 Nice-Côte d'Azur
82
Nice-St Augustin
51 Nice-Centre
Digne, Nice St Isidore 52
924
1.50 Euros - cars
2.30 Euros - caravan
Nice-Nord
54
18
Nice-Est
55

Aire du Jas Pellicot

Small, many tables and benches, exotic trees, attractive.
SOS - at the side of the rest area.

Aire de Barrière de péage (Capitou)

Two lane parking facilities.
Gendarmerie Station.
SOS - actually on the rest area.

Aire de L'Esterel

Sited on a hill, slides, swings, towers, climbing frames, tables and benches, attractive.
SOS - sited on the rest area just past the petrol station complex, another one is close to the exit from the rest area.

Aire de Belvédère du Piccolaret

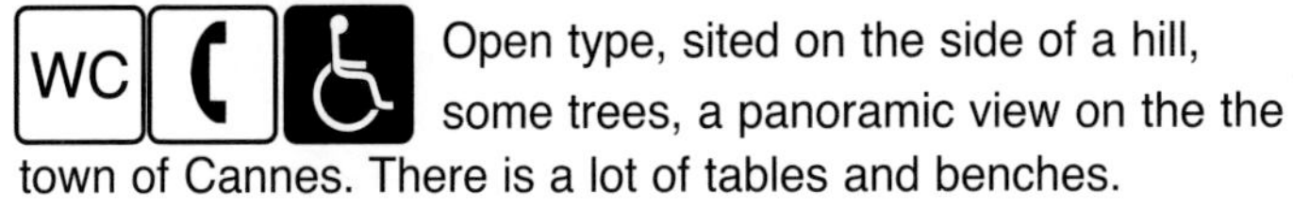

Open type, sited on the side of a hill, some trees, a panoramic view on the the town of Cannes. There is a lot of tables and benches.

SOS - actually on the rest area itself.

Aire des Bréguières-Sud

Spacious with some tables and benches.
An Automobile Museum has its place here. Both, the museum and the restaurant are accessed by the footbridge.

Aire de Barrière de péage (d'Antibes)

The rest area is sited about 200 m before the "Barrière de Péage" .

Aire de Barrière de péage (Nice St-Isidore)

Small, two lane parking facilities, just past the toll barrier.

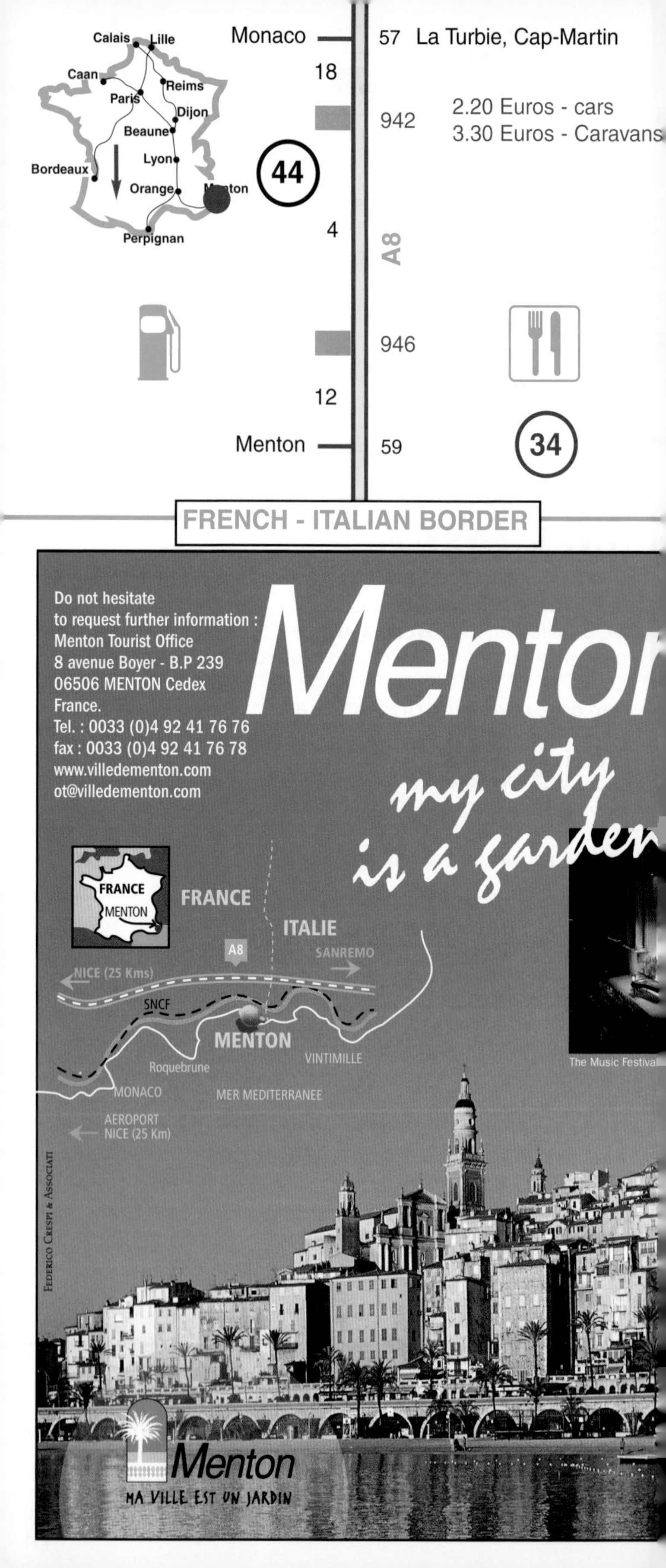
Calais
Lille
Caan
Reims
Paris
Dijon
Beaune
Lyon
Bordeaux
Orange
Menton
Perpignan
44
Monaco
57 La Turbie, Cap-Martin
18
942
2.20 Euros - cars
3.30 Euros - Caravans
4
A8
946
12
Menton
59
34
FRENCH - ITALIAN BORDER
Do not hesitate
to request further information :
Menton Tourist Office
8 avenue Boyer - B.P 239
06506 MENTON Cedex
France.
Tel. : 0033 (0)4 92 41 76 76
fax : 0033 (0)4 92 41 76 78
www.villedementon.com
ot@villedementon.com
Menton
my city
is a garden
FRANCE
MENTON
FRANCE
ITALIE
A8
SANREMO
NICE (25 Kms)
SNCF
MENTON
VINTIMILLE
Roquebrune
MONACO
MER MEDITERRANEE
AEROPORT
NICE (25 Km)
The Music Festival
FEDERICO CRESPI & ASSOCIATI
Menton
MA VILLE EST UN JARDIN

Aire de **Barrière de péage de la Turbie**

Two lane car parking facilities.

Aire de **Beausoleil**

Attractive rest area, sited on the side of a hill by the sea with a panoramic view of Monaco.
SOS - located just before the entry to the rest area.

Between the sea and the mountains...
Nestling between Monaco and the Italian Riviera, Menton is one of the rare "Towns of Art and History" on the French Riviera. Enjoying a microclimate that tends towards sub-tropical, it is famed for its exceptional gardens. This seaside resort is also ideally placed for visits to the countryside just inland from the coast, which abounds in small medieval and handicraft villages, and opportunities for sporting and cultural activities.
For a successful holiday...
Varied accommodation for all tastes with a selection of hotels of all categories, holiday residences, campsites, self-catering apartments, a youth hostel, country cottages, ... As well as a Casino, its numerous restaurants, beaches, a nautical club, ...
The Lemon Festival®
And events throughout the year...
Menton proposes a program of events, some with an international reputation, for instance "The Lemon Festival® " in February, "Garden Month" in June, "Music Festival" in August, "Mediterranean Garden Days" in September and "Christmases of the World" in December/January ...
hristmas in Menton
Reply Coupon :
Please send me further information regarding
The "Lemon Festival®"
Menton Music Festival
Christmas in Menton
Accommodation
Language, Culture & Gastronomy Courses
Other ....
Name : ....
First Name : ....
Address : ....
Tel. : ....
e-mail : ....

Menton

FROM
ORANGE
TO
FRENCH/SPANISH BORDER

Autoroute A9

Aude Hôtel

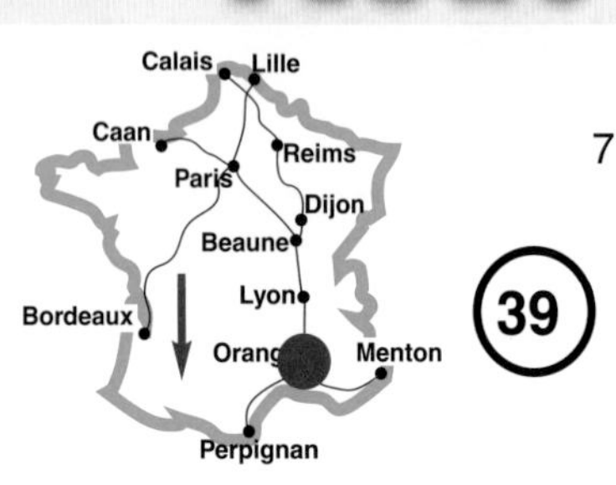

For the hotel location see page 122

7

39

A7

Bolléne — 19

643

Orange-Centre — 21 GEND

A7

9

For Marseille, Menton and Italy GOTO page 106

27

662

Roquemaure, Avignon — 22

8

A9

670

Tel.+33 (0)4-6650-3255

8

28

678

35

12

Remoulins — 23

Aude Hôtel

★★

The hotel is located In the calm setting of a popular grove in the Narbonne-Vinassan Nord service park and offers:

59 air-conditioned, sound-proofed rooms with hair dryer, direct-dialling tele-phone, satellite TV, buffet breakfast, quality restau-rant, semina facilities - groups welcome, parking facilities, garages and **courteous welcome by the hotel Reception round the clock**.

Aire de **Mornas-Village** (shown here for reference only)

Continued from page 104

Aire de **Roquemaure-Nord**

Tables and benches under trees, tidy, interesting.
SOS - actually on the rest area close to the entry slip-road.

Aire de **Tavel-Nord**

Spacious with tables and benches among trees and in the open space. Pique-nique site, forested.
SOS - located by the exit from the rest area.

Aire de **Estezargues-Nord**

Pique-nique site, some pretty spots of attractive trees.
Wooden tables and benches, spacious.
SOS - at the side of the rest area.

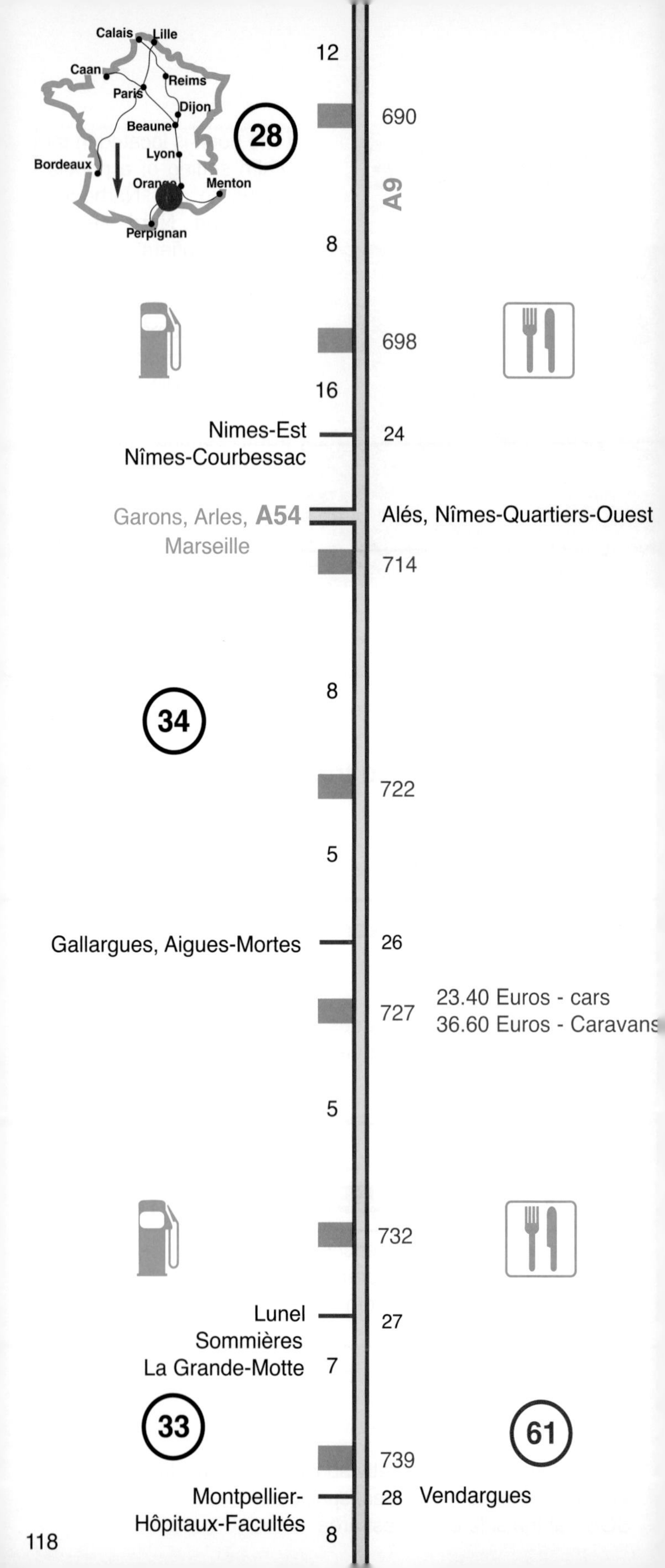
Calais
Lille
Caan
Reims
Paris
Dijon
Beaune
Lyon
Bordeaux
Orange
Menton
Perpignan
28
12
690
A9
8
698
16
Nimes-Est
Nîmes-Courbessac
24
Garons, Arles, A54
Marseille
Alés, Nîmes-Quartiers-Ouest
714
8
34
722
5
Gallargues, Aigues-Mortes
26
727
23.40 Euros - cars
36.60 Euros - Caravans
5
732
Lunel
Sommières
La Grande-Motte
27
7
33
61
739
Montpellier-
Hôpitaux-Facultés
28
Vendargues
8

Aire de **Ledenon-Nord**

Open space type of area with some tables and benches made of concrete-like material.
SOS - located just before the exit from the rest area.

Aire de **Nîmes-Marguerittes**

Open space type of site with a pique-nique site at the end of the rest area, some tables and benches.
SOS - at the end of the exit slip-road from the area.

Aire de **Milhaud-Nord**

Arranged on three levels of ground configuration.
The most upper level is best suitable for caravanners, there are table and benches.
SOS - at the side of the area, not easy to spot it.

Aire de **Vergéze-Nord**

Spacious, forested with a pique-nique site, tables and benches. Caravanners site is at the upper level with parking bays offering a degree of privacy.
SOS - conspicuously placed by the exit from the rest area.

Aire de **Barrière de péage (Monpellier 1)**

Apparent lack of facilities of any kind.

Aire d' **Ambrussum-Nord**

Caravanners site located at the end of the rest area towards the exit slip-road.
SOS - on the right hand side at the entry slip-road.

Aire de **Nabrigas**

There are tables and benches in the open space and among trees, also, swings and climbing frames.
SOS - at the side by the entry slip-road.

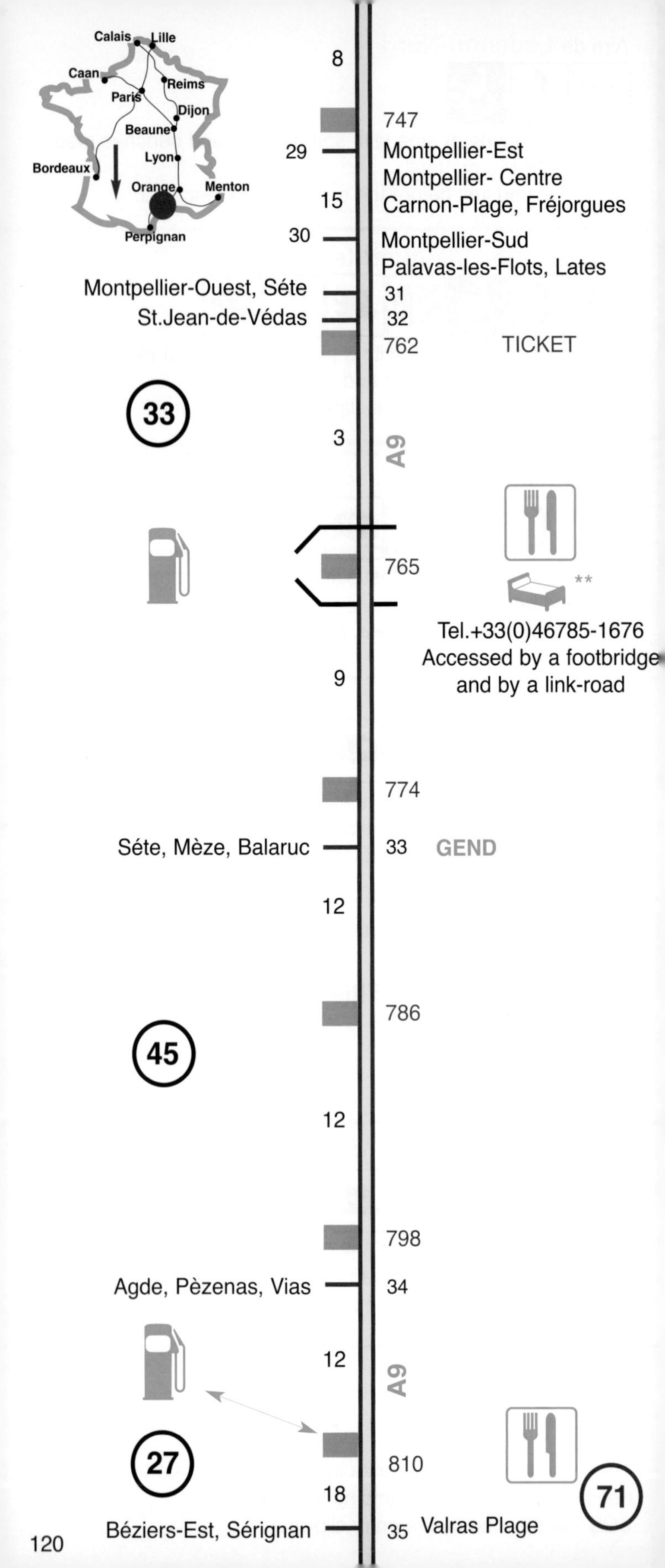
Calais
Lille
Caan
Reims
Paris
Dijon
Beaune
Lyon
Bordeaux
Orange
Menton
Perpignan
8
747
29
Montpellier-Est
Montpellier- Centre
15
Carnon-Plage, Fréjorgues
30
Montpellier-Sud
Palavas-les-Flots, Lates
Montpellier-Ouest, Séte
31
St.Jean-de-Védas
32
762
TICKET
33
3
A9
765
**
Tel.+33(0)46785-1676
Accessed by a footbridge
and by a link-road
9
774
Séte, Mèze, Balaruc
33
GEND
12
786
45
12
798
Agde, Pèzenas, Vias
34
12
A9
810
27
71
18
Béziers-Est, Sérignan
35
Valras Plage

Aire de St Aunès-Nord

Table and benches, small but pretty.
SOS - at the side of the rest area.

Aire de **Barrière de péage (Montpellier 2)**

Apparent lack of facilities of any kind

Aire de Montpellier-Fabrègues-Nord

Densely forested site with many tables and benches among trees. There is a caravenners site.
SOS - conspicuously placed at the end of the rest areay the exit slip-road.

Aire de Gigean-Nord

Open space area with some trees, tables and benches.
SOS - at the side of the rest area.

Aire de Mèze

Forested, table and benches among trees. Pique-nique site.
SOS - conspicuously placed on the rest area before the exit slip-road.

Aire de Florensac-Nord

Two lane parking facilities, some tables and benches among trees.
SOS - at the side of the rest area.

Aire de Beziérs-Montblanc-Nord

There is a caravan site at the end of the rest area.
SOS - at the side, close to the exit slip-road.

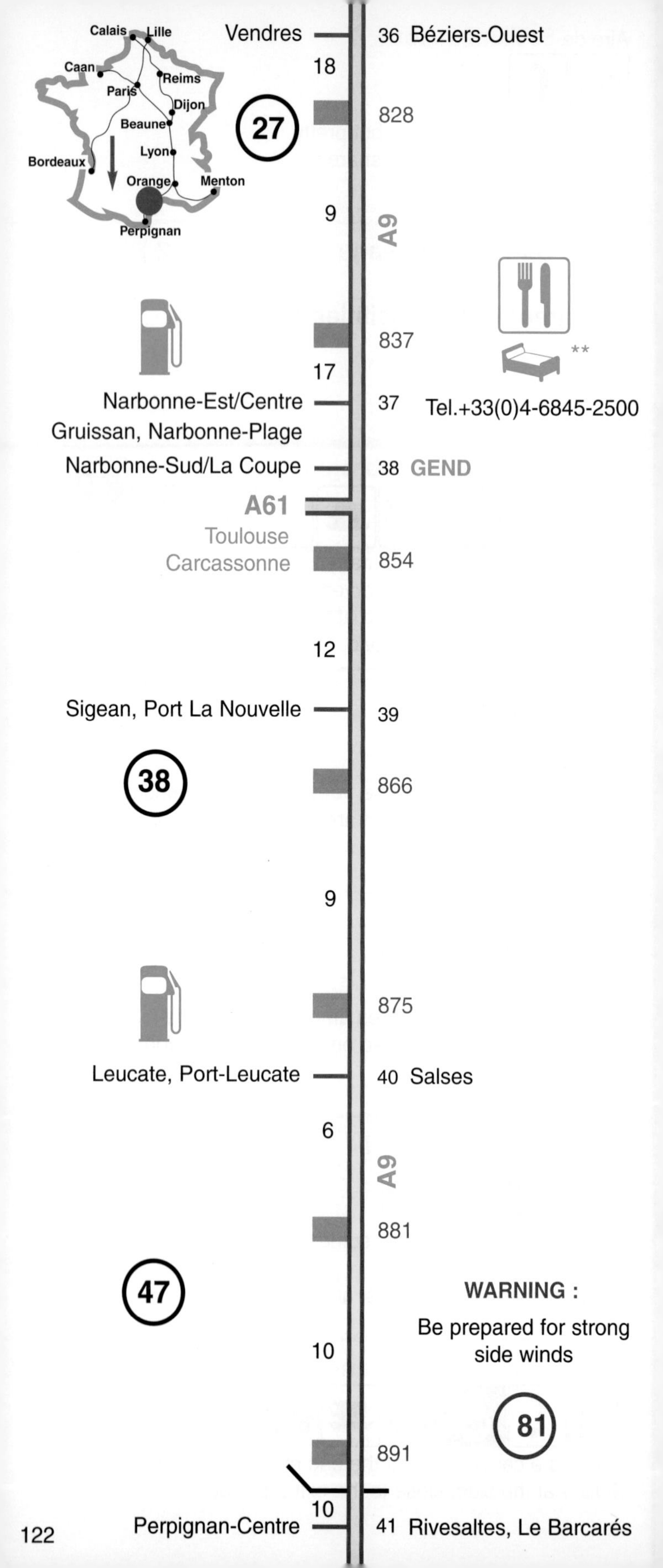

Calais
Lille
Caan
Reims
Paris
Dijon
Beaune
Lyon
Bordeaux
Orange
Menton
Perpignan
27
Vendres
36 Béziers-Ouest
18
828
9
A9
837
17
Narbonne-Est/Centre
Gruissan, Narbonne-Plage
37
Tel.+33(0)4-6845-2500
Narbonne-Sud/La Coupe
38 GEND
A61
Toulouse
Carcassonne
854
12
Sigean, Port La Nouvelle
39
38
866
9
875
Leucate, Port-Leucate
40 Salses
6
A9
881
47
WARNING :
Be prepared for strong side winds
10
81
891
10
Perpignan-Centre
41 Rivesaltes, Le Barcarés

Aire de Lespignan-Nord

There is a lot of nests of tables and benches.
SOS - at the side of the rest area.

Aire de Narbonne-Vinassan-Nord

Pique - nique jeux d'enfants, tables and benches, modest in size.
SOS - at the side of the rest area.

Aire de Prat de Cest

Slightly forested, sited on a raised ground with tables and benches among trees, incorporates a picnic site.
SOS - located actually on the rest area by the entry slip-road.

Aire des Gasparets

Arranged on two levels of the ground configuration, tables and benches among trees. There is a picnic site at the upper part of the rest area.
SOS - at the side of the rest area.

Aire de Lapalme-Ouest

Spacious with many tables and benches among trees and in the open space.
SOS - at the side of the rest area.

Aire de Fitou-Ouest

Two lane open space type of area with a few tables and benches under trees.
SOS - at the side of the rest area.

Aire de Château de Salses

Open space with bushy trees, nests of tables and benches arranged under covers. Panoramic view on the Méditerranée.
SOS - by the motorway at the end of the rest area.

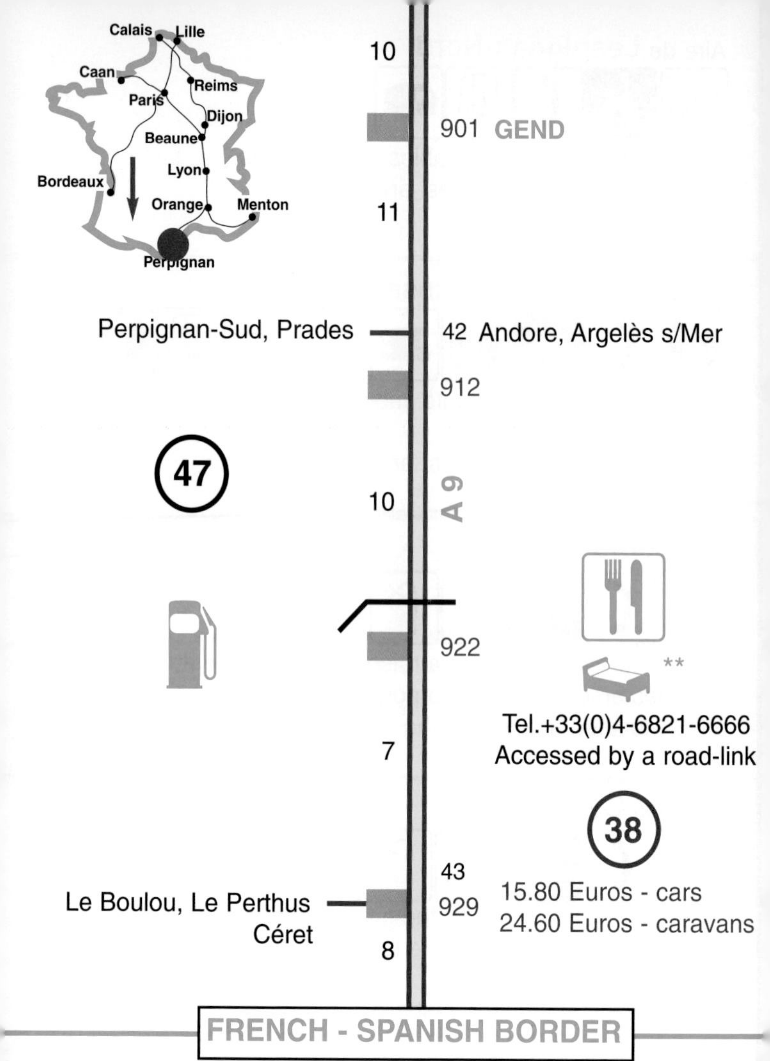
Calais
Lille
Caan
Paris
Reims
Dijon
Beaune
Lyon
Bordeaux
Orange
Menton
Perpignan
10
901 GEND
11
Perpignan-Sud, Prades
42 Andore, Argelès s/Mer
912
47
10
A 9
922
**
Tel.+33(0)4-6821-6666
Accessed by a road-link
7
38
43
Le Boulou, Le Perthus
Céret
929
15.80 Euros - cars
24.60 Euros - caravans
8
FRENCH - SPANISH BORDER

Aire de Riversaltes

Two lane parking facilities with nests of tables and benches arranged among trees, offering privacy of picnicking. Gendarmerie Station at the back of the rest area. SOS - located on the rest area by the entry slip-road.

Aire de Pavillons-Ouest

Two lane rest area with tables and benches among trees. SOS - located by the entry.

Aire du Village Catalan-Ouest

Exceptionally spacious rest area, located at the other side of the motorway, sign-posted. Large picnicking area with shops nearby accessd by the link-road.

Aire de Barrière de péage de Boulou (Perthus)

Just a car parking bay.

FROM
PARIS
TO
BORDEAUX

Autoroute A10

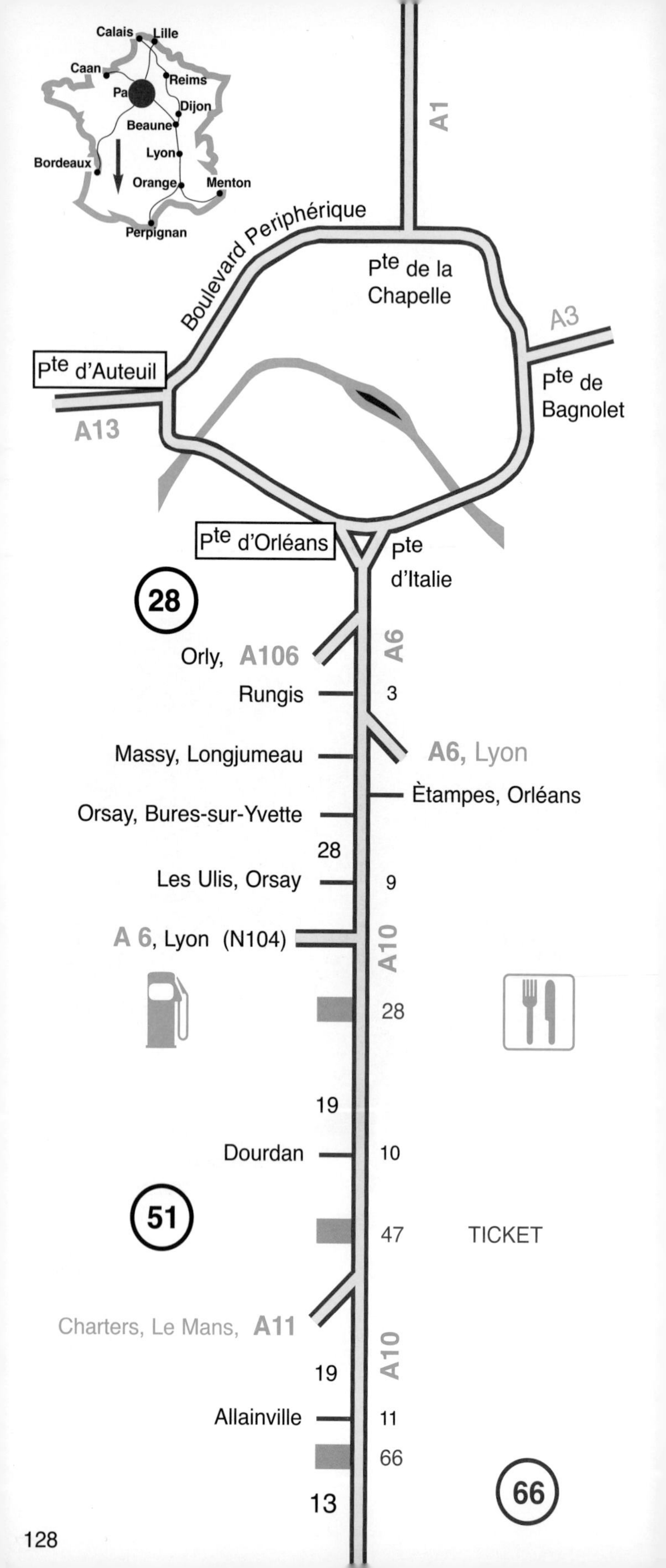
Calais
Lille
Caan
Pa
Reims
Dijon
Beaune
Bordeaux
Lyon
Orange
Menton
Perpignan
A1
Boulevard Periphérique
Pte de la Chapelle
A3
Pte d'Auteuil
Pte de Bagnolet
A13
Pte d'Orléans
Pte d'Italie
28
Orly, A106
A6
Rungis
3
Massy, Longjumeau
A6, Lyon
Ètampes, Orléans
Orsay, Bures-sur-Yvette
28
Les Ulis, Orsay
9
A 6, Lyon (N104)
A10
28
19
Dourdan
10
51
47
TICKET
Charters, Le Mans, A11
A10
19
Allainville
11
66
13
66

Aire de **Limours-Janvry**

Just parking facilities.

SOS - located by the side of the rest area.

Aire de **Barrière de péage (La Folie Bessin)**

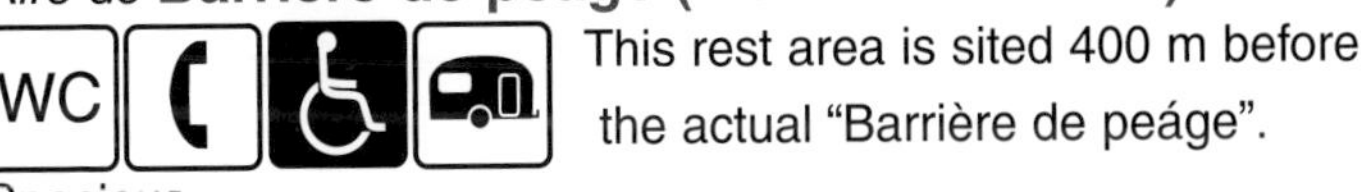

This rest area is sited 400 m before the actual "Barrière de peáge".

Spacious.

SOS - located by the entrance to the only building on the rest area.

Aire de **Boutroux**

Spacious, many sets of tables and benches in the open space and among trees offering privacy of picnicking and caravanning. Good hiding place during hot summer days.

SOS - conspicuously located by the exit slip-road.

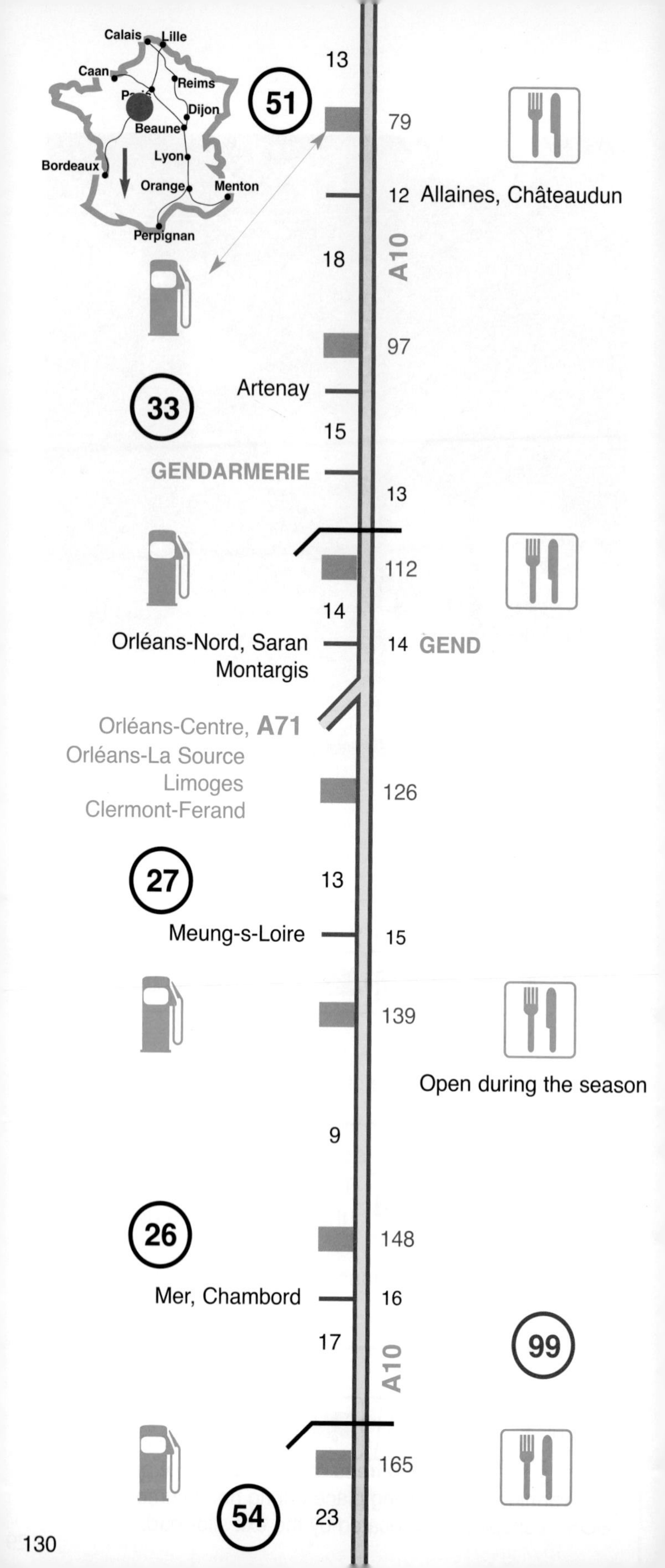
Calais
Lille
Caan
Reims
Paris
Dijon
Beaune
Lyon
Bordeaux
Orange
Menton
Perpignan
51
13
79
12 Allaines, Châteaudun
18
A10
97
Artenay
33
15
GENDARMERIE
13
112
14
Orléans-Nord, Saran
Montargis
14 GEND
Orléans-Centre, A71
Orléans-La Source
Limoges
Clermont-Ferand
126
27
13
Meung-s-Loire
15
139
Open during the season
9
26
148
Mer, Chambord
16
17
A10
99
165
54
23

Aire de Francheville

Spacious in parking facilities.

SOS - located 300 m approx. past the rest area.

Aire du Héron-Cendré

Spacious, jungle-like area with many sets of tables and benches, offering privacy of picnicking.
SOS - at the side of the rest area.

Aire d' Orléans-Saran

Just ample parking facilities.

SOS - conspicuously placed, close to the restaurant.

Aire de Bellevue

Small, open space, tables and benches. The rest area is not signed for caravanners, but it would do nicely.
SOS - conspicuously sited by the exit slip-road on the left hand side.

Aire de Meung-sur-Loire

Few tables and benches.
The restaurant doesn't operate all year round.

Aire des Fougères

Open type of site with lots of tables and benches neatly arranged among trees and in the open space.
SOS - at the side of the rest area.

Aire de Blois-Villerbon

Spacious.
SOS - located at the side of motorway close to the footbridge.
Another one sited in close proximity of the exit slip-road.

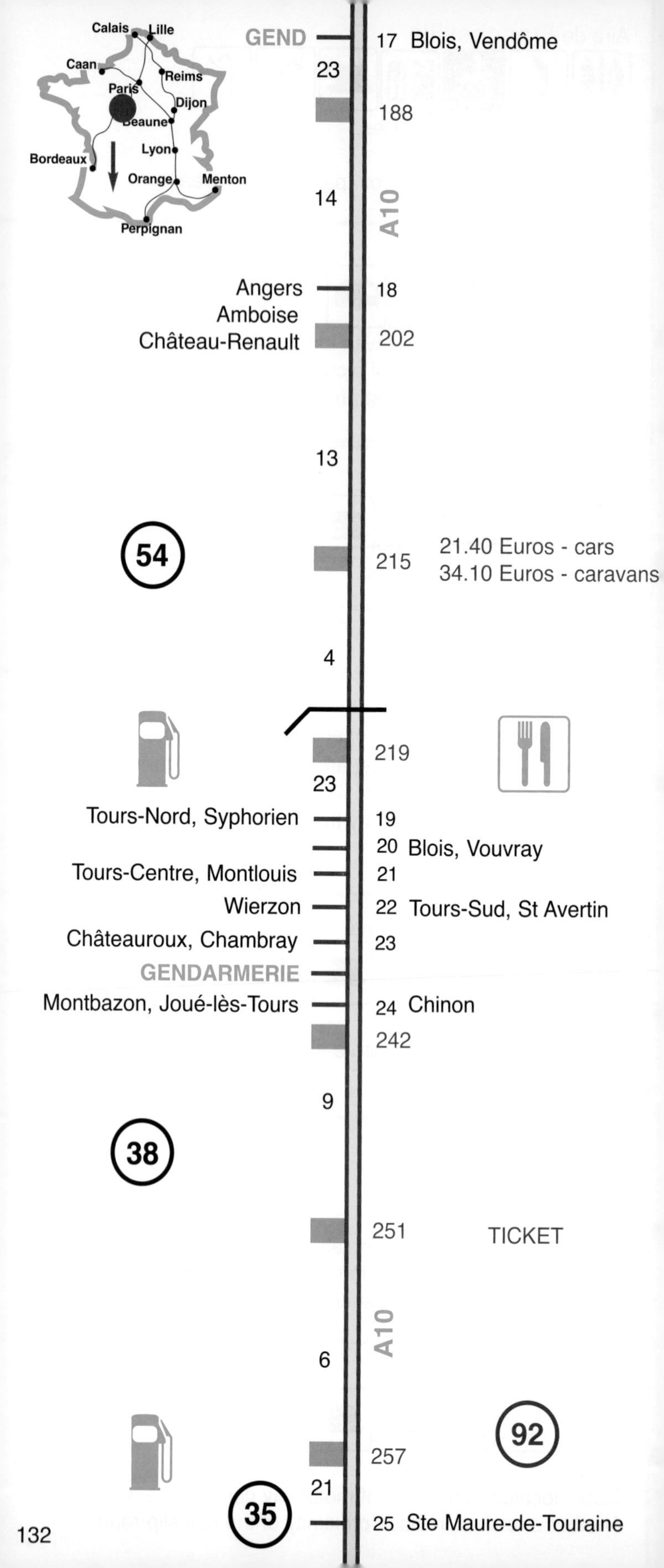
Calais
Lille
Caan
Reims
Paris
Dijon
Beaune
Lyon
Bordeaux
Orange
Menton
Perpignan
GEND
17 Blois, Vendôme
23
188
14
A10
Angers
Amboise
Château-Renault
18
202
13
54
215
21.40 Euros - cars
34.10 Euros - caravans
4
219
23
Tours-Nord, Syphorien
19
20 Blois, Vouvray
Tours-Centre, Montlouis
21
Wierzon
22 Tours-Sud, St Avertin
Châteauroux, Chambray
23
GENDARMERIE
Montbazon, Joué-lès-Tours
24 Chinon
242
9
38
251
TICKET
A10
6
92
257
21
35
25 Ste Maure-de-Touraine

Aire de la **Chatière**

Many lots of tables and benches in the open space and also among trees, offering privacy of picnicking. Good hiding place from hot weather days.
SOS - on the right hand side by the entry slip-road.

Aire de la **Courte Épée**

Plenty of nests of tables and benches among trees, many apparatus for children to keep them busy. The rest area is compatible with the one above.

Aire de **Barrière de péage (Monnaie) Tours**

Open space type of site with some tables and benches
SOS - located 300 meters approx. before the entry to the rest area.

Aire de **Tours la longue Vue**

Mostly parking facilities.
SOS - conspicuously placed by the side of area toward the exit slip-road.

Aire du **Village-Brûlé**

Forested, with a lot of tables and benches. Spacious.
SOS - at the side of the rest area, conspicuously placed.

Aire de **Barrière de péage (Sorigny) Tours**

There are some tables and benches.
There is a “Station de gonflage” offering tyre inflating facilities, free of charge.

Aire de **Ste-Maure-de-Touraine**

Mainly parking spaces.
SOS - located at the side of the rest area.

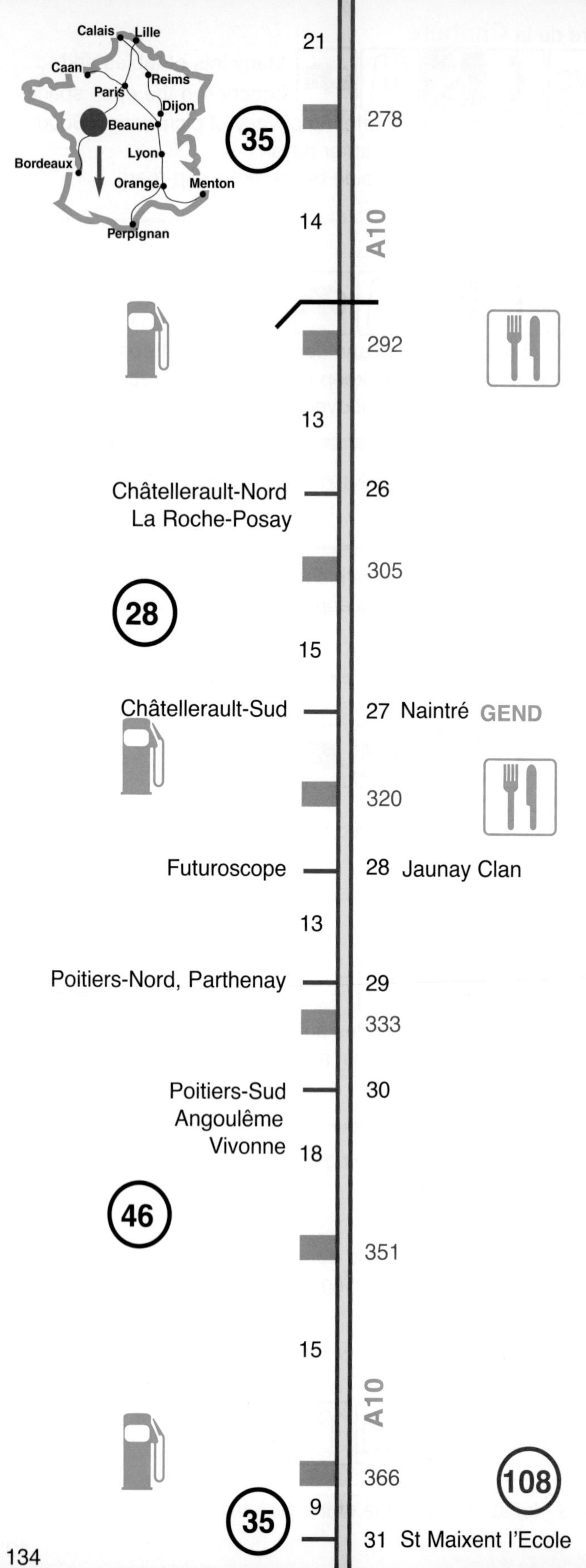
Calais
Lille
Caan
Reims
Paris
Dijon
Beaune
Lyon
Bordeaux
Orange
Menton
Perpignan
21
35
278
14
A10
292
13
Châtellerault-Nord
La Roche-Posay
26
305
28
15
Châtellerault-Sud
27 Naintré GEND
320
Futuroscope
28 Jaunay Clan
13
Poitiers-Nord, Parthenay
29
333
Poitiers-Sud
Angoulême
Vivonne
30
18
46
351
15
A10
366
108
9
35
31 St Maixent l'Ecole

Aire de Maillé

Forested with plenty of tables and benches.
SOS - located by the entry to the rest area.

Aire de Châtellerault-Antran

Just parking spaces.
Post Office Box located by the entrance to the cafeteria.
SOS - by the side of the rest area.

Aire des Meuniers

Forested, tables and benches, spacious. The telephone located on the wall by the entrance to the WC, tidy, well looked after.
SOS - at the side of the rest area.

Aire de Poitiers Jaunay-Clan

Just parking facilities. Small.

SOS - at the side towards the end of the rest area.

Aire des Cent Saptiers

Open space type of site with tables and benches.
SOS - at the side of the motorway, easily seem from the rest area.

Aire de Coulombiers-Nord

Open space site, some trees, tables and benches, tidy.
SOS - located at the side of motorway toward the entry slip-road.

Aire de Rouillé-Pamproux

Caution: small radius bend at the entry to the rest area.
Lots of tables and benches, mostly in the open space.
Parcours de santé.

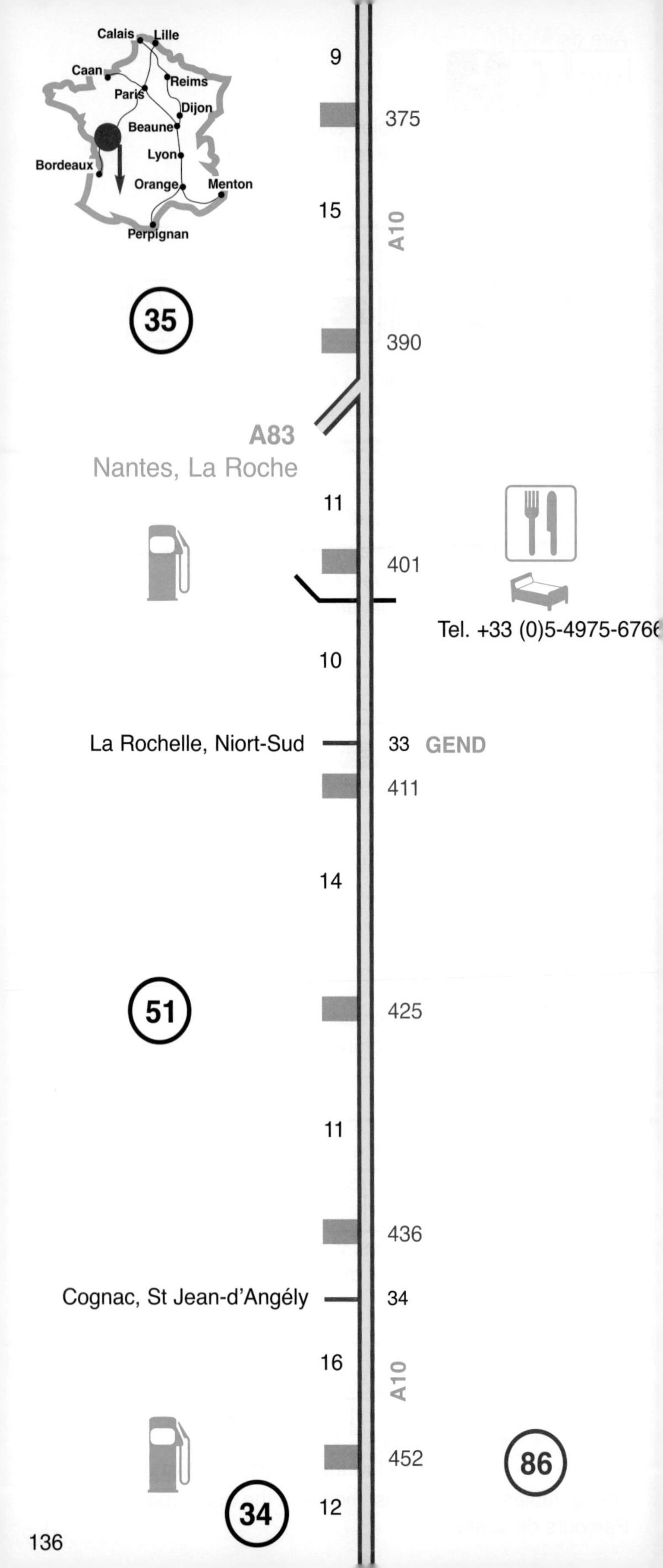
Calais
Lille
Caan
Reims
Paris
Dijon
Beaune
Lyon
Bordeaux
Orange
Menton
Perpignan
9
375
15
A10
35
390
A83
Nantes, La Roche
11
401
Tel. +33 (0)5-4975-676
10
La Rochelle, Niort-Sud
33 GEND
411
14
51
425
11
436
Cognac, St Jean-d'Angély
34
16
A10
452
86
34
12

Aire de Ste Eanne-Nord

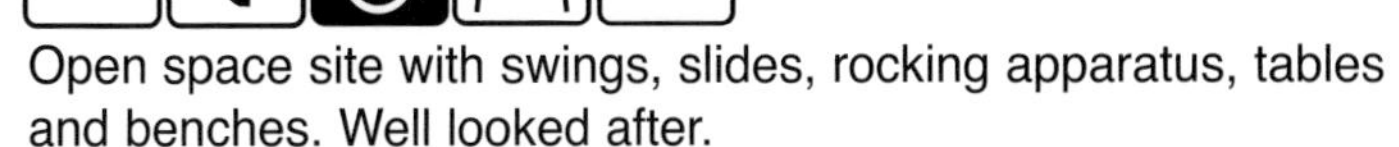

Open space site with swings, slides, rocking apparatus, tables and benches. Well looked after.
SOS - at side towards the exit from the rest area.

Aire de Ste Néomaye-Nord

Open space type of site with swings, tables and benches, some among trees.
SOS - at the side of the rest area.

Aire du Poitou-Charentes

Spacious with nests of tables and benches.
There is a “Magasine des Ruralies-Marché des Saveurs”.
SOS - on the right hand side at the entry slip-road.

Aire de Gript-Nord

Open space type of site with tables and benches.
SOS - at the side of the area towards the entry slip-road.

Aire de Dœuil s/le Mignon

Spacious with tables and benches.
SOS - at the side towards the exit from the rest area.

Aire de Lozay

Open space, lot of greenery, tables and benches, spacious.
“ **Decouverte d’art Roman en Saintonge. Visite gratuite.** ”
SOS - at the side, close to the entry slip-road.

Aire de Fenioux

Spacious with tables and benches among trees at the upper part of the rest area, swings, slides.
SOS - at the side of the rest area.

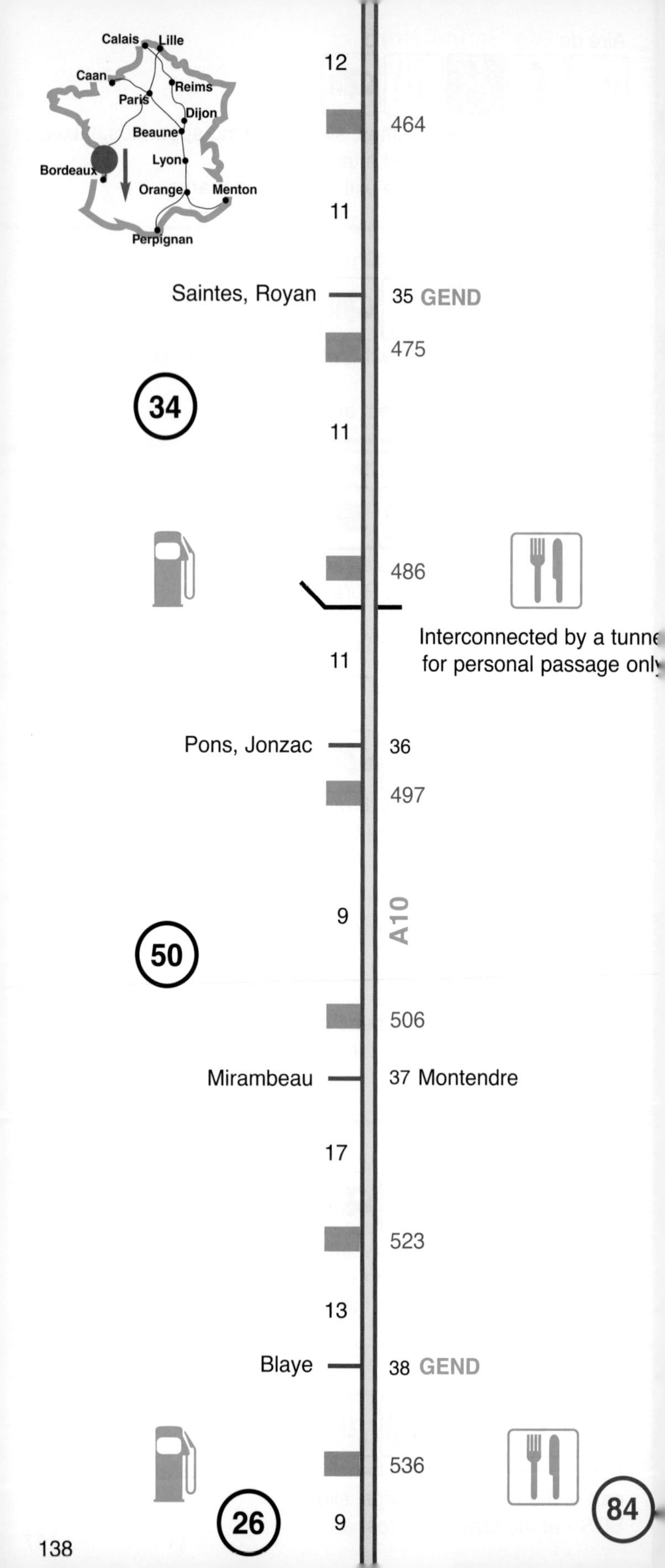
Calais
Lille
Caan
Reims
Paris
Dijon
Beaune
Lyon
Bordeaux
Orange
Menton
Perpignan
12
464
11
Saintes, Royan
35 GEND
475
34
11
486
Interconnected by a tunne
for personal passage onl
11
Pons, Jonzac
36
497
9
A10
50
506
Mirambeau
37 Montendre
17
523
13
Blaye
38 GEND
536
26
9
84

Aire de **Port d'Envaux**

Arranged in two parts: grassy, open space and also a forested one. There are tables and benches.
SOS - located by the entry slip-road.

Aire de **Chermignac**

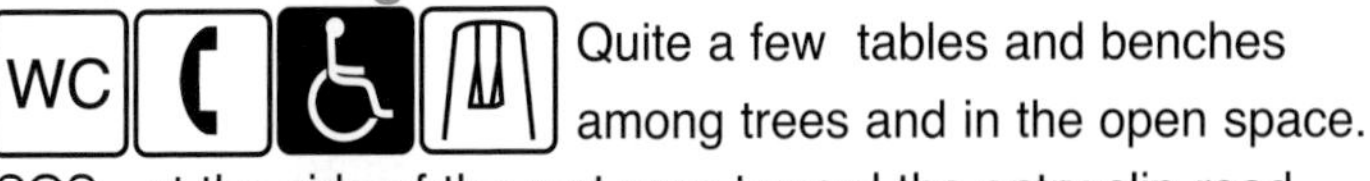

Quite a few tables and benches among trees and in the open space.
SOS - at the side of the rest area toward the entry slip-road.

Aire de **St-Léger**

Exceptionally spacious offering a picnicking area with lots of nests of tables and benches among trees, swings, climbing frames and more. Restaurant is sited far away from the petrol service station, towards the exit from the rest area.
SOS - at the side of motorway.

Aire de **St-Palais**

Tables and benches provided in both, the open space and among trees.
SOS - located in close proximity of the entry to the rest area.

Aire de **St-Ciers**

Lots of tables and benches among trees and in the open space.
SOS - located close to the entry slip-road.

Aire de **St-Caprais**

Tables and benches among trees and in the open space.
SOS - at the side of the rest area close to the entry slip-road.

Aire de **Saugon**

As above.
SOS - at the side of the rest area, not accessible from the rest area.

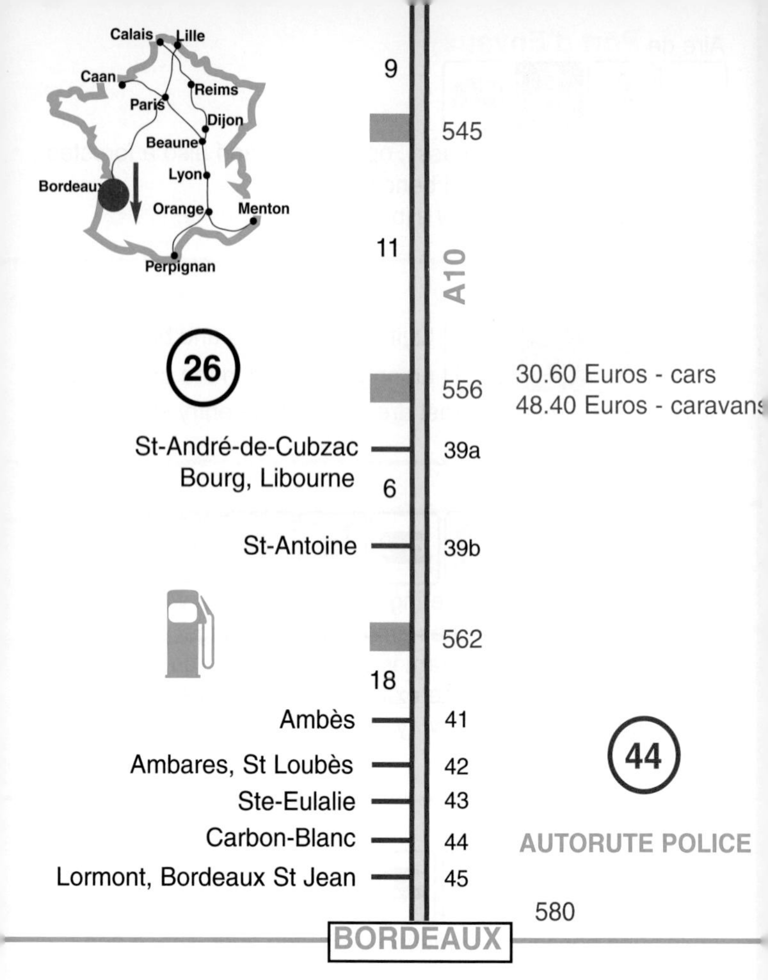
Calais
Lille
Caan
Paris
Reims
Dijon
Beaune
Lyon
Bordeaux
Orange
Menton
Perpignan
9
545
11
A10
26
556
30.60 Euros - cars
48.40 Euros - caravans
St-André-de-Cubzac
Bourg, Libourne
39a
6
St-Antoine
39b
562
18
Ambès
41
Ambares, St Loubès
42
44
Ste-Eulalie
43
Carbon-Blanc
44
AUTORUTE POLICE
Lormont, Bordeaux St Jean
45
580
BORDEAUX

Aire de **St Cristoly**

Tables and benches among trees and in the open space.
Spacious.
SOS - at the side toward the exit from the rest area.

Aire de **Barrière de péage de Virsac**

Just parking spaces.

GENDARMERIE

Aire de **l'Estalot**

Just parking facilities.

SOS - 400 metres before the entry to the rest area.

The Autoroutes Going North

FROM
SPANISH/FRENCH BORDER
TO
ORANGE - LYON - PARIS

Autoroutes A9, A7 & A6

Aire de **Pia**

Few tables and benches, some among trees.
SOS - at the side of the rest area conspicuously positioned.

Aire des **Pavillons-Est**

Forested, with a few benches, pleasant.
SOS - located at the side of the rest area close to the entry slip-road.

Aire du **Village Catalan-Est**

Exceptionally spacious offering high degree of privacy.
Unusually large picnicking area with shops nearby.

Aire de **Barrière de péage de Boulou, Perthus**

Car parking spaces, *station de gonflage,* offering tyre inflating facilities free of charge.

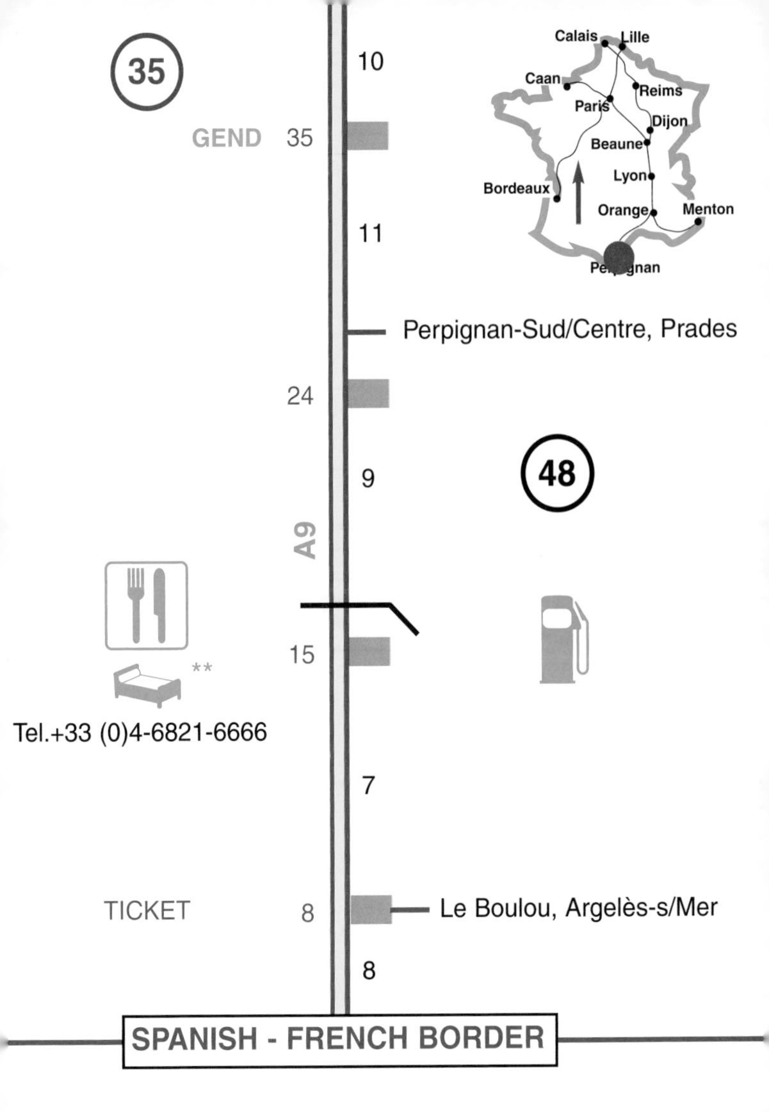
35
10
GEND 35
11
Calais
Lille
Caan
Reims
Paris
Dijon
Beaune
Lyon
Bordeaux
Orange
Menton
Perpignan-Sud/Centre, Prades
24
9
48
A9
15
**
Tel.+33 (0)4-6821-6666
7
TICKET
8
Le Boulou, Argelès-s/Mer
8
SPANISH - FRENCH BORDER

Aire de Lespignan-Sud

Tables and benches, some trees.
SOS - at the side of the rest area, not easy to spot it.

Aire de Narbonne-Vinassan-Sud

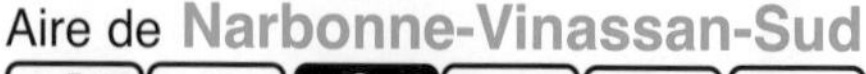

Pique - nique jeux d'enfants, located on raised ground, many nests of table and benches, lot of trees, exceptionally large.

Aire de Bages

Spacious, grassy, tables and benches.
SOS - located by the motorway in close proximity of the exit slip-road.

Aire de Sigean

Incorporates a picnic area at the exit end of the rest area, tables and benches among trees.
SOS - conspicuously placed, accessed by steps.

Aire de Lapalme-Est

Open space, some trees, tables and benches.

SOS - at the side of the rest area.

Aire de Fitou-Est

This rest area offers panoramic views on the Médinterranée.
SOS - conspicuously placed at the end of the rest area.

Aire de Château de Salses

This rest area offers panoramic views on the Méditeranée.
SOS - at the side of the rest area towards the exit slip-road.

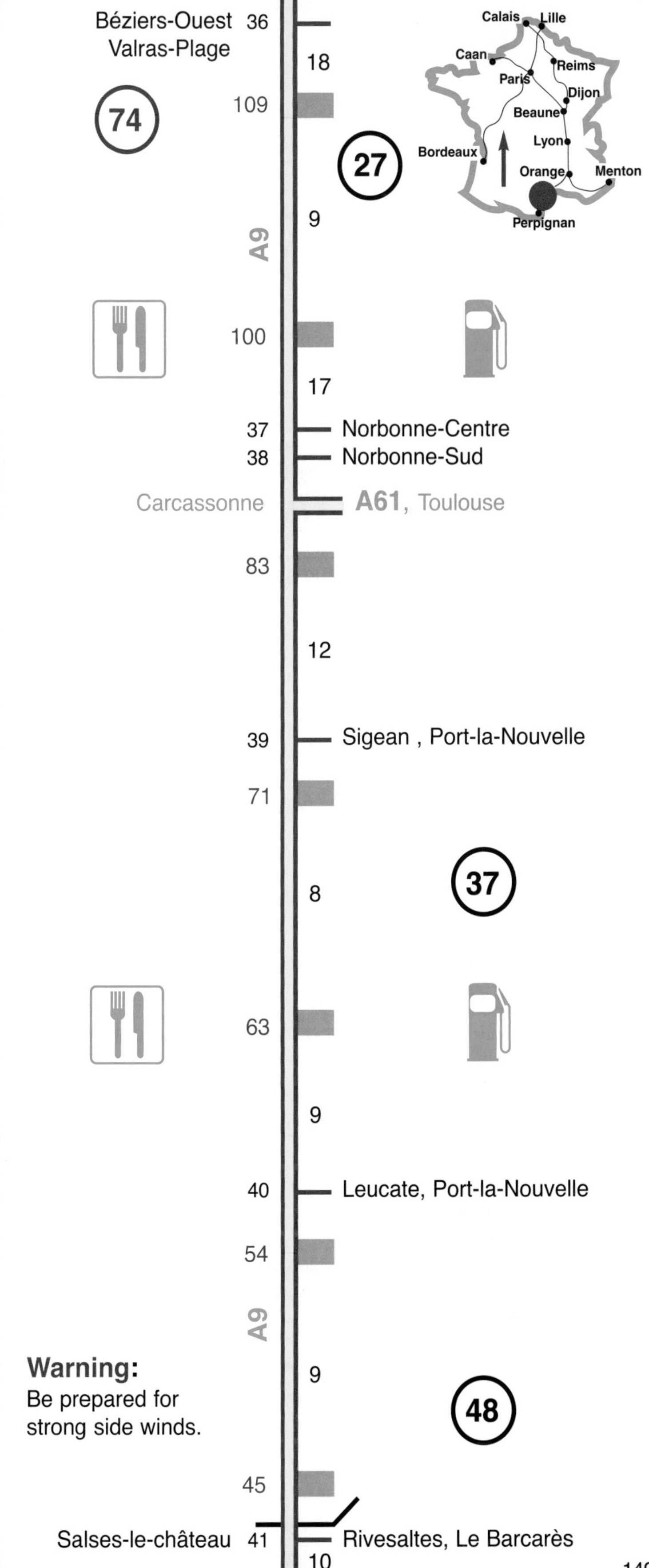
Béziers-Ouest
Valras-Plage
36
18
74
109
27
9
A9
100
17
37
Norbonne-Centre
38
Norbonne-Sud
Carcassonne
A61, Toulouse
83
12
39
Sigean , Port-la-Nouvelle
71
8
37
63
9
40
Leucate, Port-la-Nouvelle
54
A9
Warning:
Be prepared for strong side winds.
9
48
45
Salses-le-château
41
Rivesaltes, Le Barcarès
10
Calais
Lille
Caan
Reims
Paris
Dijon
Beaune
Lyon
Bordeaux
Orange
Menton
Perpignan

Aire de Saint Aunès-Sud

Stone-made tables and benches, few trees, small and pretty.

SOS - at the side of the rest area.

Aire de **Barrière de péage (Montpellier 2)**

No facilities of any kind

Aire de Montpellier-Fabrègues-Sud

Spacious, forested, mainly parking spaces. The PO Box is placed by the entrance to the restaurant.
SOS - Located towards the exit slip-road.

Aire de Gigean-Sud

Mainly car parking spaces with few tables and benches.
SOS - at the side toward the exit from the rest area.

Aire de Loupian

Open space with some tables and benches, incorporates a picnic area.
SOS - located by the exit from the rest area.

Aire de Florensac-Sud

Two lane rest area with some tables and benches among trees.
SOS - sited in close proximity of the entry slip-road.

Aire de Béziers-Montblanc-Sud

Spacious in parking facilities. There are some benches.
SOS - located by the motorway close to the entry slip-road.

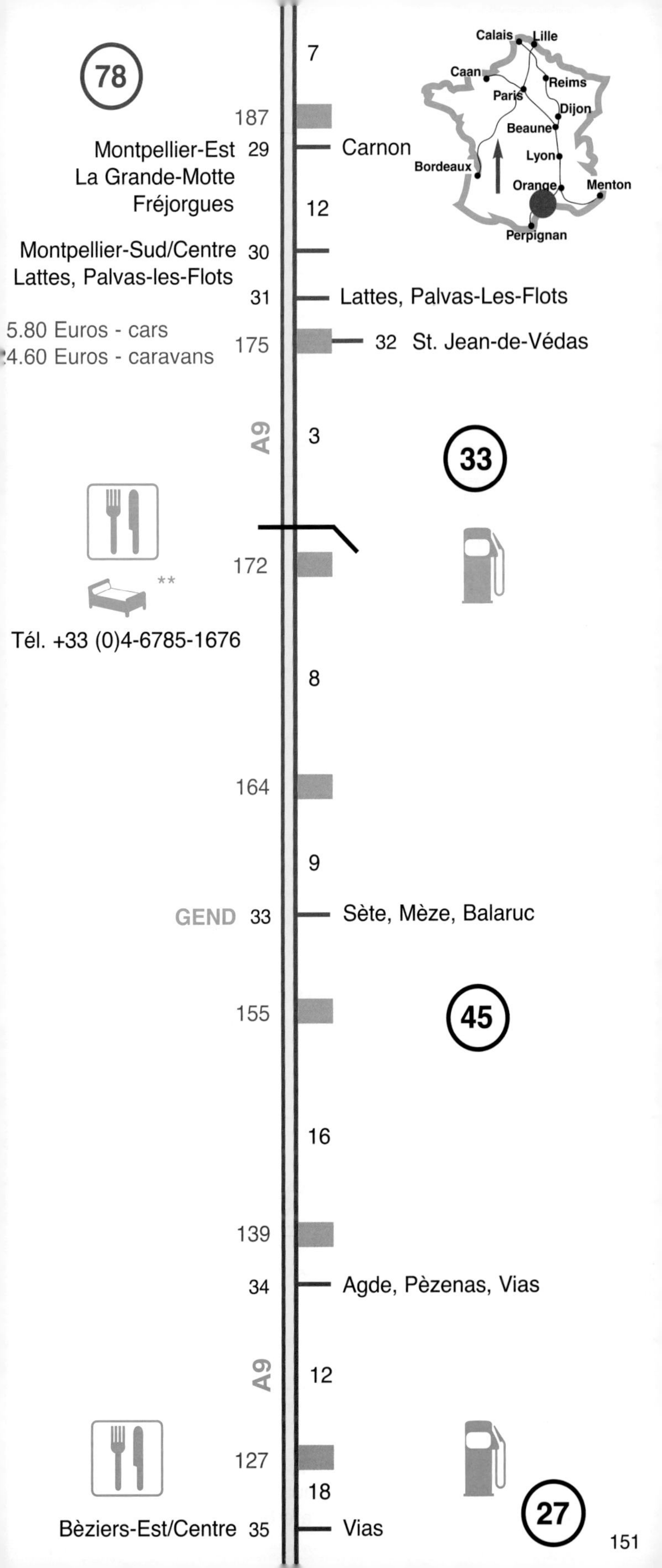

78
7
Calais
Lille
Caan
Reims
Paris
Dijon
Beaune
Bordeaux
Lyon
Orange
Menton
Perpignan
187
Montpellier-Est 29
Carnon
La Grande-Motte
Fréjorgues
12
Montpellier-Sud/Centre 30
Lattes, Palvas-les-Flots
31
Lattes, Palvas-Les-Flots
5.80 Euros - cars
4.60 Euros - caravans
175
32 St. Jean-de-Védas
A9
3
33
172
**
Tél. +33 (0)4-6785-1676
8
164
9
GEND 33
Sète, Mèze, Balaruc
155
45
16
139
34
Agde, Pèzenas, Vias
A9
12
127
18
27
Bèziers-Est/Centre 35
Vias

Aire de **Ledenon-Sud**

Open space, stone-made tables and benches, small, pretty.

SOS - at the side of the rest area.

Aire de **Nimes-Marguerittes (Sud)**

Ample parking facilities, tables and benches.
SOS - located at the exit from the ret area.

Aire de **Milhaud-Sud**

Small, one lane rest area with quite a few tables and benches in a row set among trees
SOS - at the side toward the exit slip-road

Aire de **Vèrgeze-Sud**

The rest area is sited on three levels, forested, picnic area with a lot of nests of tables and benches, neatly set among trees.

SOS - located actually on the rest area.

Aire de **Barrière de péage "Montpellier 1"**

There are two telephone cubicals and the site has nothing more to offer.

Aire d ' **Ambrussum-Sud**

Mainly car parking facilities. Cafeteria.
SOS - at the end of the rest area on the left hand side of the exit slip-road.

Aire de **Mas du Roux**

Pique-nique jeux d'en fants, tables and benches among trees and in the open space too. Not marked, as suitable for caravanners but would do nicely.
SOS - at the side of the rest are by the entry slip-road.

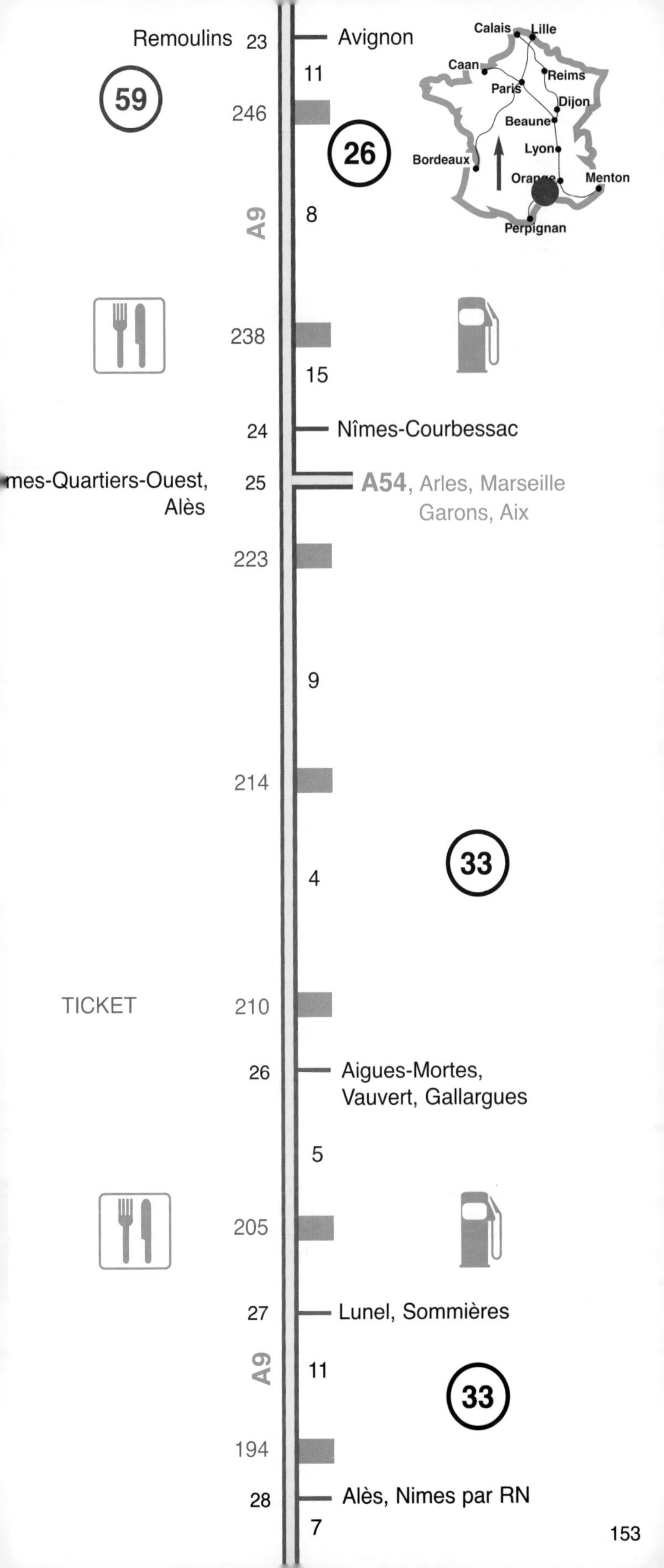

Remoulins
23
Avignon
11
59
246
26
Calais
Lille
Caan
Reims
Paris
Dijon
Beaune
Lyon
Bordeaux
Menton
Perpignan
A9
8
238
15
24
Nîmes-Courbessac
mes-Quartiers-Ouest,
Alès
25
A54, Arles, Marseille
Garons, Aix
223
9
214
33
4
TICKET
210
26
Aigues-Mortes,
Vauvert, Gallargues
5
205
27
Lunel, Sommières
A9
11
33
194
28
Alès, Nimes par RN
7

Aire de **Mornas-les-Adrets**

(This rest area is shown here for your reference only)

To continue for Lyon and Paris
GOTO page 165

Aire de **Roquemaure-Sud**

Two lane rest area with quite a few tables and benches among trees. Small and pretty.
SOS - located by the exit from the rest area.

Aire de **Tavel-Sud**

       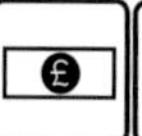   

Large with a caravanners site at the end of the rest area. Tables and benches in the open space and under trees.
SOS - by the exit slip-road.

Aire de **Estezargues-Sud**

Spacious, arranged on three levels with bushy trees, a lot of tables and benches in the open space and under trees.
SOS - at the side of the rest area toward the exit slip-road.

VENT VIOLENT
SOYEZ PRUDENTS

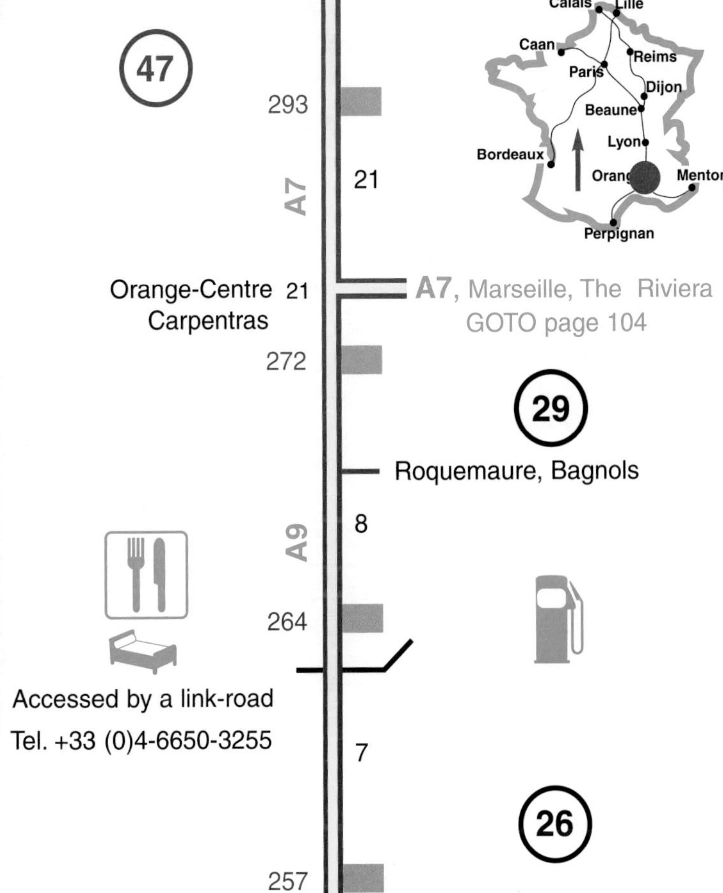
47
293
A7
21
Calais
Lille
Caan
Reims
Paris
Dijon
Beaune
Lyon
Bordeaux
Orang
Menton
Perpignan
Orange-Centre 21
Carpentras
A7, Marseille, The Riviera
GOTO page 104
272
29
Roquemaure, Bagnols
A9
8
264
Accessed by a link-road
Tel. +33 (0)4-6650-3255
7
26
257
11

FROM
ITALIAN/FRENCH BORDER
TO
ORANGE - LYON - PARIS - CALAIS
(LILLE - BELGIAN/FRENCH BORDER)
{VALENCIENNE}

Autoroutes A8, A7, A6, A1, A26, {A2}

Aire de **Bréguières-Nord**

Spacious site which is not apparent at first.
There is a Musée de l'Automobiliste. Some tables and benches.
SOS - they are located in close proximity to both, the entry and exit slip- roads.

Aire de **Barrière de péage (d'Antibes)**

One lane parking facilities, small.
SOS - located at the exit from the rest area.

Aire de **Barrière de péage (Nice St-Isidore)**

Just car parking facilities.
SOS - located on the rest area itself. Gendarmerie Station.

Aire de **Barrière de péage (de la Turbie)**

Small, one lane parking facilities.

SOS - 200 m past the rest area.

Aire de la **Scoperta**

Mainly open space with tables and benches among trees, all in the picnicking part of the area.

SOS - at the side of the rest area. There is another one sited on the rest area itself by the WC housing.

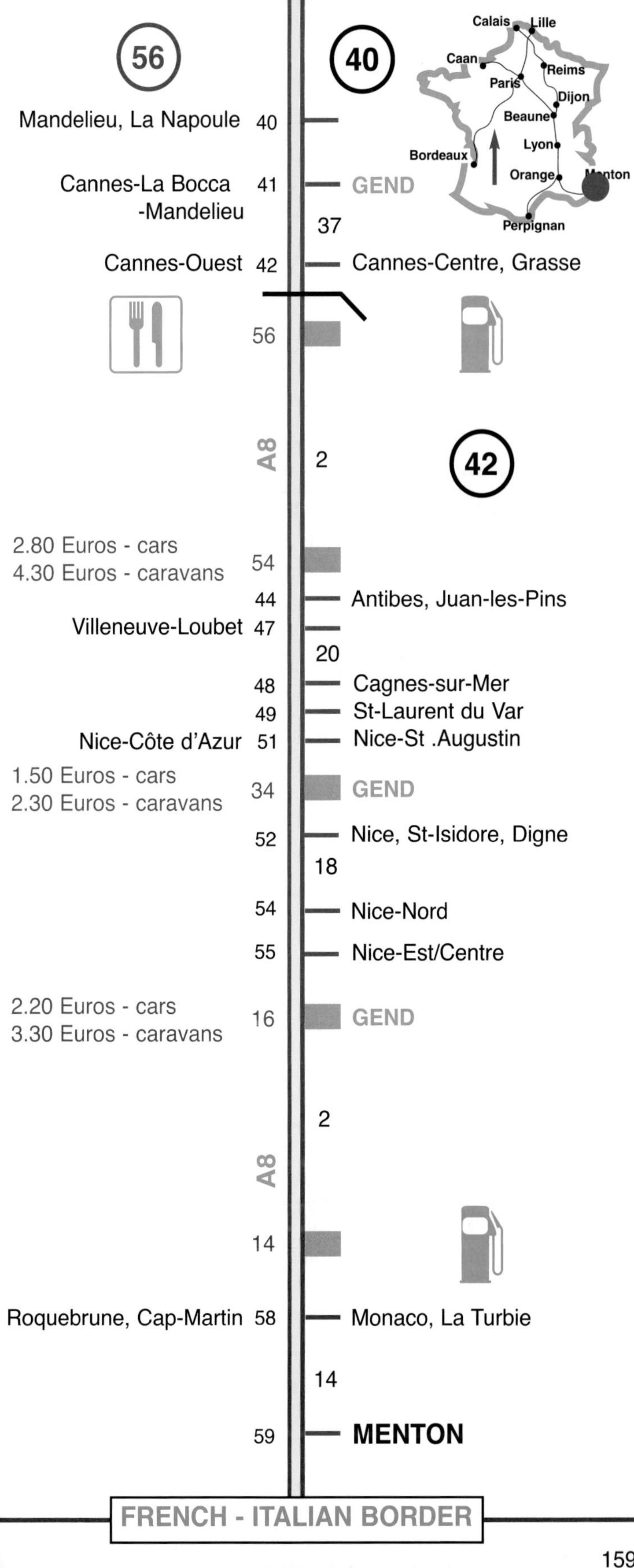
56
40
Calais
Lille
Caan
Reims
Paris
Dijon
Beaune
Lyon
Bordeaux
Orange
Perpignan
Mandelieu, La Napoule 40
Cannes-La Bocca
-Mandelieu 41
GEND
37
Cannes-Ouest 42
Cannes-Centre, Grasse
56
A8
2
42
2.80 Euros - cars
4.30 Euros - caravans
54
44
Antibes, Juan-les-Pins
Villeneuve-Loubet 47
20
48
Cagnes-sur-Mer
49
St-Laurent du Var
Nice-Côte d'Azur 51
Nice-St .Augustin
1.50 Euros - cars
2.30 Euros - caravans
34
GEND
52
Nice, St-Isidore, Digne
18
54
Nice-Nord
55
Nice-Est/Centre
2.20 Euros - cars
3.30 Euros - caravans
16
GEND
2
A8
14
Roquebrune, Cap-Martin 58
Monaco, La Turbie
14
59
MENTON
FRENCH - ITALIAN BORDER

Aire de **Rousset**

Open space type of site, mostly parking spaces, some tables and benches.
SOS - at the side of the rest area.

Aire de **St-Hilaire**

Two lane, open space type of area, yet with tables and benches among trees.
SOS - located by the rest area's entry slip-road.

Aire de **Cambarette-Nord**

Open space with a few tables and benches
SOS - located at the side toward the exit from the rest area.

Aire de **Candumy**

Sited on a hill at two levels of ground configuration. It is forested with quite a few nests of tables and benches.
SOS - located close to the entry slip-road and another one located at the upper level of the rest area.

Aire de **Vidauban-Nord**

Mostly parking facilities with some tables and benches among trees.
SOS - by the exit from the rest area.

Aire du **Canaver**

Spacious with many nests of tables and benches among trees.
SOS - located by the exit from the rest area.

Aire de **Barrière de péage (Le Capitou)**

Two lane rest area with some tables and benches.
SOS - actually on the rest area itself.

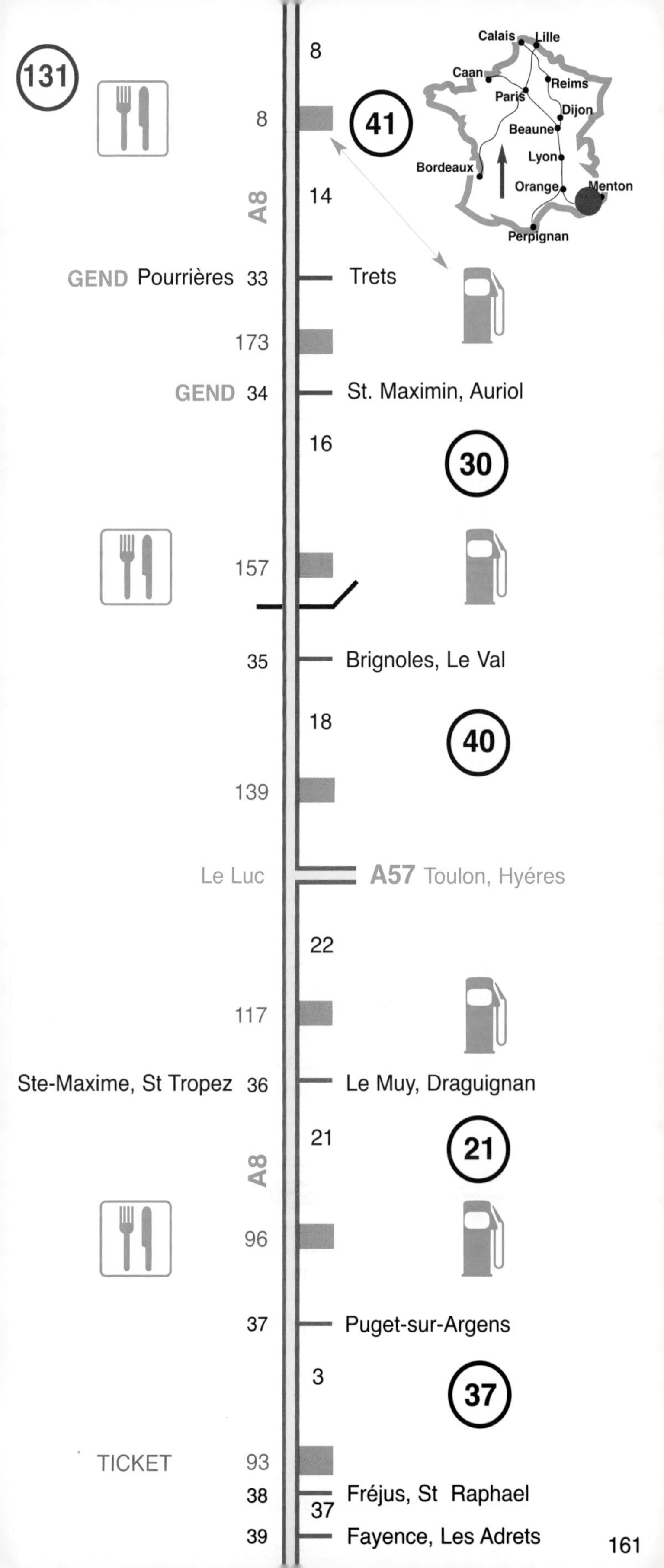

131
Calais
Lille
Caan
Reims
Paris
Dijon
Beaune
Lyon
Bordeaux
Orange
Menton
Perpignan
8
8
41
A8
14
GEND Pourrières 33
Trets
173
GEND 34
St. Maximin, Auriol
16
30
157
35
Brignoles, Le Val
18
40
139
Le Luc
A57 Toulon, Hyéres
22
117
Ste-Maxime, St Tropez 36
Le Muy, Draguignan
21
21
A8
96
37
Puget-sur-Argens
3
37
TICKET
93
38
Fréjus, St Raphael
37
39
Fayence, Les Adrets

Aire de **Cavaillon-Plan d'Orgon**

Open type of area, sited on a hill by a water reservoir, small.
SOS - 300 m approx. before the entry to the rest area.

Aire de **Sénas**

Two lane parking facilities with some tables and benches, very small, tidy and interesting.
SOS - located by the entry to the area.

Aire de **Lamanon**

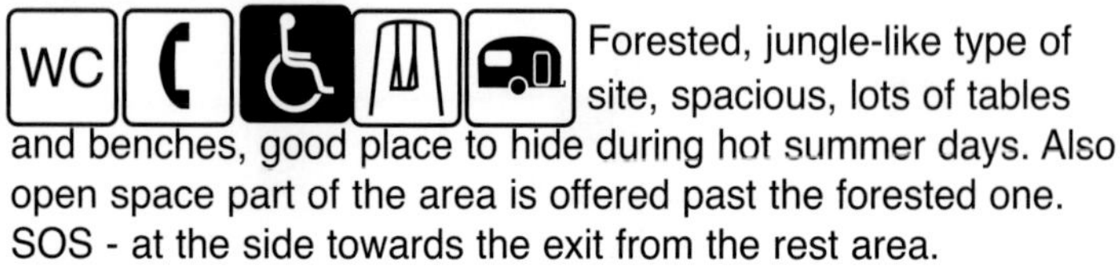

Forested, jungle-like type of site, spacious, lots of tables and benches, good place to hide during hot summer days. Also open space part of the area is offered past the forested one.
SOS - at the side towards the exit from the rest area.

Aire de **Barrière de péage (Lançon de Provence)**

One lane parking bay. There is a "station de gonflage" - tyre inflating facilities free of charge
SOS - located on the rest area by the telephone cubicals.

Aire de **Lançon de Provence-Est**

Spacious, tables and benches among trees.
SOS - actually on the rest area located close to the entrance of the services housing (the footbridge).

Aire de **Ventabren-Nord**

There are two sites for caravanners with many nests of tables and benches, one by the entry to the rest area and the other one by the exit from the rest area.
SOS - not far from the exit slip-road

Aire de **Barriére de pèage (Aix-en-Provence)**

Two lane parking facilities, smart. Gendarmerie Station.
SOS - Located on the rest area by an office building there.

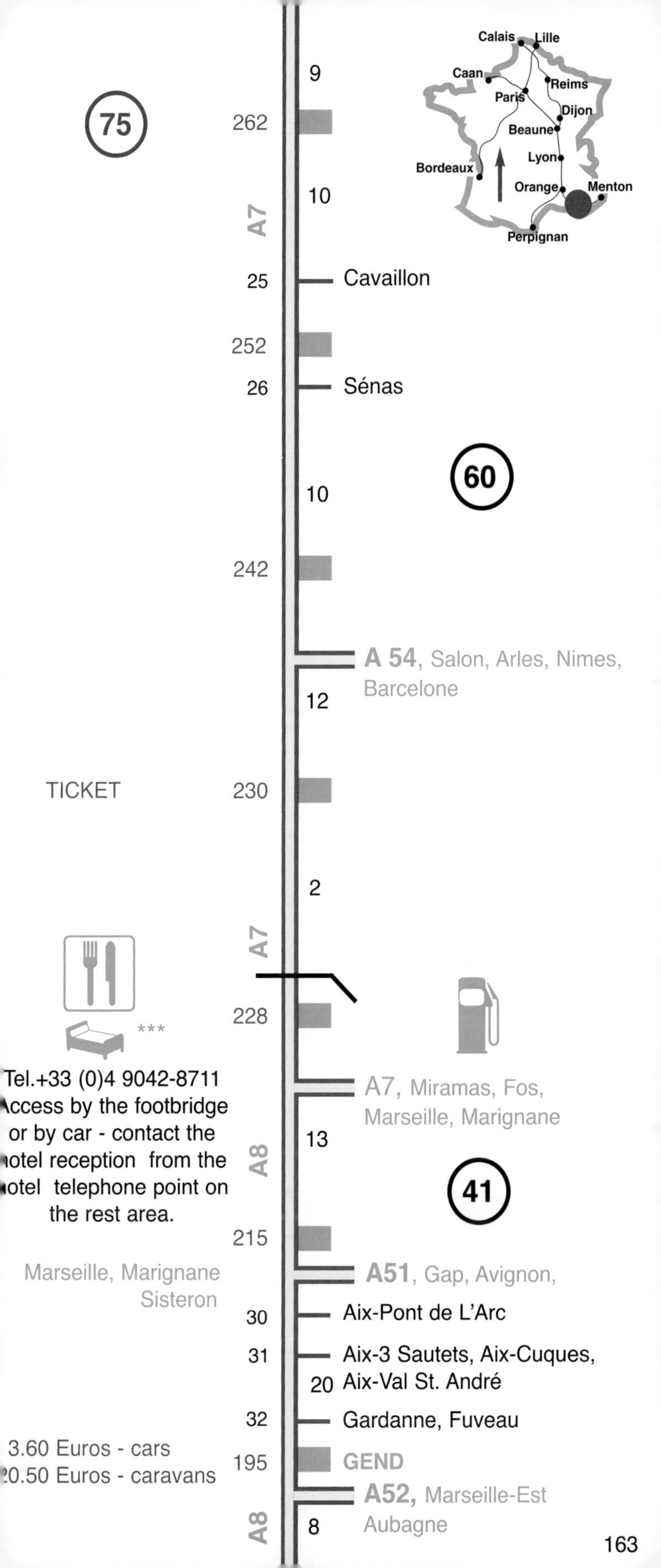

75
262
9
10
A7
Calais
Lille
Caan
Reims
Paris
Dijon
Beaune
Lyon
Bordeaux
Orange
Menton
Perpignan
25
Cavaillon
252
26
Sénas
10
60
242
A 54, Salon, Arles, Nimes, Barcelone
12
TICKET
230
2
A7
228
***
Tel.+33 (0)4 9042-8711
Access by the footbridge or by car - contact the hotel reception from the hotel telephone point on the rest area.
A7, Miramas, Fos, Marseille, Marignane
13
A8
41
215
Marseille, Marignane
Sisteron
A51, Gap, Avignon,
30
Aix-Pont de L'Arc
31
Aix-3 Sautets, Aix-Cuques, Aix-Val St. André
20
32
Gardanne, Fuveau
3.60 Euros - cars
20.50 Euros - caravans
195
GEND
A52, Marseille-Est
Aubagne
A8
8

Aire de **Montélimar**

Pique-nique jeux d'enfants. Large with nests of tables and benches in the open space and among trees.
SOS - at the side of the rest area and another one located on the rest area by the footbridge.

Aire de **Donzère**

Open space type of site with tables and benches, some are among trees.
SOS - at the side of the rest area.

Aire de **Tricastin**

Small, elegant place with tables and benches.
SOS - 400 metres approx. past the rest area.

Aire de **Mornas-les-Adrets**

Spacious, tables and benches mostly in the open space. Simple.
SOS - at the side of the rest area.

Aire d ' **Orange-le-Coudoulet**

Large, elegant with a site of pique-nique jeux d'enfants.
SOS - 200 metres past the rest area.

Aire de **Sorgues**

Pigue-nique d'enfants, well looked after site for caravanners, spacious, a lot of tables and benches among trees.
SOS - at the side of the rest area.

Aire de **Novés**

Two lane, open space type of area with tables and benches.
SOS- at the side by the entry to the rest area.

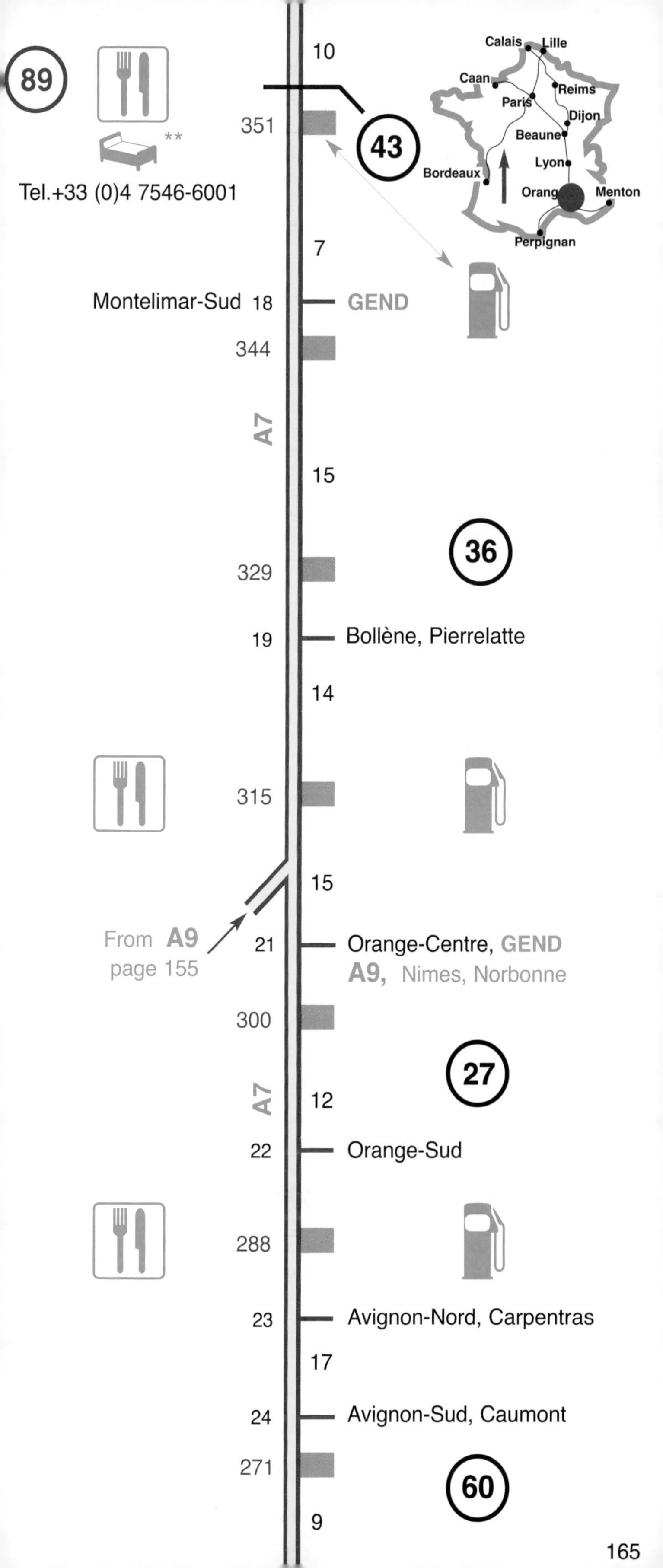
89
Tel.+33 (0)4 7546-6001
10
351
43
Calais
Lille
Caan
Reims
Paris
Dijon
Beaune
Lyon
Bordeaux
Orang
Menton
Perpignan
7
Montelimar-Sud 18
GEND
344
A7
15
36
329
19
Bollène, Pierrelatte
14
315
15
From A9
page 155
21
Orange-Centre, GEND
A9, Nimes, Norbonne
300
27
A7
12
22
Orange-Sud
288
23
Avignon-Nord, Carpentras
17
24
Avignon-Sud, Caumont
271
60
9

Aire de la **Bouterne**

Open space site with many tables and benches among trees, pique-nique jeux d'enfants, spacious.
SOS - actually on the rest area, conspicuously placed.

Aire de **Latitude 45**

Open type of site with some trees, tables and benches arranged neatly in a row separated by hedges, thus, offering more privacy for travellers, spacious. PO BOX located inside the cafeteria.
SOS - located at the side of the rest area.

Aire de **Portes-les-Valence**

Open type of site, pique-nique jeux d'enfants. Not designated for caravans but might do.
SOS - at the side of the rest area.

Aire de **Livron**

Small, lot of tables and benches under trees and in the open space.
SOS - at the side of the area.

Aire de **Saulce-sur-Rhône**

Pique-nique jeux d'enfants, small, well cared for with tables and benches under tree crowns and in the open space.
SOS - just past the exit from the rest area.

Aire du **Logis-Neuf**

Pique-nique jeux d'enfants, with tables and benches in the open space and under trees, tidy, well cared for. Spacious.
SOS - located by the entry to the rest area.

Aire du **Roubion**

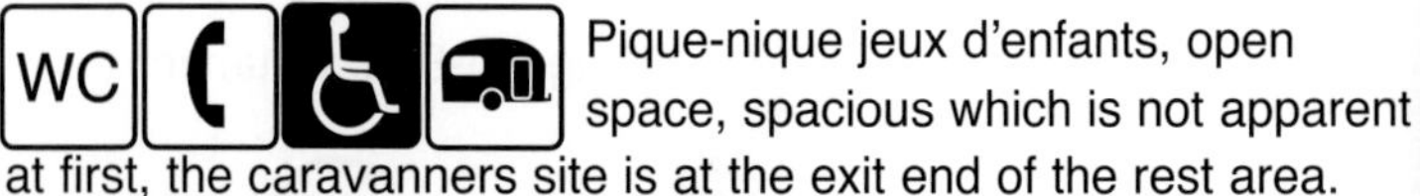

Pique-nique jeux d'enfants, open space, spacious which is not apparent at first, the caravanners site is at the exit end of the rest area. There are tables and benches.
SOS - located by the entry to the rest area.

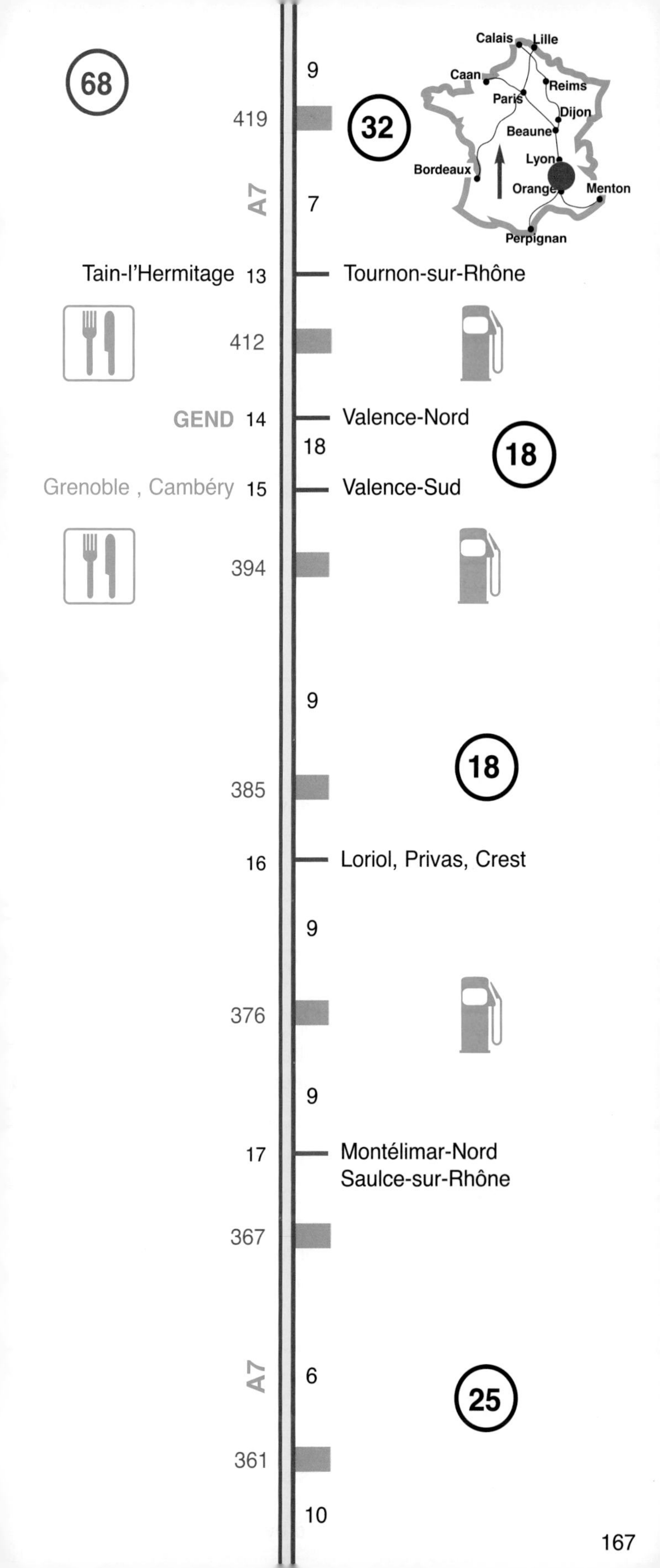
68
9
419
32
Calais
Lille
Caan
Reims
Paris
Dijon
Beaune
Lyon
Bordeaux
Orange
Menton
Perpignan
A7
7
Tain-l'Hermitage 13
Tournon-sur-Rhône
412
GEND 14
Valence-Nord
18
18
Grenoble , Cambéry 15
Valence-Sud
394
9
385
18
16
Loriol, Privas, Crest
9
376
9
17
Montélimar-Nord
Saulce-sur-Rhône
367
A7
6
25
361
10

Aire de **Pierre-Bénite**

There are tables and benches.

Aire de **Sérézin du Rhône**

Spacious in car parking facilities, grill and sandwich bar.

Aire de **Barrière de péage (de Vienne)**

Spacious,some tables and benches.
Autoroute Police.

Aire de la **Grande Borne**

Pique - nique jeux d ‘enfants. Plenty of nests of tables and stools mostly among trees. Caravan site.
SOS - located just before the entry to the rest area.

Aire de **St-Rambert d’Albon**

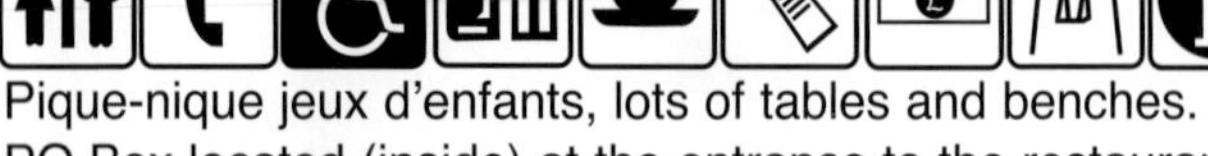

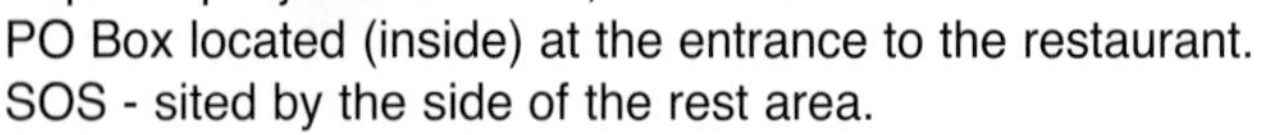

Pique-nique jeux d’enfants, lots of tables and benches.
PO Box located (inside) at the entrance to the restaurant.
SOS - sited by the side of the rest area.

Aire de la **Combe Tourmente**

Pique-nique jeux d’enfants. lots of tables and benches under trees and in the open space. Large grassy area.
SOS - at the side of the rest area.

Aire de la **Galaure**

Small, two lane rest area with nests of tables and benches among trees, well looked after.
SOS - conspicuously placed by the exit from the rest

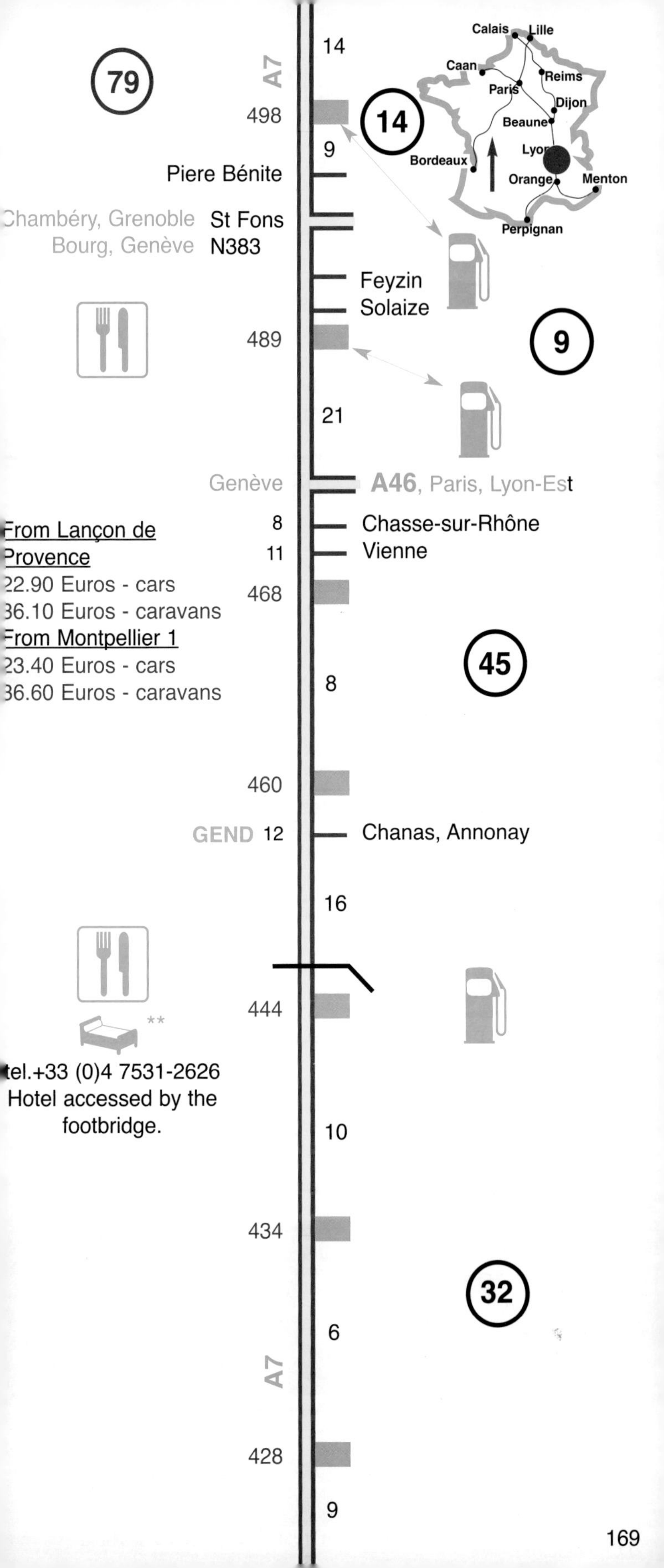
79
A7
14
498
14
9
Piere Bénite
Chambéry, Grenoble
Bourg, Genève
St Fons
N383
Feyzin
Solaize
489
9
21
Genève
A46, Paris, Lyon-Est
Calais
Lille
Caan
Reims
Paris
Dijon
Beaune
Lyon
Bordeaux
Orange
Menton
Perpignan
From Lançon de Provence
22.90 Euros - cars
36.10 Euros - caravans
From Montpellier 1
23.40 Euros - cars
36.60 Euros - caravans
8
Chasse-sur-Rhône
11
Vienne
468
45
8
460
GEND 12
Chanas, Annonay
16
444
tel.+33 (0)4 7531-2626
Hotel accessed by the footbridge.
10
434
32
6
A7
428
9

Aire de **Taponas**

`there are tables and benches.
SOS - at the end of the rest area by the exit slip-road.

Aire de **Boitray**

Exceptionally spacious, located by a water reservoir, tables and benches, coffee bar.
SOS - conspicuously placed at the entry slip-road and one more located some 200 m before the entry to the rest area.

Aire de **Barrière de péage (Villafranche-Limas-Est)**

Basically car parking spaces.
There is a *Station de Ganflage* - tyre inflating facilities, free of charge.

Aire de **Chères**

Spacious with tables and benches.
SOS - located by the the exit slip-road.

Aire de **Paisy**

Generally, car parking facilities, some tables and benches.

The “Mushroom” rest area, page 95

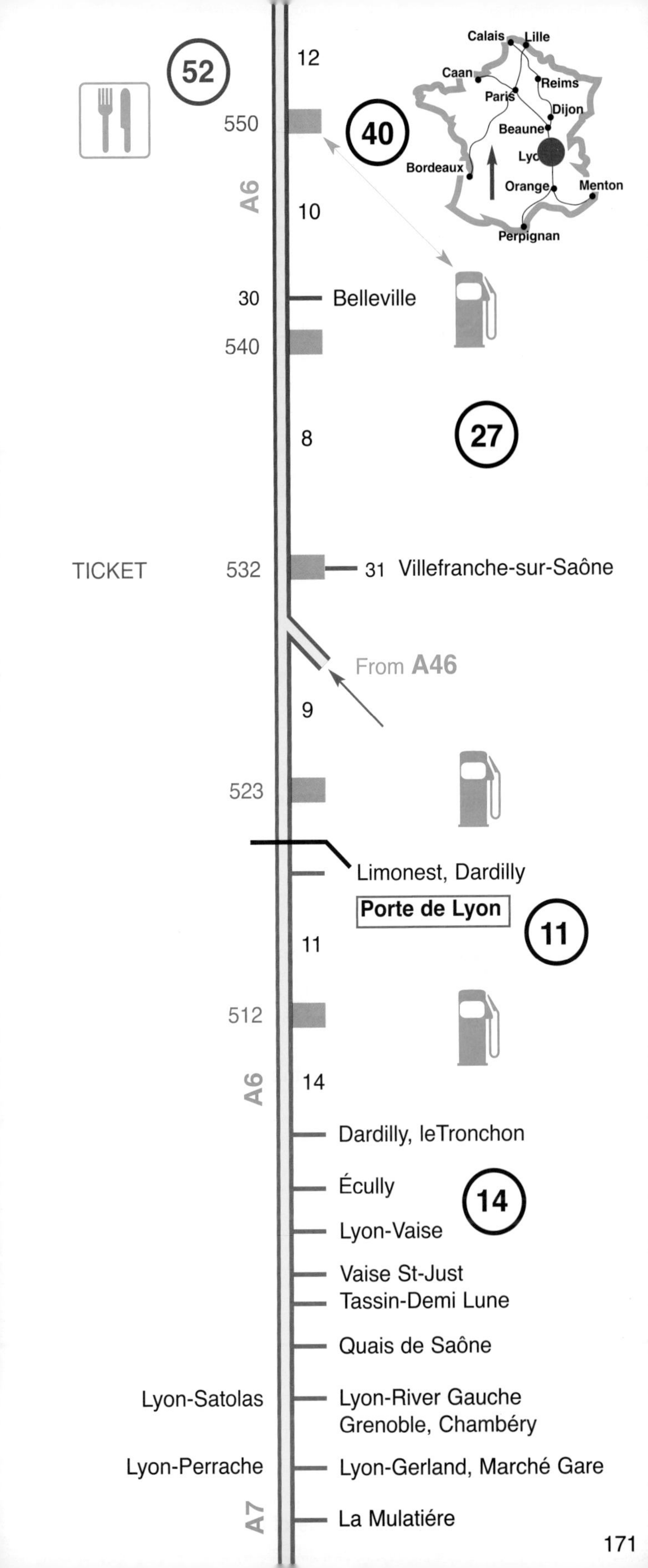
52
12
550
40
Calais
Lille
Caan
Reims
Paris
Dijon
Beaune
Lyon
Bordeaux
Orange
Menton
Perpignan
A6
10
30
Belleville
540
27
8
TICKET
532
31
Villefranche-sur-Saône
From A46
9
523
Limonest, Dardilly
Porte de Lyon
11
11
512
A6
14
Dardilly, leTronchon
Écully
14
Lyon-Vaise
Vaise St-Just
Tassin-Demi Lune
Quais de Saône
Lyon-Satolas
Lyon-River Gauche
Grenoble, Chambéry
Lyon-Perrache
Lyon-Gerland, Marché Gare
A7
La Mulatiére

Aire de la Loyère

Smart, lots of tables and benches in the open space and also in the forested part of the area. Swings, see-saws, slides.
SOS - by the side of the motorway at the very end of the area.

Aire de St-Ambreuil

Spacious. At the exit end of the area there is a site for caravanners, a wide range of services offered.
SOS - at the side of the rest area.

Aire de Boyer

Small, an open space grassy area, a lot of greenery, many tables and benches.
SOS - at the side of the rest area, close to entry slip-road.

Aire d ' Uchizy

Small, pretty with tables and benches neatly arranged in a row under trees.
SOS - at the side of the rest area..

Aire de Mâcon-la-Salle

A wide range of services offered, many nests of tables and benches.
SOS - located at the side toward the exit from the rest area.

Aire des Sablons

The rest area differs from others in the sense of design origination. Tables and benches among trees.
SOS - located at the side of the rest area.

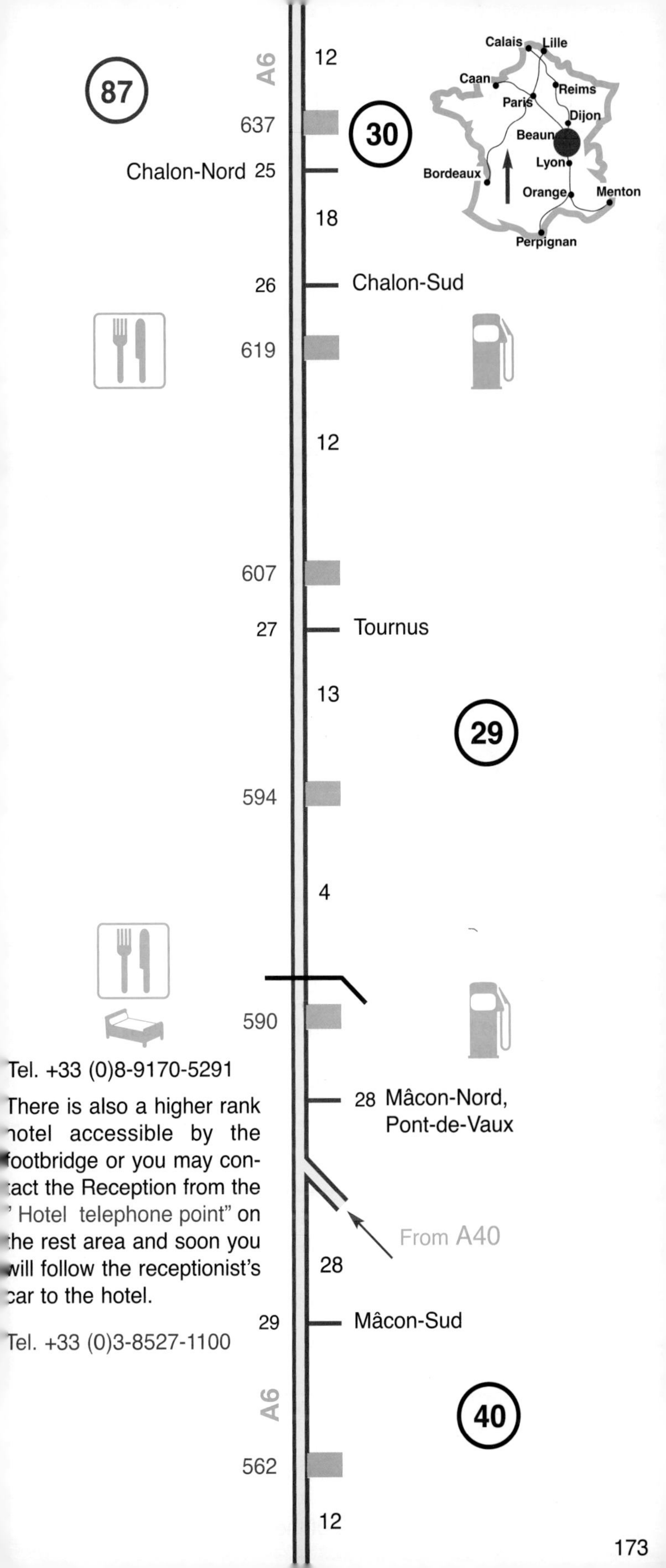

Tel. +33 (0)8-9170-5291

There is also a higher rank hotel accessible by the footbridge or you may contact the Reception from the "Hotel telephone point" on the rest area and soon you will follow the receptionist's car to the hotel.

Tel. +33 (0)3-8527-1100

Aire de Marcigny

WC

Forested, tables and benches, pretty.

SOS - at the side of the rest area, conspicuously placed toward the exit slip-road..

Aire des Lochères

Spacious with tables and benches.

There s a site for caravanners.

SOS - located on the right hand side by the exit slip-road.

Aire de la Rèpote

Small, two lane parking facilities, tables and benches, simple.

SOS - located by the entry to the rest area.

Aire du Creux Moreau

Elegant place with tables and benches.

SOS - at the side of the rest area and another one located in close proximity of the exit slip-road.

Aire du Bois des Corbeaux

Arranged in two parts: forested and open space sites, both, with tables and benches.

SOS - at the side of the rest area.

Aire de Savigny-les-Beaune

WC

Open space type of area with tables and benches neatly arranged in a row. It offers a panoramic view of the countryside. There are concrete-made stools and tables along the line of viewing.

SOS - conspicuously located at the side of the rest area.

Aire de Beaune-Merceuil

Ample car parking facilities. P.O. Box by the entrance to the petrol station boutique.

SOS - located at the side of the rest area.

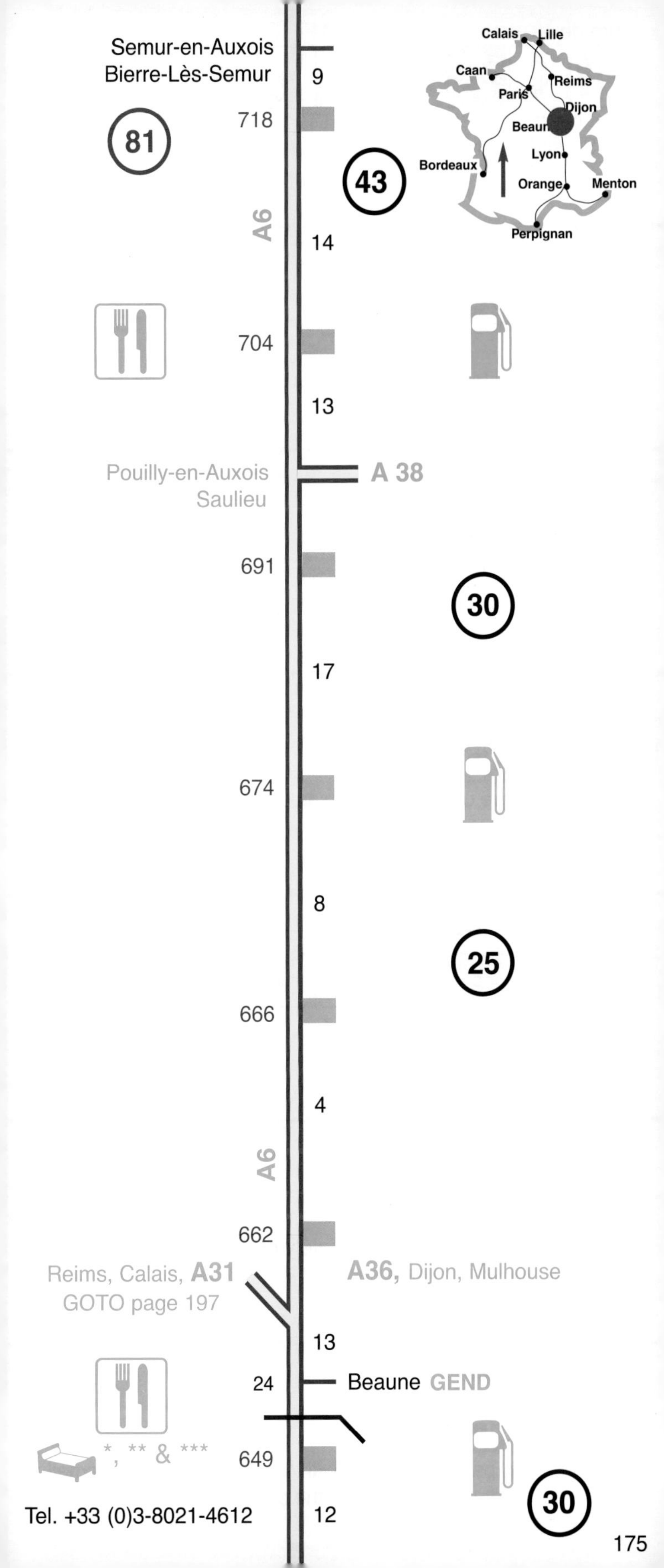
Semur-en-Auxois
Bierre-Lès-Semur
9
81
718
43
Calais
Lille
Caan
Reims
Paris
Dijon
Beaun
Lyon
Bordeaux
Orange
Menton
Perpignan
A6
14
704
13
Pouilly-en-Auxois
Saulieu
A 38
691
30
17
674
8
25
666
4
A6
662
Reims, Calais, A31
GOTO page 197
A36, Dijon, Mulhouse
13
24
Beaune GEND
*, ** & ***
649
Tel. +33 (0)3-8021-4612
12
30

Aire de Venoy-Soleil Levant

Just car parking spaces.
SOS - sited at the very end of the rest area.

Aire du Buisson Rond

As below.
SOS - located by the entry to the area.

Aire du Cherveuil

Lot of nests of table and benches among trees, forested.

SOS - at the side of the rest area.

Aire d' Hevaux

Jungle-like type of site, with tables and benches among trees. Spacious.
SOS - located at the very end of the rest area

Aire de Maison-Dieu

Exceptionally spacious rest area.
SOS - at the side of the rest area.

Aire de Toutry-Genetoy

Some tables or benches, completely open site.
SOS - at the side the rest area.

Aire de la Côme

Just one lane parking facilities with tables and benches, small.
SOS - located by the exit from the area.

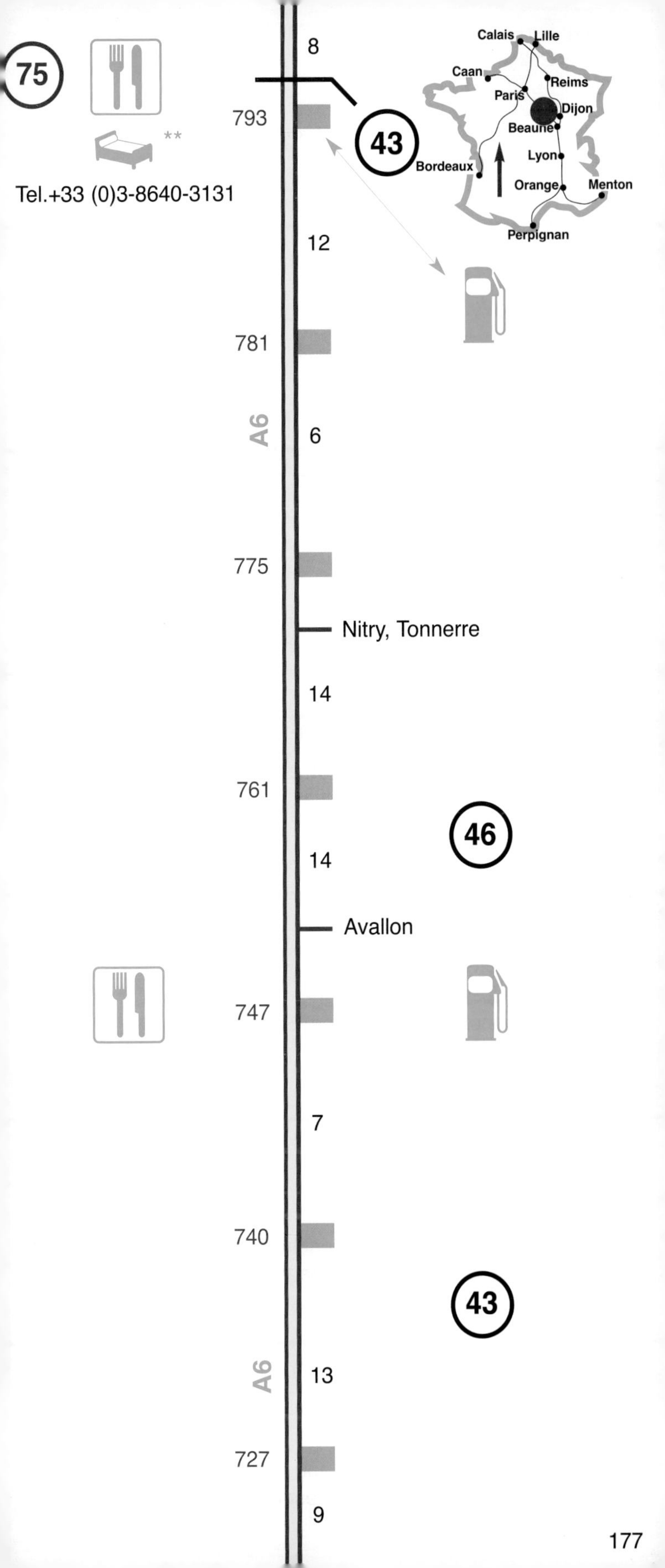
75
**
Tel.+33 (0)3-8640-3131
8
793
43
Calais
Lille
Caan
Reims
Paris
Dijon
Beaune
Lyon
Bordeaux
Orange
Menton
Perpignan
12
781
A6
6
775
Nitry, Tonnerre
14
761
46
14
Avallon
747
7
740
43
A6
13
727
9

Aire d' Égreville

Generally, open space type of area, partly forested. There are tables and benches.
SOS - located at the side of the rest area

Aire de la Roche

Forested, tables and benches, well looked after.
SOS - at the side of the rest area.

Aire de la Couline

Basically, just car parking facilities.
SOS - at the side of the rest area.

Aire de la Loupière

Tables and benches among trees. Small.
SOS - at the side of the rest area.

Aire des Pâtures

Small, simple with tables and benches among trees.
SOS - located by the entry slip-road.

Aire de Bois du Thureau

Small, simple with some tables and benches among trees.
SOS - located at the side of the rest area.

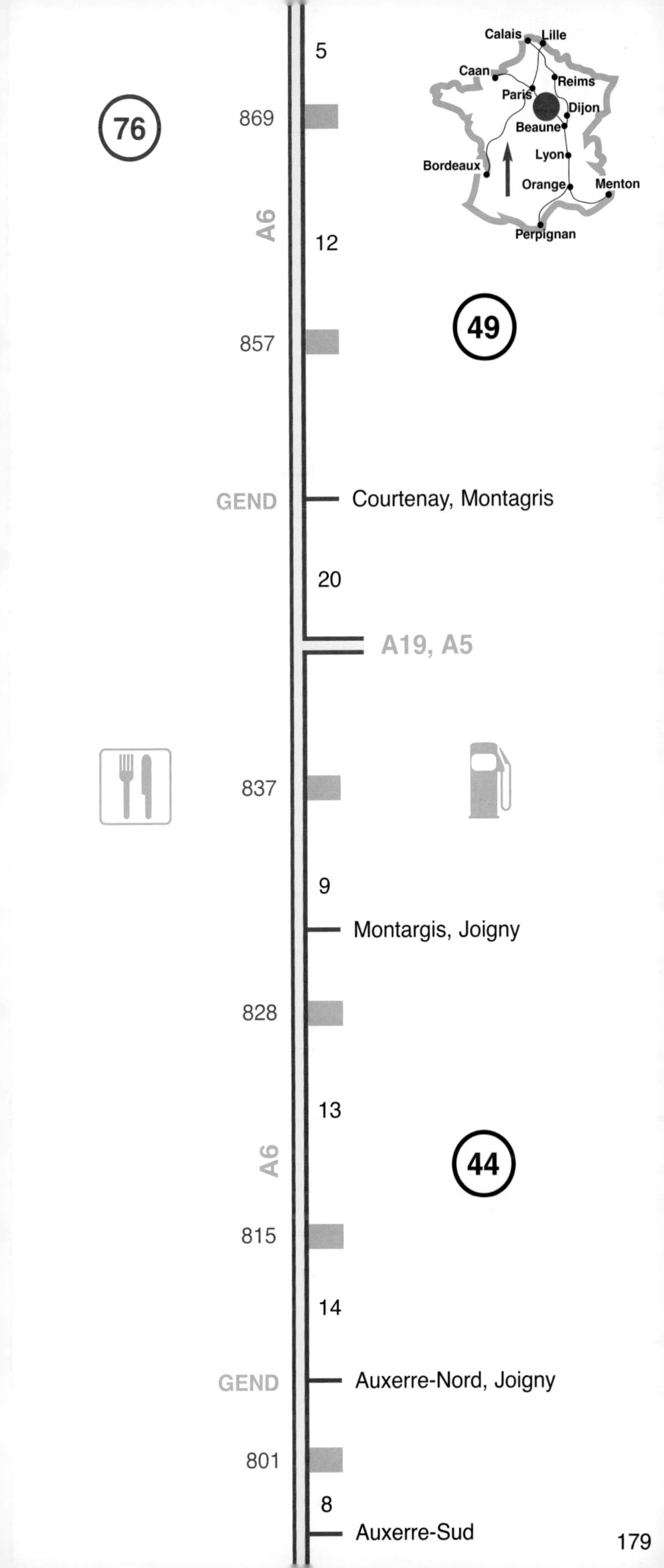

Calais
Lille
Caan
Reims
Paris
Dijon
Beaune
Bordeaux
Lyon
Orange
Menton
Perpignan
76
869
5
A6
12
857
49
GEND
Courtenay, Montagris
20
A19, A5
837
9
Montargis, Joigny
828
13
A6
44
815
14
GEND
Auxerre-Nord, Joigny
801
8
Auxerre-Sud

Aire de Villabé

Just car parking spaces. Mostly occupied by lorries.
SOS - at the side of the rest area

Aire de Nainville

SOS - at the side of the rest area.

Aire de **Barrière de péage (de Fleury, Paris)**

Just car parking spaces.
Gendarmerie Station.

Aire d' Arbonne

There are few tables and benches among trees.
SOS - at the side of the rest area.

Aire d' Achères

Small, simple with tables and benches.
SOS - located at the side of the rest area.

Aire de Darvault (Nemours)

Ample range of quality services.
SOS - located on the rest area itself.

Aire de Floée

One lane parking area, small with few tables and benches.
SOS - at the side of the rest area.

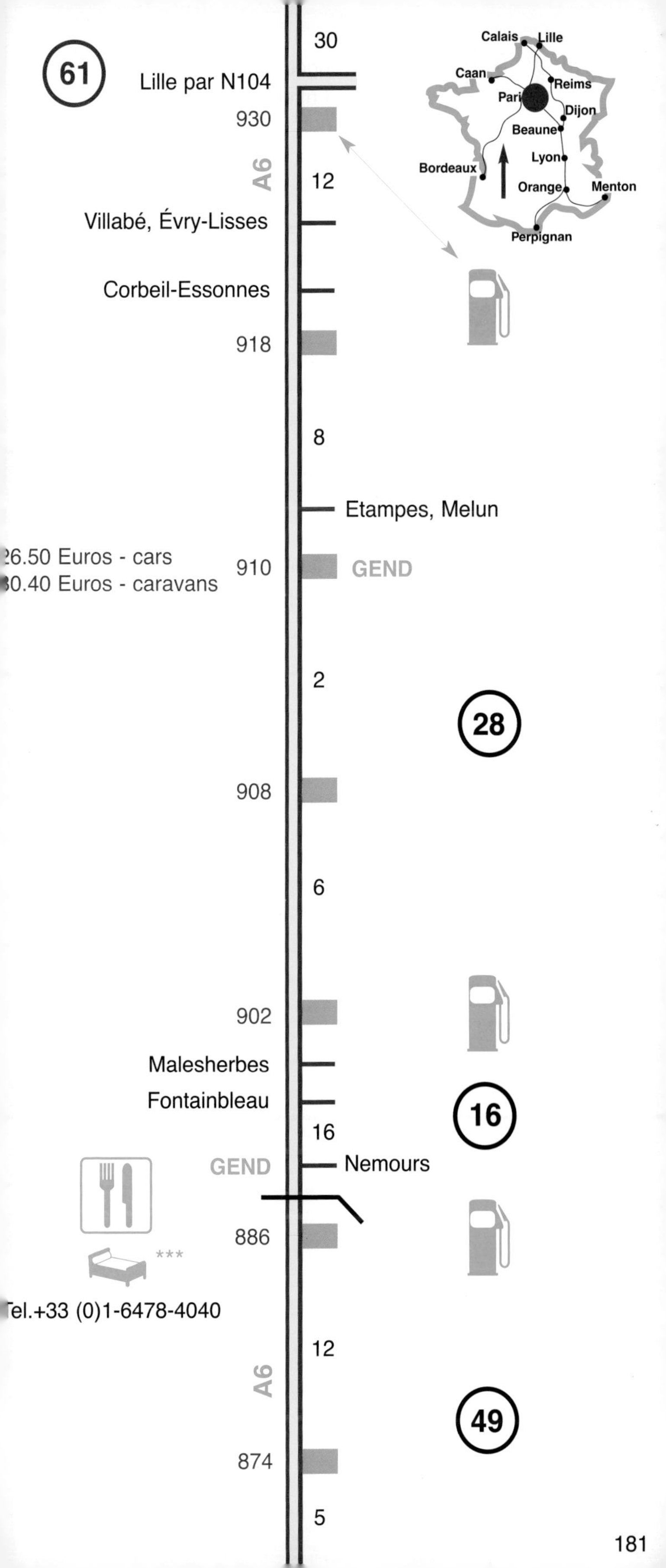
61
Lille par N104
30
930
A6
12
Villabé, Évry-Lisses
Corbeil-Essonnes
918
8
Etampes, Melun
26.50 Euros - cars
30.40 Euros - caravans
910
GEND
2
28
908
6
902
Malesherbes
Fontainbleau
16
16
GEND
Nemours
886
***
Tel.+33 (0)1-6478-4040
12
A6
49
874
5
Calais
Lille
Caan
Reims
Dijon
Beaune
Lyon
Bordeaux
Orange
Menton
Perpignan
28

Aire de Roberval-Est

Arranged on two levels, the upper level offers a lot of tables and benches, slides, swings and various rocking apparatus for children to play.
SOS - located by the entry to the rest area.

Aire de Barrière de Péage de Charmant, Paris

SOS - located on the parking area itself, another one is sited in close proximity of the exit slip-road.

Aire de Vemars-Est

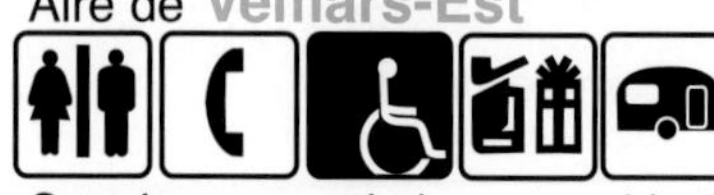

Spacious, mostly in car parking facilities.

In November 2010 the hotel was closed. Redevelopment of the Rest area takes place.

Aire de Villeron

Open space, mostly grassy at the top level of the rest area, few tables and benches.
SOS - by the motorway easily seen from the rest area.

La Courneuve

Just car parking facilities.

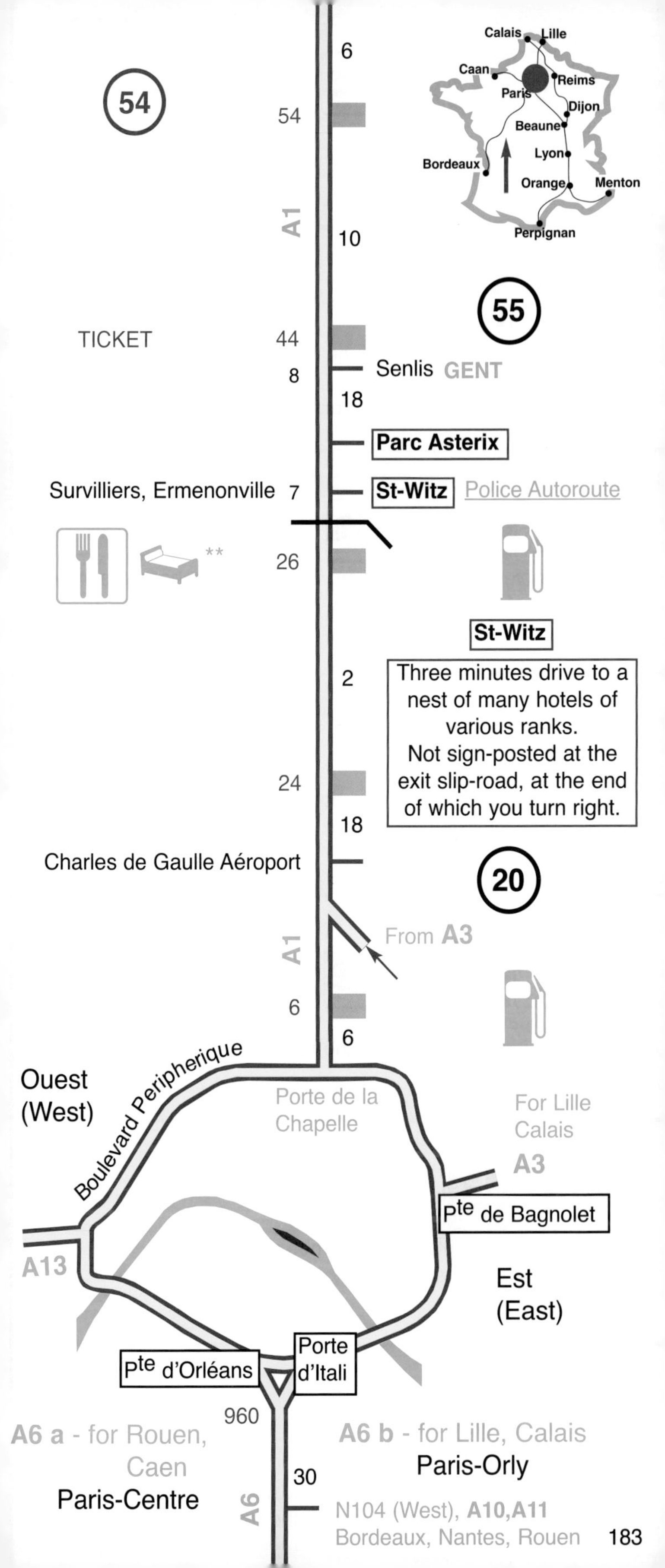
54
6
54
A1
10
Calais
Lille
Caan
Reims
Paris
Dijon
Beaune
Lyon
Bordeaux
Orange
Menton
Perpignan
55
TICKET
44
8
Senlis GENT
18
Parc Asterix
Survilliers, Ermenonville 7
St-Witz
Police Autoroute
**
26
St-Witz
2
Three minutes drive to a nest of many hotels of various ranks.
Not sign-posted at the exit slip-road, at the end of which you turn right.
24
18
Charles de Gaulle Aéroport
20
From A3
A1
6
6
Boulevard Peripherique
Ouest (West)
Porte de la Chapelle
For Lille Calais
A3
Pte de Bagnolet
A13
Est (East)
Porte d'Itali
Pte d'Orléans
960
A6 a - for Rouen, Caen
Paris-Centre
A6 b - for Lille, Calais
Paris-Orly
30
A6
N104 (West), A10,A11
Bordeaux, Nantes, Rouen

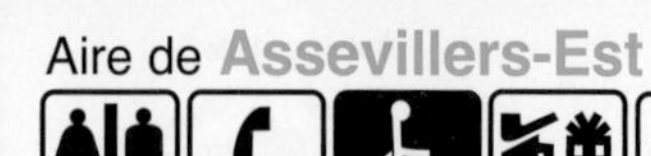

Aire de **Assevillers-Est**

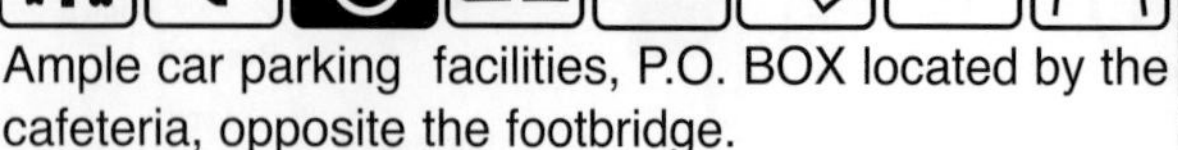

Ample car parking facilities, P.O. BOX located by the cafeteria, opposite the footbridge.
SOS - located by the entry to the rest area.

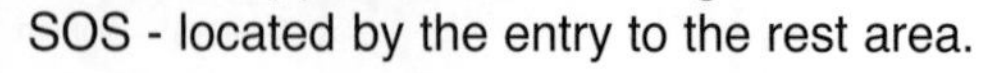

Aire de **Fonches**

Open space type of area with nests of tables and benches. There are telephone cabins.
SOS - at the side, close to the exit slip-road.

Aire de **Goyencourt-Est**

Nests of tables and benches among trees, telephone mounted on the wall of WC housing by the entrance.
SOS - in close proximity of the entry slip-road.

Aire de **Tilloloy-Est**

There are plenty of tables and benches among trees.
SOS - at the side of the rest area.

Aire de **Ressons-Est**

Mostly car parking facilities.
SOS - located by the entry to the rest area.

Aire de **Remy**

There are lots of tables and benches among trees.
SOS - located in close proximity of the entry slip-road.

Aire de **Chevrières**

Spacious with some tables and benches among trees. The telephone is mounted on the WC housing wall by the entrance.
SOS - located 200 m past the rest area.

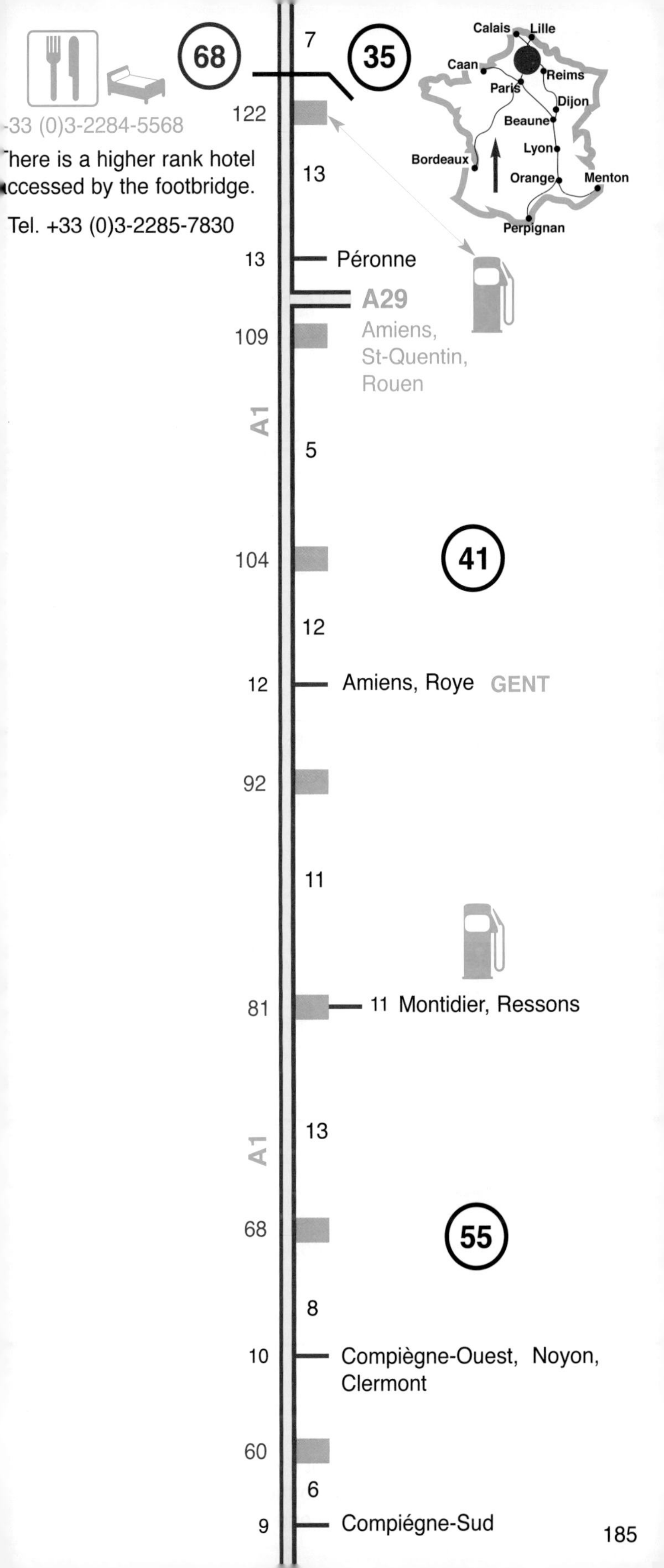
68
7
35
Calais
Lille
Caan
Reims
Paris
Dijon
Beaune
Lyon
Bordeaux
Orange
Menton
Perpignan
-33 (0)3-2284-5568
122
'here is a higher rank hotel
ccessed by the footbridge.
Tel. +33 (0)3-2285-7830
13
13
Péronne
A29
109
Amiens,
St-Quentin,
Rouen
A1
5
104
41
12
12
Amiens, Roye
GENT
92
11
81
11 Montidier, Ressons
13
A1
68
55
8
10
Compiègne-Ouest, Noyon,
Clermont
60
6
9
Compiégne-Sud

Aire de la Grande Bucaille

There are tables and benches, small and simple.
SOS - at the side of the area and also on the rest area itself.

Aire d' Angres

Spacious, few tables and benches in the open and under trees, well looked after, inviting.
SOS - at the side of motorway, easily seen from the rest area, just past the service station complex.

Aire de la Cressonnière

Open space, two lane parking area, couple of tables and benches, simple.
SOS - at the side toward the entry to the area.

Aire de Wancourt-Est

The caravenners site is located at the end of the rest area by the exit, some tables and benches in the open space and under trees. SOS - at the side of the rest area.

Aire de Croisilles

Some tables and benches well screened by bushes at the upper level of the rest area.
SOS - at the side.

Aire de Beaulencourt

Small with few tables and benches.
SOS - at the side of the rest area.

Aire de Feuillères

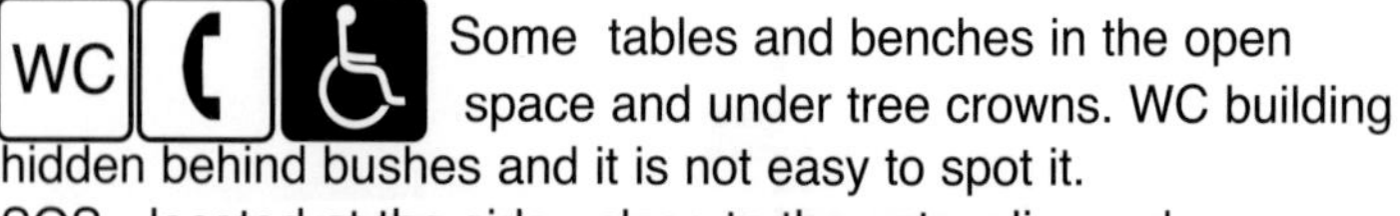

Some tables and benches in the open space and under tree crowns. WC building hidden behind bushes and it is not easy to spot it.
SOS - located at the side, close to the entry slip-road. Another one is sited at the end of the exit slip-road.

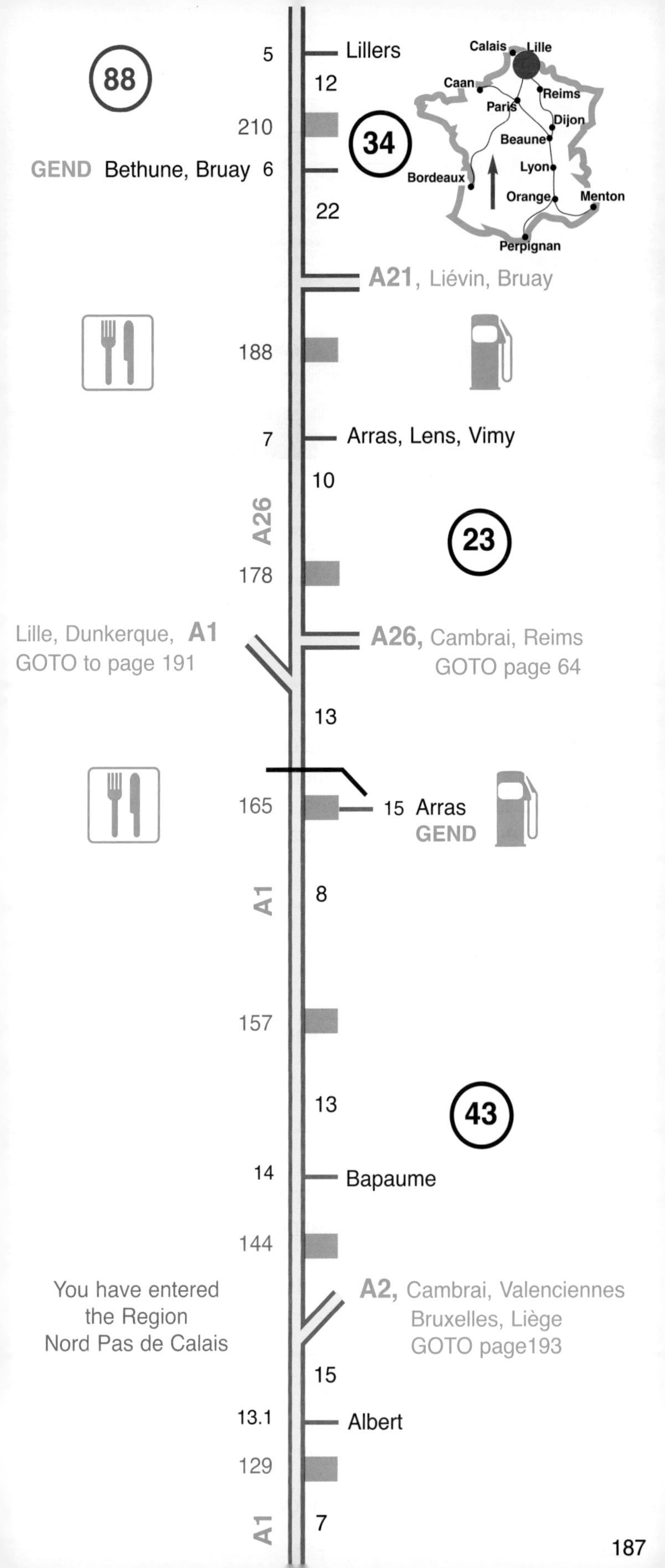
88
5
Lillers
12
210
34
GEND Bethune, Bruay 6
22
Calais
Lille
Caan
Reims
Paris
Dijon
Beaune
Bordeaux
Lyon
Orange
Menton
Perpignan
A21, Liévin, Bruay
188
7
Arras, Lens, Vimy
10
A26
23
178
Lille, Dunkerque, A1
GOTO to page 191
A26, Cambrai, Reims
GOTO page 64
13
165
15 Arras
GEND
A1
8
157
13
43
14
Bapaume
144
You have entered
the Region
Nord Pas de Calais
A2, Cambrai, Valenciennes
Bruxelles, Liège
GOTO page193
15
13.1
Albert
129
A1
7

Port Calais

Aire de Nortkerque

There are tables and benches arranged in a manner offering a degree of privacy, tidy, well cared for.

SOS - located at the side by the motorway and another one is located on the rest area.

Aire de Barrière de péage de Setques

Open space parking area with some tables and benches. Smart.

GEND

Aire de Villefleur

Open space type of site with tables and benches offering privacy of picnicking.

SOS - at the side of the rest area. It is difficult to spot it, as it is embedded by bushy trees.

Aire de Hilaire-Cottes

Spacious, grassy with some tables and benches arranged neatly in a row.

SOS - at the side of the rest area towards the exit slip-road.

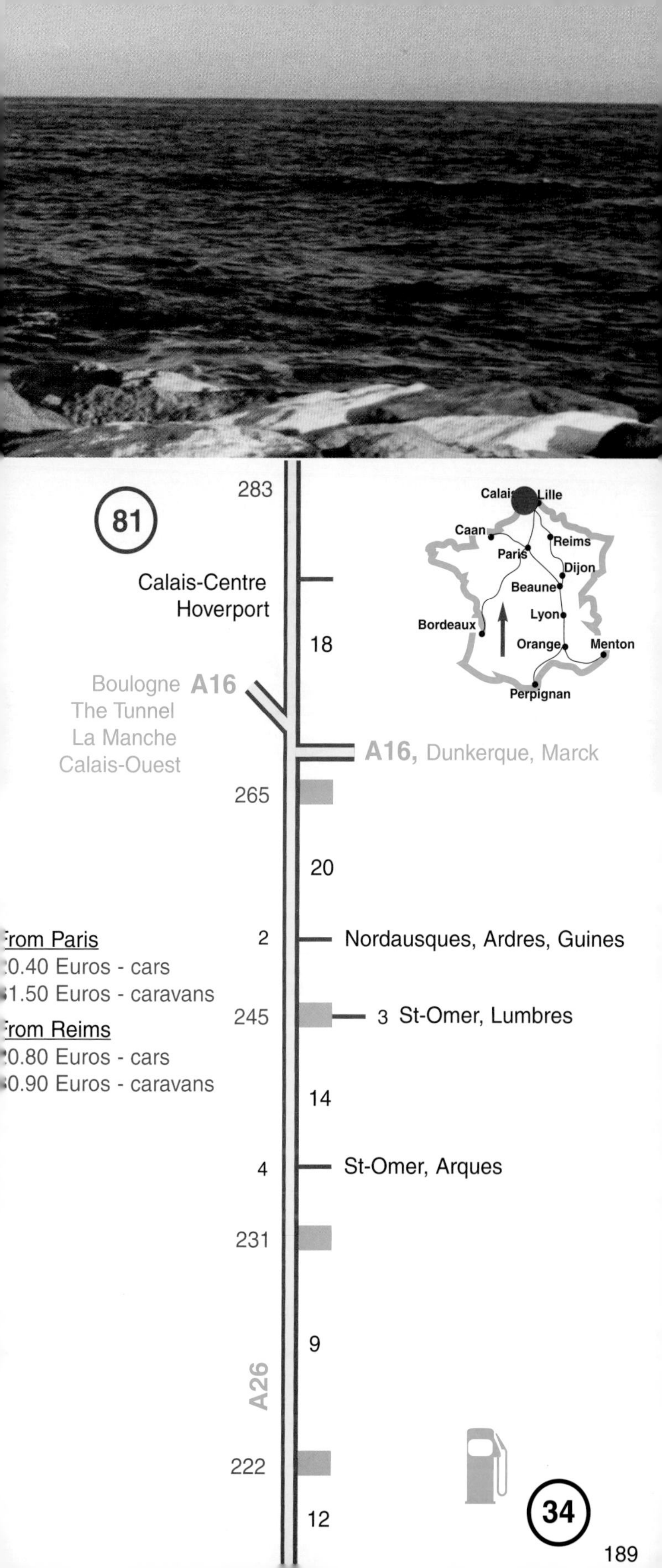
81
283
Calais-Centre
Hoverport
18
Boulogne A16
The Tunnel
La Manche
Calais-Ouest
A16, Dunkerque, Marck
265
20
From Paris
0.40 Euros - cars
1.50 Euros - caravans
2
Nordausques, Ardres, Guines
245
3 St-Omer, Lumbres
From Reims
0.80 Euros - cars
0.90 Euros - caravans
14
4
St-Omer, Arques
231
9
A26
222
12
34
Calais
Lille
Caan
Reims
Paris
Dijon
Beaune
Lyon
Bordeaux
Orange
Menton
Perpignan

Aire de **Phalempin-Est**

Just car parking facilities.
SOS - located by the motorway, just past the exit slip-road.

Aire de **Barrière de péage de Fresnes, Lille**

Spacious in car parking facilities.
GEND
SOS - located actually on the parking area.

Aire de **Wancourt-Est** (shown here for reference)

SOS - at the side of the rest area.

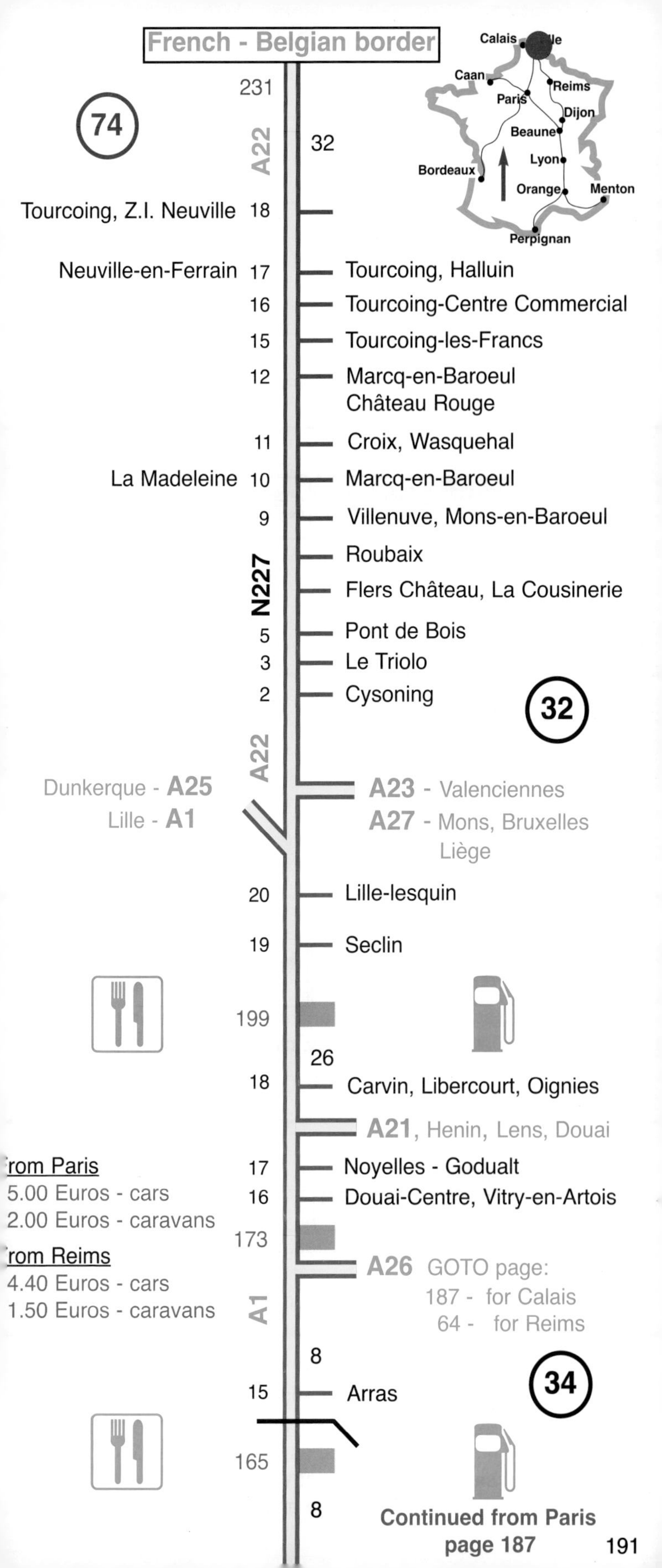
French - Belgian border
Calais
Caan
Paris
Reims
Dijon
Beaune
Lyon
Bordeaux
Orange
Menton
Perpignan
74
231
A22
32
Tourcoing, Z.I. Neuville 18
Neuville-en-Ferrain 17
Tourcoing, Halluin
16 Tourcoing-Centre Commercial
15 Tourcoing-les-Francs
12 Marcq-en-Baroeul
Château Rouge
11 Croix, Wasquehal
La Madeleine 10
Marcq-en-Baroeul
9 Villenuve, Mons-en-Baroeul
N227
Roubaix
Flers Château, La Cousinerie
5 Pont de Bois
3 Le Triolo
2 Cysoning
32
A22
Dunkerque - A25
Lille - A1
A23 - Valenciennes
A27 - Mons, Bruxelles
Liège
20 Lille-lesquin
19 Seclin
199
26
18 Carvin, Libercourt, Oignies
A21, Henin, Lens, Douai
rom Paris
5.00 Euros - cars
2.00 Euros - caravans
rom Reims
4.40 Euros - cars
1.50 Euros - caravans
17 Noyelles - Godualt
16 Douai-Centre, Vitry-en-Artois
173
A26 GOTO page:
187 - for Calais
64 - for Reims
A1
8
15 Arras
34
165
8
Continued from Paris
page 187

Rest area at the French - Belgian border

Limited rest area facilities.

Aire d' Emblise

NO FACILITIES

Two lane parking with no facilities of any kind.

SOS - located at the very end of the exit slip-road.

Aire de la Sentinelle

Basically parking spaces. Spacious.
SOS - at the side of the rest area towards the entry slip-road, just past the footbridge.

Aire de Barrière de péage de Hordain

Just parking spaces.
Gendarmerie.

Aire d' Havrincourt

Open space, small with tables and benches, cafeteria, bar.
SOS - by the side of the mtorway, close to the exit slip-road.

Aire de Rocquigny

A lot of sets of tables and benches, mostly under trees, small and smart
SOS - at the side of the rest area, not easy to spot it.

Aire de Feuilléres (Shown here for reference)

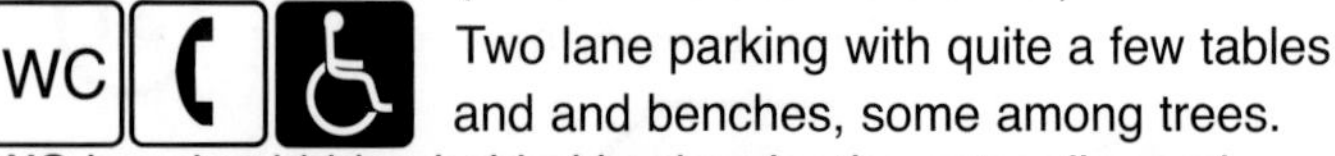

Two lane parking with quite a few tables and and benches, some among trees.
WC housing hidden behind bushes by the entry slip-road.
SOS - at the side, close to the entry slip-road.
Another one located at the end of the exit slip-road.

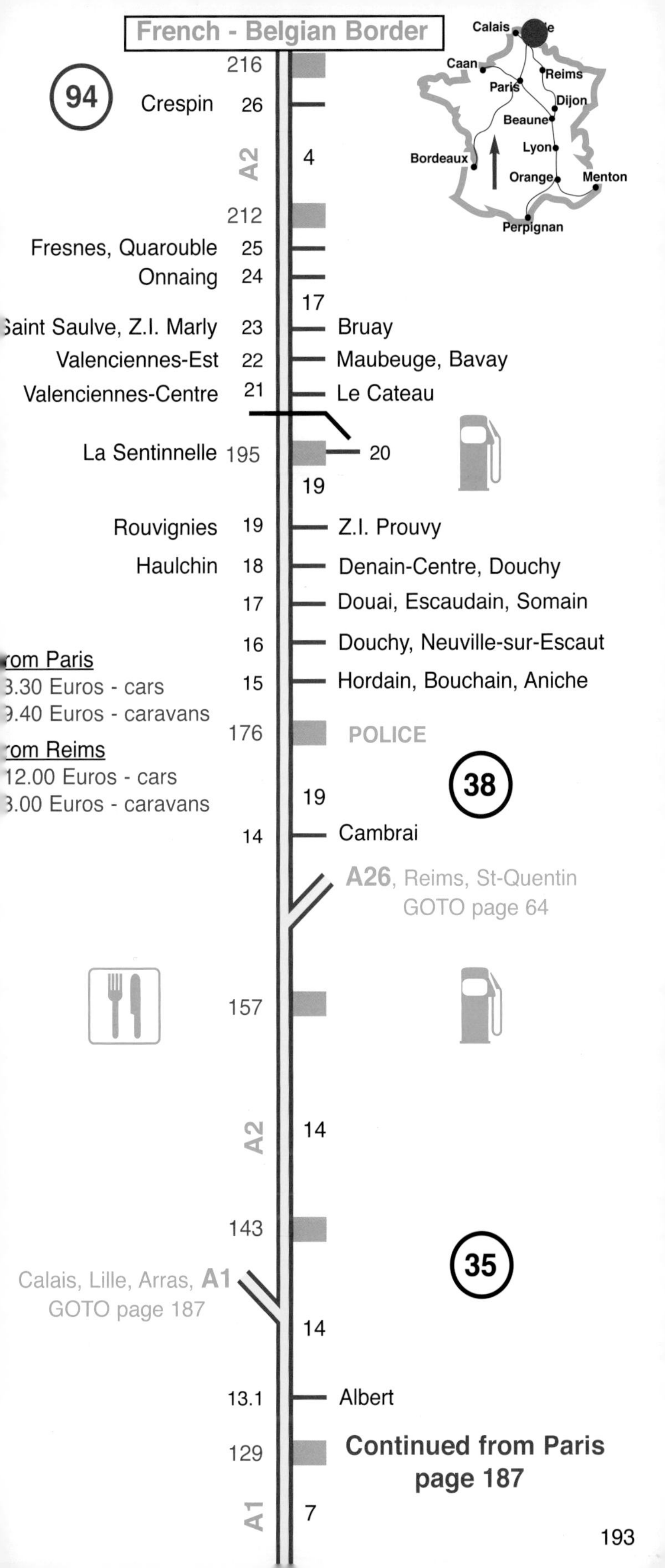
French - Belgian Border
Calais
Caan
Reims
Paris
Dijon
Beaune
Lyon
Bordeaux
Orange
Menton
Perpignan
94
216
Crespin 26
A2
4
212
Fresnes, Quarouble 25
Onnaing 24
17
Saint Saulve, Z.I. Marly 23 Bruay
Valenciennes-Est 22 Maubeuge, Bavay
Valenciennes-Centre 21 Le Cateau
La Sentinnelle 195 20
19
Rouvignies 19 Z.I. Prouvy
Haulchin 18 Denain-Centre, Douchy
17 Douai, Escaudain, Somain
16 Douchy, Neuville-sur-Escaut
15 Hordain, Bouchain, Aniche
rom Paris
3.30 Euros - cars
9.40 Euros - caravans
176 POLICE
rom Reims
12.00 Euros - cars
3.00 Euros - caravans
38
19
14 Cambrai
A26, Reims, St-Quentin
GOTO page 64
157
A2
14
143
35
Calais, Lille, Arras, A1
GOTO page 187
14
13.1 Albert
129
Continued from Paris
page 187
A1
7

FROM
(LYON) - BEAUNE
TO
CALAIS (PARIS BY-PASS)

Autoroutes
A6, A31, A5, A26, A4 & A26

Aire de la Villa-des-Tuillières

There are tables and benches and a site for caravanners.

Aire de Dijon-Spoy

Spacious with nests of tables and benches.
The services, as shown, are available at the other side of the motorway only and accessed by car.

Aire de Pre d'Azur

Spacious, a lot of greenery with a site for caravanners.
SOS - at the side of the rest area.

Aire de Gevrey-Chambertin

Spacious, many nests of tables and benches and a caravan site.
SOS - 300 m before the entry slip-road. Another one is located at the side of the motorway easily seen from the rest area.

Aire de Boncourt-le-Bois

Densely forested area with nests of tables an benches among trees.

Aire de Corgolin

One lane parking facilities with tables and benches among trees.

Aire de Beaune-Merceuil

This rest area is shown here for your reference only.

Continued from page 174

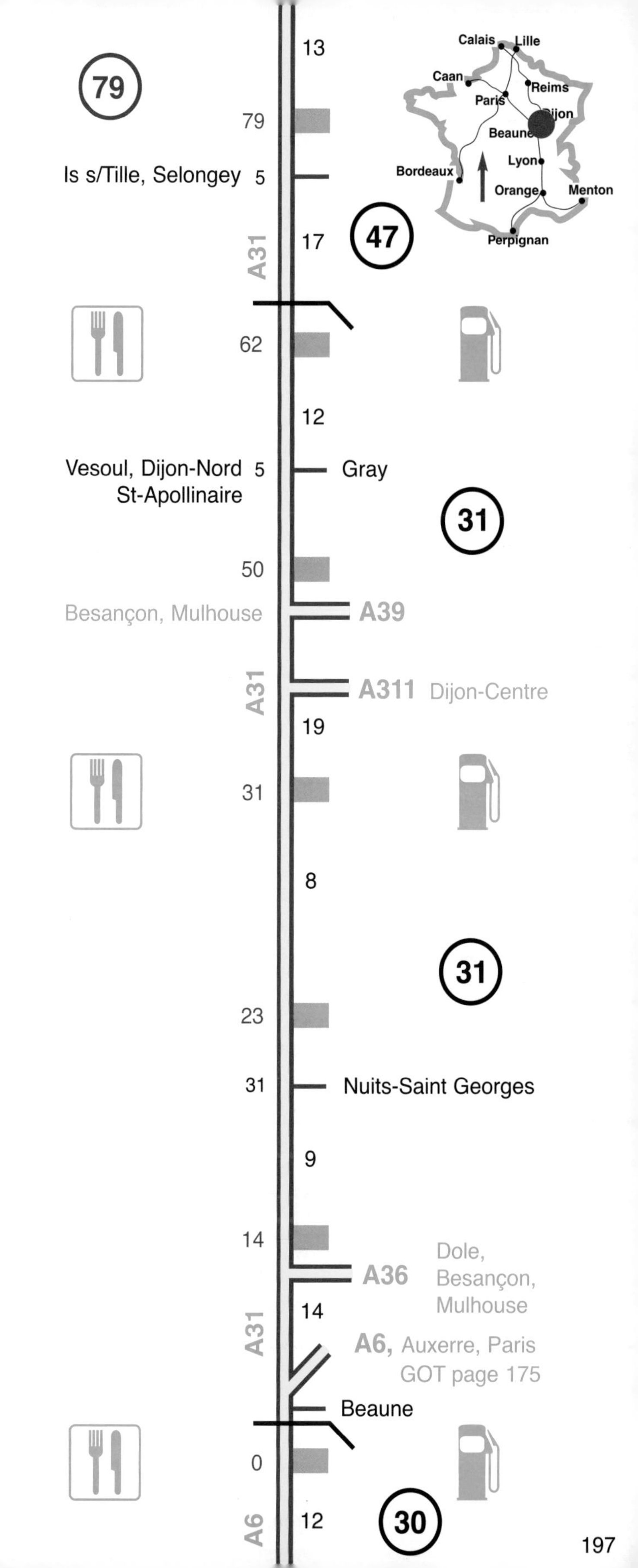

Calais
Lille
Caan
Reims
Paris
Dijon
Beaune
Lyon
Bordeaux
Orange
Menton
Perpignan
79
13
79
Is s/Tille, Selongey 5
47
17
A31
62
12
Vesoul, Dijon-Nord 5
St-Apollinaire
Gray
31
50
Besançon, Mulhouse
A39
A31
A311 Dijon-Centre
19
31
8
31
23
31
Nuits-Saint Georges
9
14
A36
Dole,
Besançon,
Mulhouse
14
A31
A6, Auxerre, Paris
GOT page 175
Beaune
0
30
A6
12

Aire des Crocs de la Terre

Two lane rest area with a few tables and benches. Public telephone mounted on the WC building wall by the entrance.
SOS - by the side of the rest area.

Aire de Troyes-Le-Plessis

Spacious, tables and benches, well looked after.
SOS- actually on the rest area, opposite the entry to the footbridge and another one located by the exit from the rest area.

Aire de Champignol

There are couple of nests of tables and stools.
SOS - located by the exit from the rest area.

Aire de Châteauvillain-Orges

Spacious in parking facilities with some tables and benches.
The P.O.BOX located inside the restaurant by the boutique.

Aire du Champ à la Croix

Two lane rest area with a couple of tables and benches among trees. The public telephone is located by the WC entrance.
SOS - sited by the m-way at the exit from the area.

Aire de Langres-Noidant

There is a site for caravanners with some tables and benches.

SOS - located at the side of the rest area.

Aire de Combe-Suzon

WC

There are some tables and benches.
SOS - by the side of the motorway accessed from the rest area through a recess in the tree-line screen separating the motorway from the rest area.

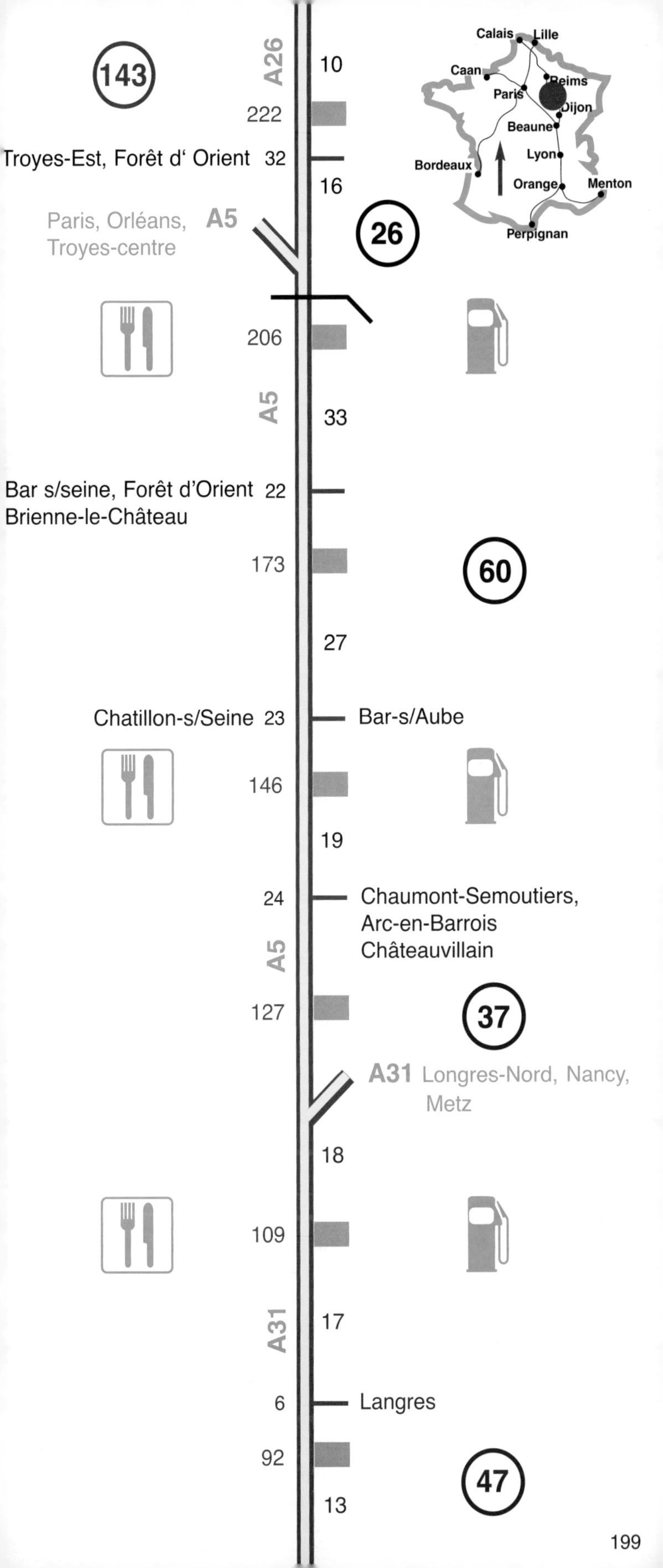

143
A26
10
222
Troyes-Est, Forêt d' Orient 32
16
Paris, Orléans, Troyes-centre A5
26
206
A5
33
Bar s/seine, Forêt d'Orient 22
Brienne-le-Château
173
60
27
Chatillon-s/Seine 23
Bar-s/Aube
146
19
24
Chaumont-Semoutiers, Arc-en-Barrois Châteauvillain
A5
127
37
A31 Longres-Nord, Nancy, Metz
18
109
A31
17
6
Langres
92
47
13
Calais
Lille
Caan
Reims
Paris
Dijon
Beaune
Lyon
Bordeaux
Orange
Menton
Perpignan

Aire de la **Vesle**

Small. Some tables and benches made of concrete neatly arranged under trees.
SOS - located at the side of the rest area.

Aire de **Reims Champagne-Nord**

Facilities accessible by car from the other side of the motorway
SOS - on the right hand side at the entry slip-road.

Aire des **Grands Traquiers**

Tables and benches.
SOS - one is located at the side of the rest area and another one actually on the rest area itself.

Aire de la **Bardolle**

There are some tables and benches.
SOS - one is sited at the side of the rest area and another one actually on the rest area.

Aire de **Sommesous**

Some tables and benches among trees and in the open space.
Entry to the area and the exit slip-road, as one.
SOS - located by the entry to the rest area. Garage assistance available e.g. tyres.

Aire de **Champ-l'Épée**

Small, yet with many nests of tables and benches in the open space, a lot of bushes, some trees.
SOS - at the side of the rest area, another one conspicuously placed on the rest area itself.

Aire de **Charmont**

Open space rest area with a couple of tables and benches.
Petrol available from automatic distribution pumps, operated by credit cards. Also accessed from the other side of motorway.
SOS - at the side of the rest area.

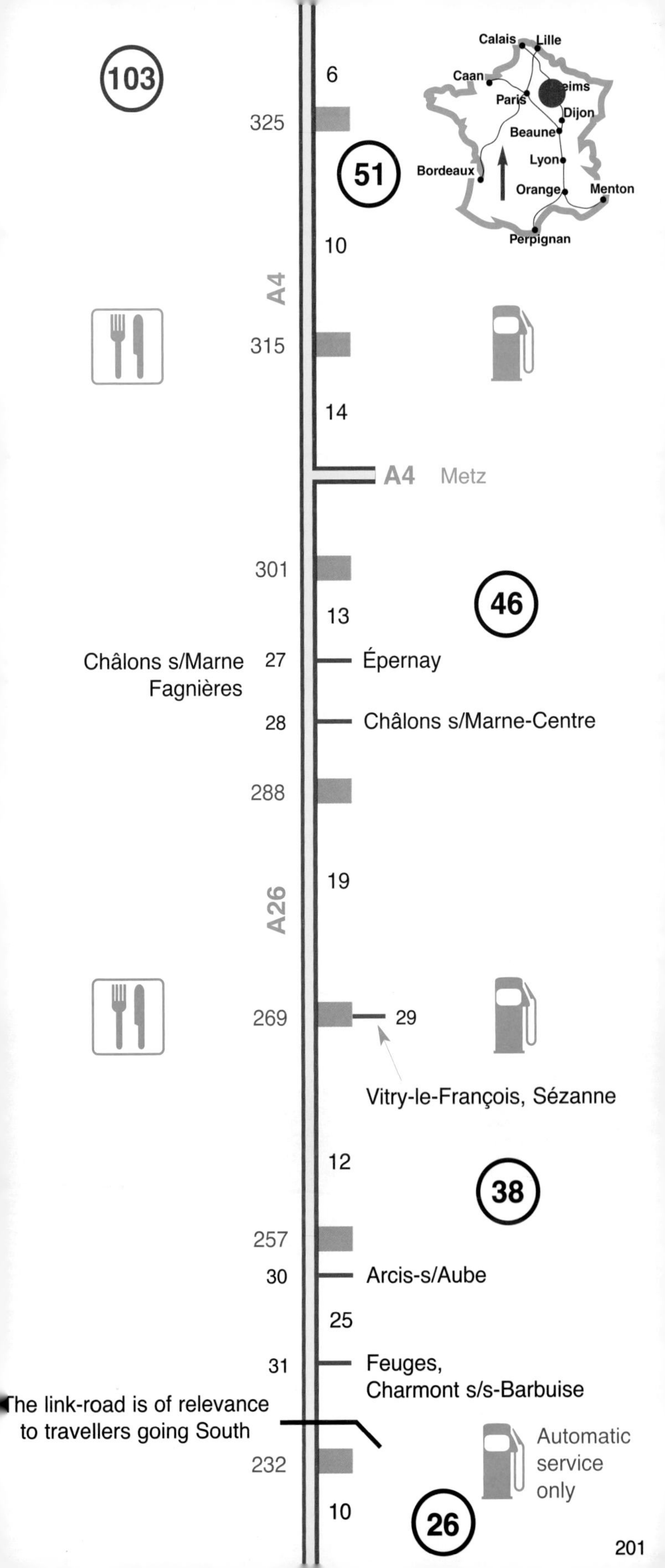
103
6
325
51
Calais
Lille
Caan
Paris
Dijon
Beaune
Lyon
Bordeaux
Orange
Menton
Perpignan
10
A4
315
14
A4 Metz
301
46
13
Châlons s/Marne
Fagnières
27
Épernay
28
Châlons s/Marne-Centre
288
19
A26
269
29
Vitry-le-François, Sézanne
12
38
257
30
Arcis-s/Aube
25
31
Feuges,
Charmont s/s-Barbuise
The link-road is of relevance
to travellers going South
232
Automatic
service
only
10
26

Aire de les **Pélerins**

Spacious, mostly open plan area with tables and benches at various parts of the area.

SOS - close to the entry slip-road to the rest area, another one actually on the rest area itself.

Aire de le **Champ Roland**

There are quite a few nests of tables and benches.

SOS - located at the side of the rest area.

Aire de **Loivre**

One lane rest area with a couple of tables and benches in the open space. It is marked with a caravan sign but, in fact, offers limited facilities.

SOS - there are two SOS telephones, one at the side of the rest area and the other one on the rest area itself.

Aire de **Barrière de péage de Coyrcy, Reims**

Spacious in car parking facilities.

***Aire de* Barrière de Péage de Taissy, Reims**

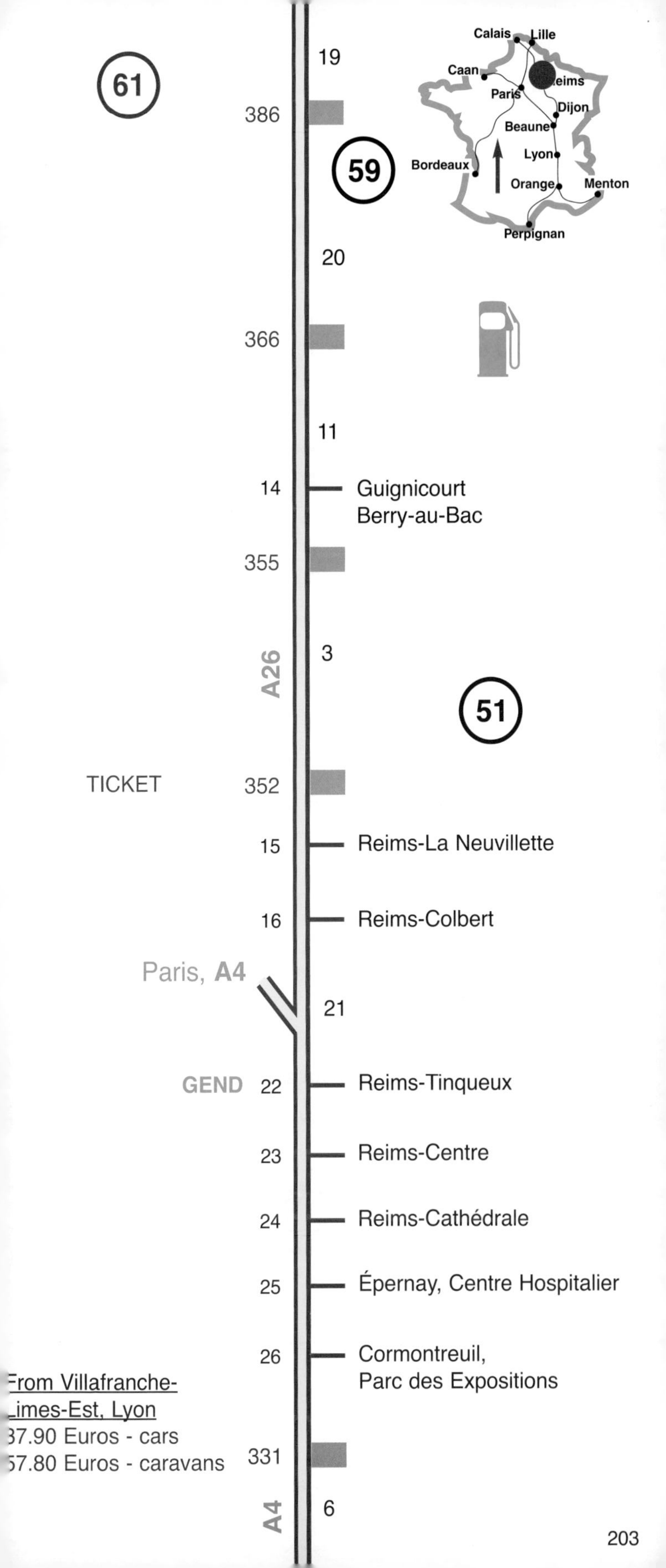
61
19
386
59
Calais
Lille
Caan
Reims
Paris
Dijon
Beaune
Lyon
Bordeaux
Orange
Menton
Perpignan
20
366
11
14
Guignicourt
Berry-au-Bac
355
A26
3
51
TICKET
352
15
Reims-La Neuvillette
16
Reims-Colbert
Paris, A4
21
GEND
22
Reims-Tinqueux
23
Reims-Centre
24
Reims-Cathédrale
25
Épernay, Centre Hospitalier
26
Cormontreuil,
Parc des Expositions
From Villafranche-
Limes-Est, Lyon
37.90 Euros - cars
57.80 Euros - caravans
331
A4
6

Aire de la Cressonnière

This rest area is shown here for your reference only.

Aire de Bonnettes

Couple of tables and benches.
WC - scruffy looking inside (October 2002).
SOS - located at the entry to the rest area.

To continue for Calais GOTO page 187

Aire de Rumaucourt

There are some tables and benches.

SOS - located at the entry slip-road.

Aire du Plateau

Some tables and benches, all offer privacy of picnicking.
SOS - located close to the entry slip-road.

Aire de la Haute Bruyère

Tables and benches in the open space and under trees with a lot of apparatus for children.
SOS - actually sited on the rest area.

Aire d' Urvillers

Spacious. Post Office Box located by the entrance to the cafeteria.
SOS - located in close proximity of the entry slip-road.

Aire du Broyon

Open space, small, a lot of grassy area, a few nests of tables and benches.
SOS - close to the entry slip-road and another one on the rest area itself.

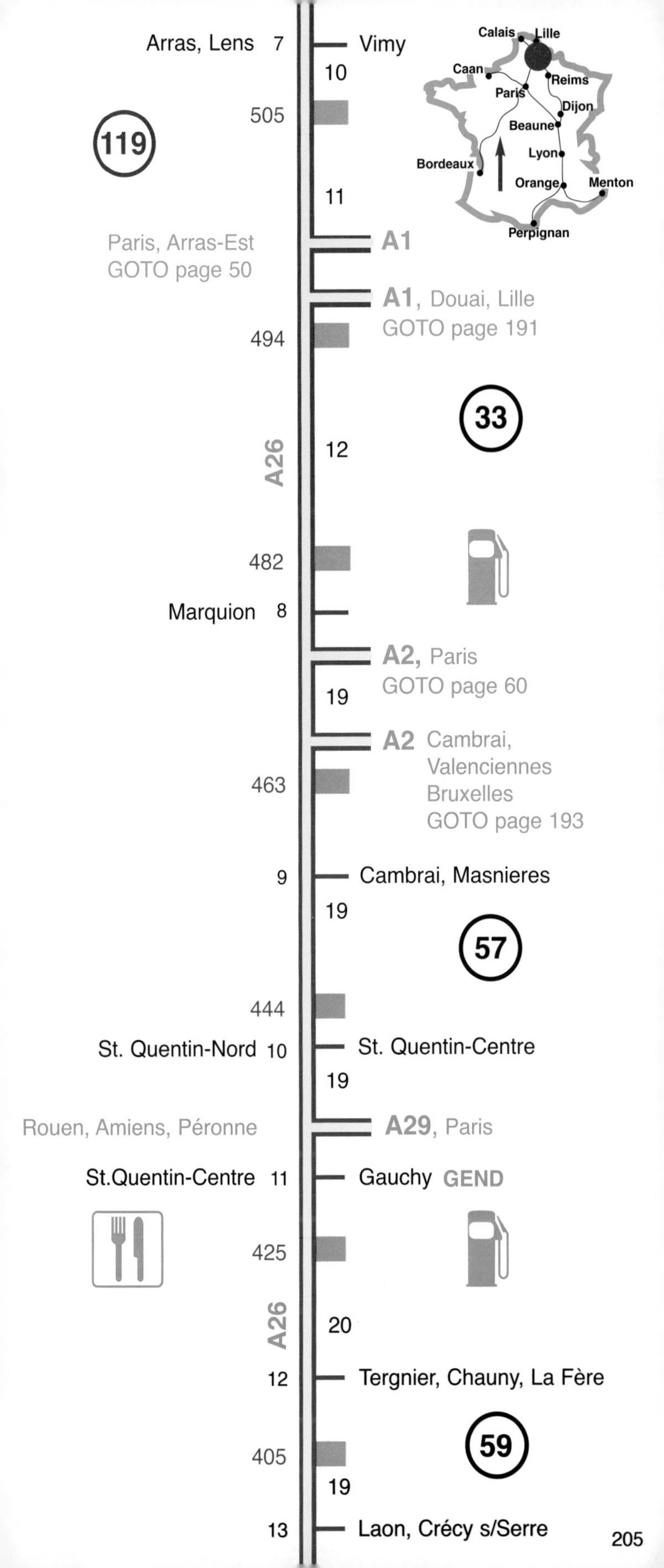

Arras, Lens 7
Vimy
10
505
119
Calais
Lille
Caan
Reims
Paris
Dijon
Beaune
Bordeaux
Lyon
Orange
Menton
Perpignan
11
Paris, Arras-Est
GOTO page 50
A1
A1, Douai, Lille
GOTO page 191
494
33
A26
12
482
Marquion 8
A2, Paris
GOTO page 60
19
A2 Cambrai,
Valenciennes
Bruxelles
GOTO page 193
463
9
Cambrai, Masnieres
19
57
444
St. Quentin-Nord 10
St. Quentin-Centre
19
Rouen, Amiens, Péronne
A29, Paris
St.Quentin-Centre 11
Gauchy GEND
425
A26
20
12
Tergnier, Chauny, La Fère
59
405
19
13
Laon, Crécy s/Serre

FROM
BORDEAUX
TO
PARIS

Autoroute A10

Aire de Boisredon

Tables and benches, mostly in the open space..
SOS - located at the side close to the entry slip-road.

Aire de Saugon

Tables and benches, spacious. “ Parcours de santé ”
SOS - at the side of the rest area. Access from the rest area is difficult.

Aire de Cézac

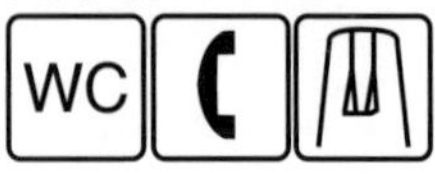

Spacious, forested, tables and benches, suitable for picnicking.

Aire de Barrière de péage de Virsac, Bordeaux

Small with few benches.

Aire de Meillac

Just parking facilities.

SOS - located 200 m approx. before the entry to the rest area.

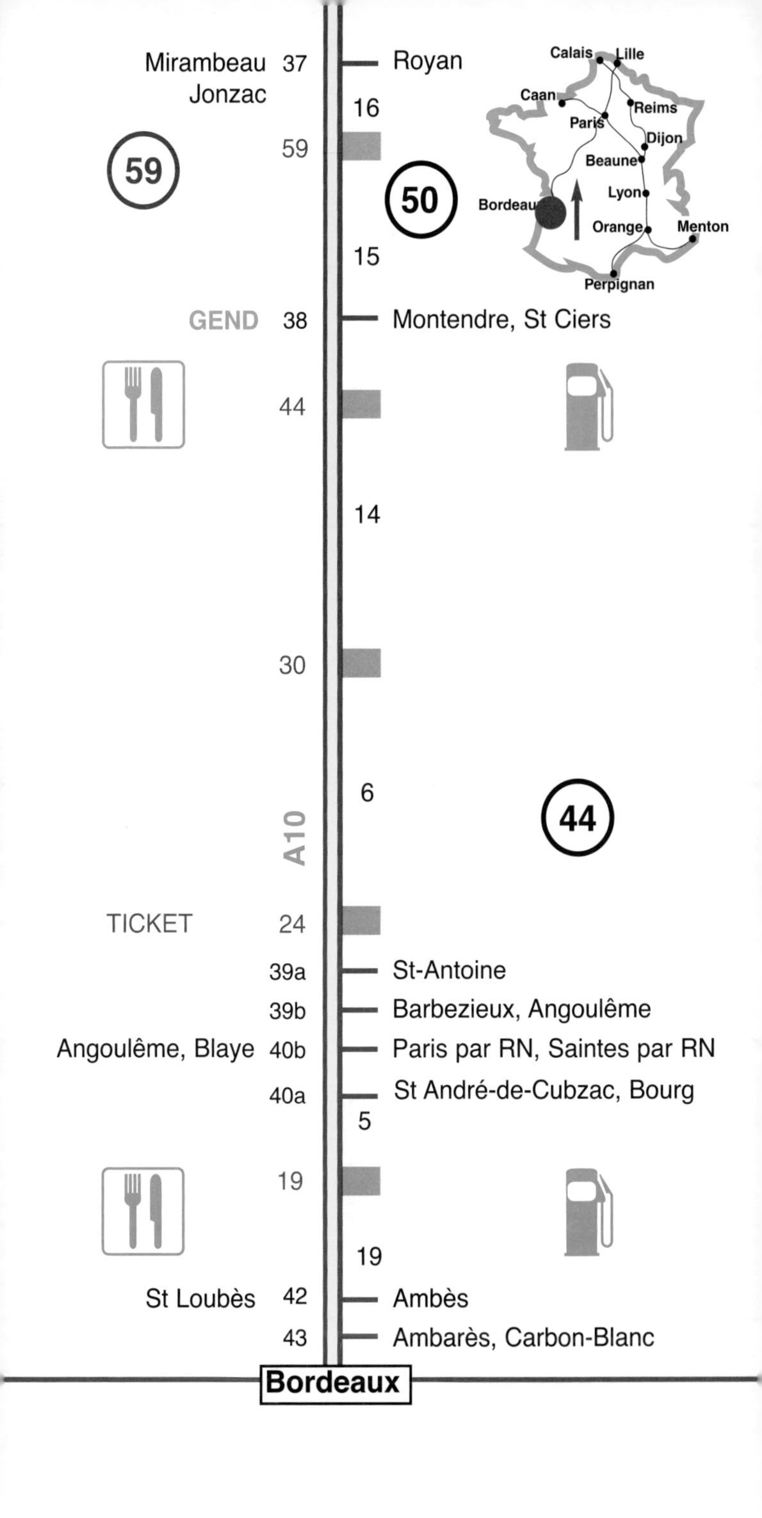
Mirambeau 37 Royan
Jonzac
16
59
59
50
Calais
Lille
Caan
Paris
Reims
Dijon
Beaune
Bordeaux
Lyon
Orange
Menton
Perpignan
15
GEND 38 Montendre, St Ciers
44
14
30
6
44
A10
TICKET 24
39a St-Antoine
39b Barbezieux, Angoulême
Angoulême, Blaye 40b Paris par RN, Saintes par RN
40a St André-de-Cubzac, Bourg
5
19
19
St Loubès 42 Ambès
43 Ambarès, Carbon-Blanc
Bordeaux

Aire de la Benâte

Large with tables and benches in the open space and among trees.
SOS - located on the rest area.

Aire de Fenioux

Open space type of area with climbing frames and swings.
Caravanners site entrance, by the exit from the rest area.
SOS - at the side of the rest area.

Aire de Port d' Envaux

Tables and benches among trees and in the open space, also climbing frames and swings. Small.
SOS - located on the left hand side by the entry slip-road.

Aire de Chermignac

There are tables and benches among trees.
SOS - at the side of motorway, easily seen from the rest area.

Aire de Saint-Léger

Tables and benches, slides, swings, see-saws.
There is another picnicking site accessed by the exit from the rest area.
SOS - located by the exit from the rest area.

Aire de St Palais

Tables and benches in the open space and among trees, suitable for picnicking.
SOS - at the side of the rest area.

Aire de St Ciers

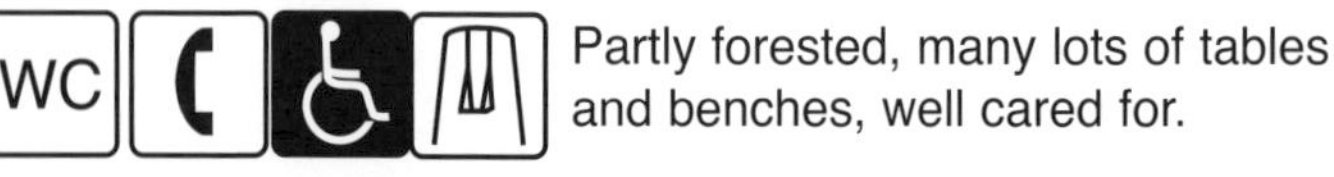

Partly forested, many lots of tables and benches, well cared for.

SOS - located by the entry to the rest area.

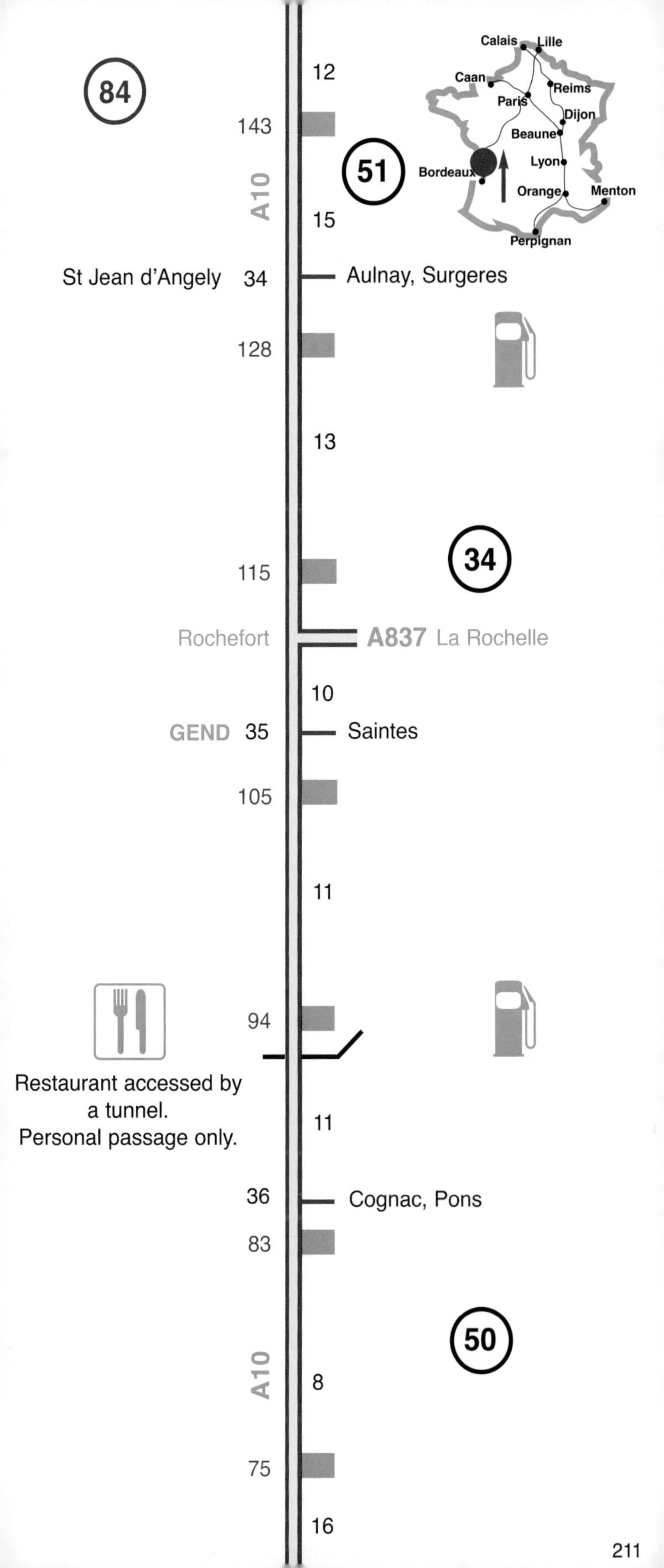
84
12
143
51
Calais
Lille
Caan
Reims
Paris
Dijon
Beaune
Lyon
Bordeaux
Orange
Menton
Perpignan
A10
15
St Jean d'Angely
34
Aulnay, Surgeres
128
13
115
34
Rochefort
A837
La Rochelle
10
GEND
35
Saintes
105
11
94
Restaurant accessed by a tunnel.
Personal passage only.
11
36
Cognac, Pons
83
50
A10
8
75
16

Aire de Coulombiers-Sud

Open space type of site with tables and benches and a lot of grassy spots.
SOS - at the side of the rest area.

Aire de Rouillé-Pamproux

Tables and benches in the open space and shady spots, a lot of grassy area with a site for caravanners at the exit end of the rest area offering privacy of picnicking.
SOS - at the side of the rest area.

Aire de Ste Eanne-Sud

Tables and benches, swings, climbing frames, some shady spots.
SOS - at the side of the rest area.

Aire de Ste Néomaye-Sud

Open space type of site, with few tables and benches.
SOS - 100 m before the entry to the rest area and another one by the side of motorway, close to entry slip-road.

Aire du Poitou-Charentes

There is a “Magasine des Ruralies-Marché des Saveurs”.
There are tables and benches, spacious.
SOS - close to the entry slip-road accessed by a footpath.

Aire de Gript-Sud

Tables and benches in the open space and under trees, slides, swings, climbing apparatus of various kinds.
SOS - conspicuously sited by the exit from the rest area.

Aire de Dœuil s/le Mignon

Tables and benches, climbing frames, shady spots.
SOS - located by the exit from the rest area.

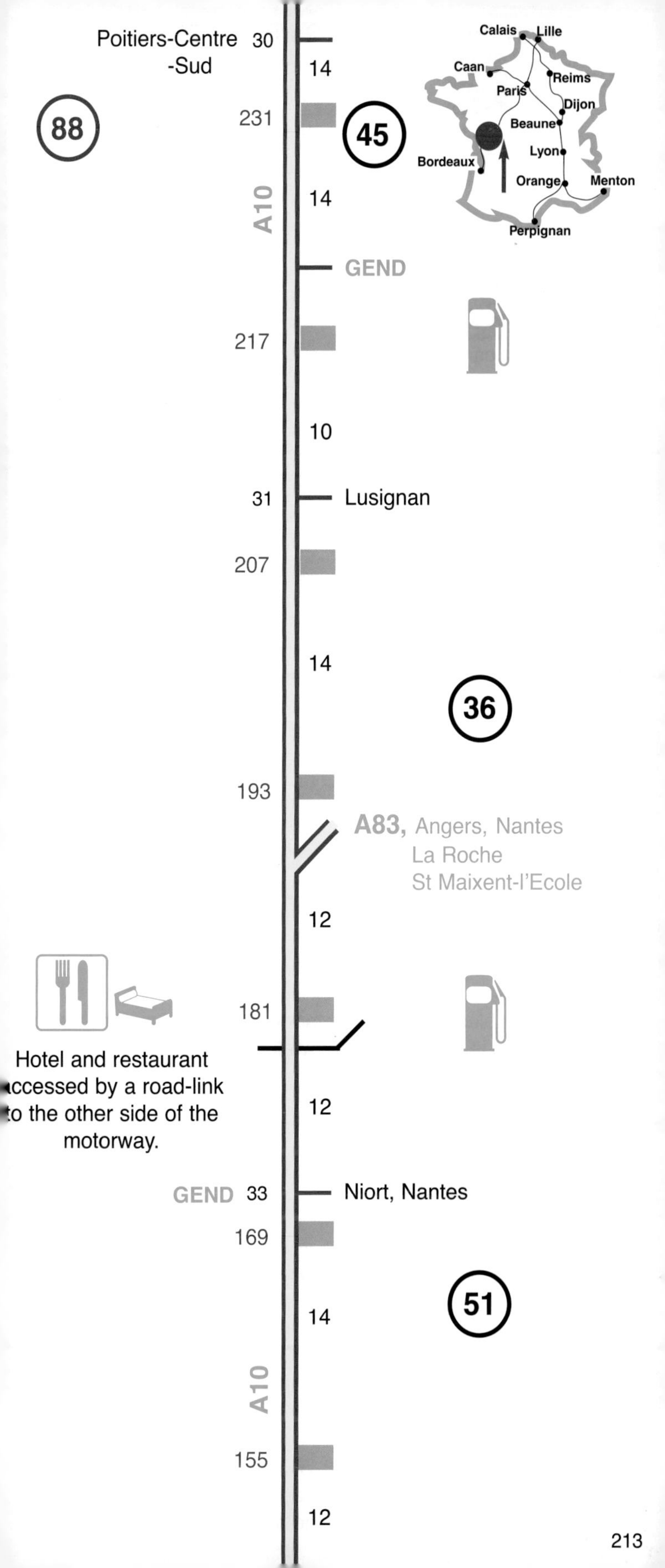

Poitiers-Centre
-Sud
30
14
88
231
45
Calais
Lille
Caan
Reims
Paris
Dijon
Beaune
Lyon
Bordeaux
Orange
Menton
Perpignan
A10
14
GEND
217
10
31
Lusignan
207
14
36
193
A83, Angers, Nantes
La Roche
St Maixent-l'Ecole
12
181
Hotel and restaurant
accessed by a road-link
to the other side of the
motorway.
12
GEND
33
Niort, Nantes
169
51
14
A10
155
12

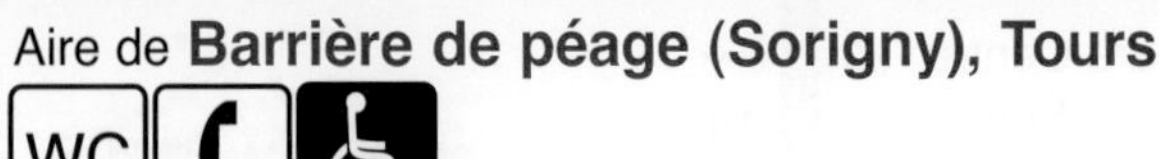

Aire de Barrière de péage (Sorigny), Tours

Few tables and benches,grassy spots. GENDARMERIE
SOS - just past the rest area.

Aire de la Fontaine-Colette

Basically, just car parking facilities, buffet, bar.
SOS - at the side of the rest area.

Aire de Nouâtre

Few tables and benches among trees.
SOS - conspicuously placed at the side, easily seen from the rest area.

Aire de Châtellerault-Usseau

  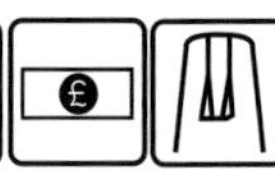

Mainly car parking facilities.
SOS - at the side of the rest area.

Aire des Chagnats

Quite a few tables and benches in the wooded part of the area.
The telephone is mounted on the wall by the entrance to WC.
SOS - at the side of the rest area.

Aire de Poitiers-Chincé

Just car parking spaces.
Post Office Box located by the entrance to the restaurant.
SOS - at the side, close to the exit from the rest area.

Aire des Quatre Vents

There are quite a few tables and benches at the upper part of the rest area. The telephone is located by the entrance to the WC housing.
SOS - at the end of the exit slip-road, and another one is sited 200 m approx. further up the route.

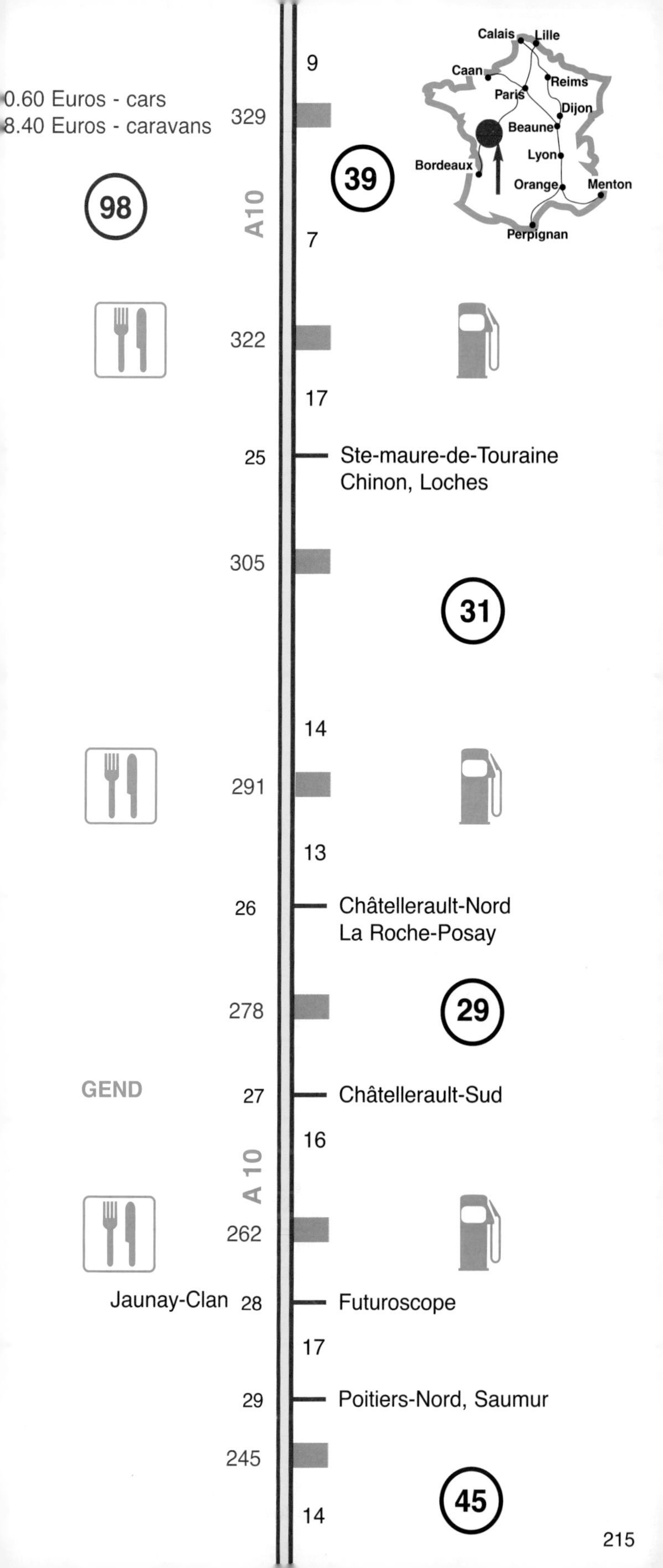

0.60 Euros - cars
8.40 Euros - caravans
329
9
98
39
A10
7
322
17
25
Ste-maure-de-Touraine
Chinon, Loches
305
31
14
291
13
26
Châtellerault-Nord
La Roche-Posay
278
29
GEND
27
Châtellerault-Sud
16
A 10
262
Jaunay-Clan
28
Futuroscope
17
29
Poitiers-Nord, Saumur
245
45
14
Calais
Lille
Caan
Reims
Paris
Dijon
Beaune
Bordeaux
Lyon
Orange
Menton
Perpignan

Aire de **Brusolle**

WC — One lane rest area with many tables and benches along the length of the area, some under trees. Telephone mounted on the wall by WC entrance.

SOS - conspicuously placed at the side of the rest area.

Aire de **Blois Ménars**

Just car parking spaces. There is a site for caravanners.
Cafeteria with slides for children at the side.
SOS - some 200 m before the entry to the rest area.

Aire des **Bruères**

Tables and benches mostly among trees. The site for caravanners is sign-posted.
SOS - located some 300 m approx. before the entry to the rest area. Another one is found at the end of exit slip-road.

Aire de la **Picardière**

Lots of nests of tables and benches among trees, offering privacy of picnicking. The rest area is located in a little forest.
SOS - located in close proximity of the entry slip-road

Aire de **Barrière de péage de Monnaie, Tours**

Just parking facilities. There is a "Station de Gonflage" - tyre inflating facilities, free of charge. GENDARMERIE

Aire de **Tours-Val-de-Loire**

Spacious, mostly car parking facilities.
SOS - at the side of the motorway, opposite the Service Station complex, easily seen from the rest area.

Aire du **Moulin Rouge**

Forested, tables and benches among trees, lot of grassy area and also a good hiding place during hot weather days.
SOS - at the side of the rest area towards the entry slip-road.

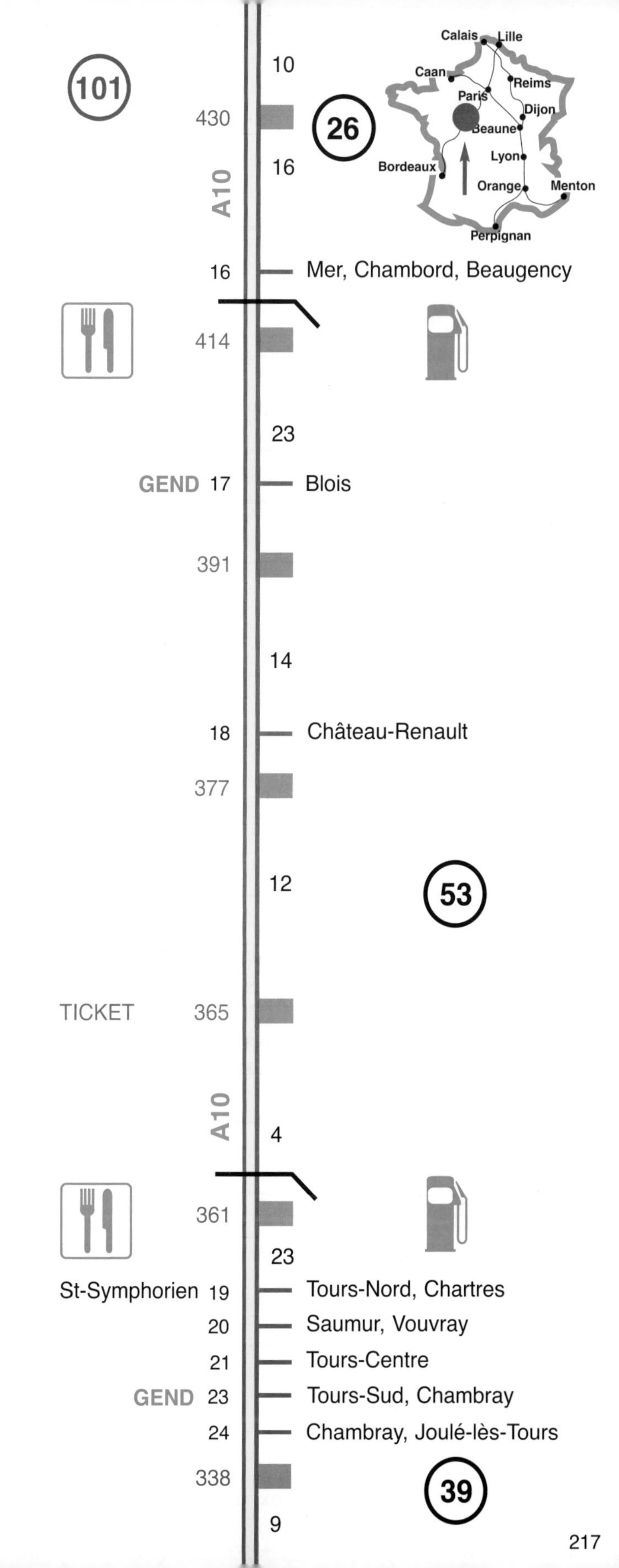
101
10
430
26
16
A10
Calais
Lille
Caan
Reims
Paris
Dijon
Beaune
Lyon
Bordeaux
Orange
Menton
Perpignan
16
Mer, Chambord, Beaugency
414
23
GEND 17
Blois
391
14
18
Château-Renault
377
12
53
TICKET
365
A10
4
361
23
St-Symphorien 19
Tours-Nord, Chartres
20
Saumur, Vouvray
21
Tours-Centre
GEND 23
Tours-Sud, Chambray
24
Chambray, Joulé-lès-Tours
338
39
9

Aire de **Barrière de péage de Folie Bassin, Paris**

Spacious in parking spaces.
SOS - it is here on the rest area itself.

Aire de **Marnières**

Large, open space with quite a few nests of tables and benches. There is a site for caravanners.
SOS - at the side of the rest area by the exit slip-road.

Aire du **Val Neuvy**

Just parking facilities.

Aire de la **Dauneuse**

It is a dense forest with tables and benches within.
SOS - at the side, close to the entrance to the rest area.

Aire d' **Orléans-Gidy**

Mostly parking facilities and provision for caravanners.
SOS - at the side of the rest area, just past the footbridge.

Aire des **Chauvry**

Small, one lane rest area with many tables and benches, some shady spots. Well looked after.
SOS - located by the entrance to the rest area

Aire de **Beaugency-Messas**

Just parking spaces.
SOS - located some 100 m approx. past the exit slip-road.

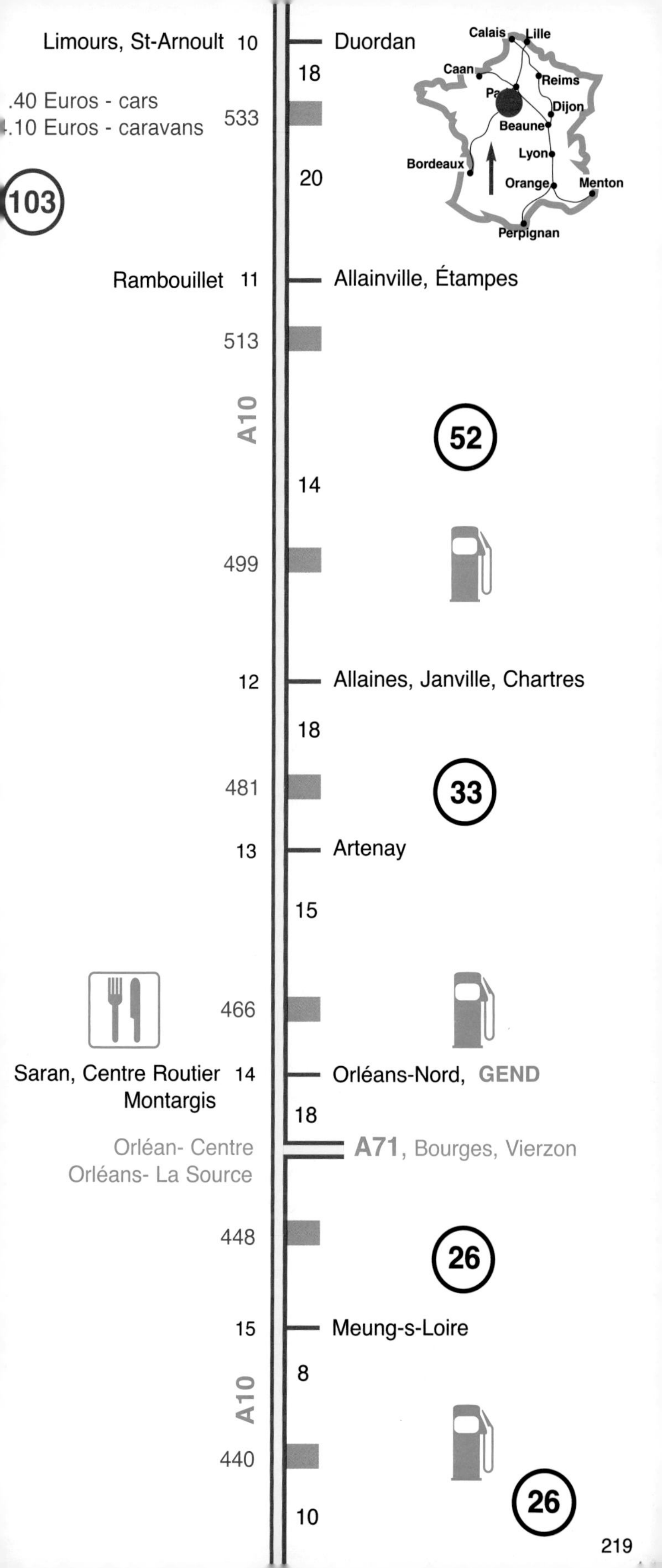

Limours, St-Arnoult 10
Duordan
18
.40 Euros - cars
.10 Euros - caravans
533
20
103
Calais
Lille
Caan
Reims
Dijon
Beaune
Lyon
Bordeaux
Orange
Menton
Perpignan
Rambouillet 11
Allainville, Étampes
513
A10
52
14
499
12
Allaines, Janville, Chartres
18
481
33
13
Artenay
15
466
Saran, Centre Routier 14
Montargis
Orléans-Nord, GEND
18
Orléan- Centre
Orléans- La Source
A71, Bourges, Vierzon
448
26
15
Meung-s-Loire
8
A10
440
26
10

Approaching the Boulevard Periphérique from the direction of the Autoroute A6 which is applicable to both, coming from Bordeaux and from Lyon, and depending on your intended destination, you continue your journey using the following information accordingly:
Before you reach Boulevard Periphérique the Autoroute A6 becomes two separate autoroutes. One, as A6b leading for Lille, Calais and Paris-Orly, and the other, A6a leading for Rouen, Caen and Paris-Centre.
In case you missed it, there will be another choice of the same, but, this time the alternatives are more specific: "A6a Pte d'Orléans" and "A6b Pte d'Italie".
The same option will be offered once again, soon after that, before you enter the Boulevard Periphérique round Paris.

The above information and the diagrammatically shown the Boulevard Periphérique on the next page are complementary and will help you through, nicely.

For CAEN you follow the sign "ROUEN" and for CALAIS you follow the sign "LILLE" while on the Boulevard Periphérique.

Aire de Limours-Briis-s/s-Forges

Just parking facilities provided.
SOS - at the side of the rest area.

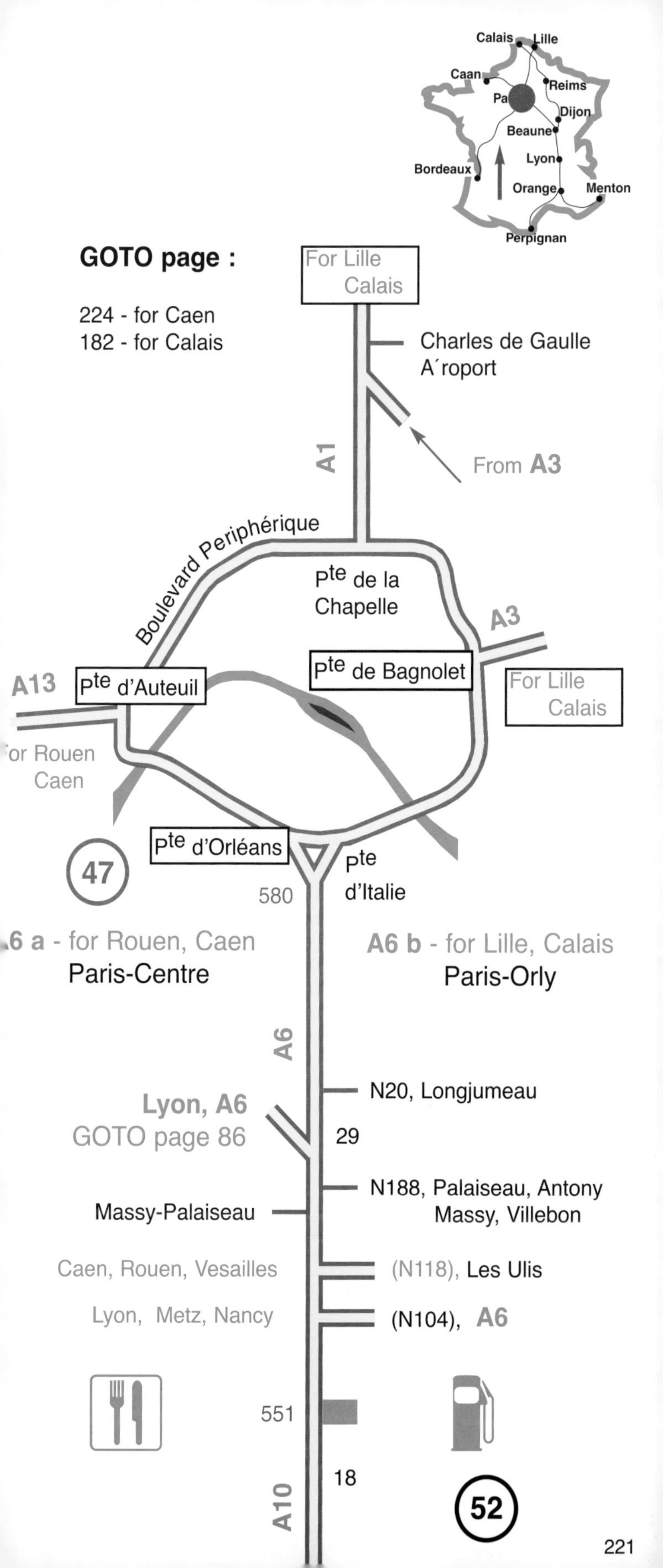
Calais
Lille
Caan
Pa
Reims
Dijon
Beaune
Lyon
Bordeaux
Orange
Menton
Perpignan
GOTO page :
224 - for Caen
182 - for Calais
For Lille
Calais
Charles de Gaulle
A´roport
A1
From A3
Boulevard Periphérique
Pte de la
Chapelle
A3
Pte de Bagnolet
A13
Pte d'Auteuil
For Lille
Calais
or Rouen
Caen
Pte d'Orléans
Pte
d'Italie
47
580
6 a - for Rouen, Caen
Paris-Centre
A6 b - for Lille, Calais
Paris-Orly
A6
N20, Longjumeau
Lyon, A6
GOTO page 86
29
N188, Palaiseau, Antony
Massy, Villebon
Massy-Palaiseau
Caen, Rouen, Vesailles
(N118), Les Ulis
Lyon, Metz, Nancy
(N104), A6
551
18
A10
52

FROM
PARIS
TO
CAEN

Autoroute A13

Aire de Guerville

This rest area is meant for lorries only

SOS - at close proximity of the entry slip-road to the rest area.

Aire de Épône-Nord

Just car parking facilities.

SOS - actually on the rest area by the WC building.

Aire de Morainvilliers-Nord

Spacious in parking facilities. Letter Box located by the entrance to the restaurant.
SOS - sited at close proximity of the entry slip-road.

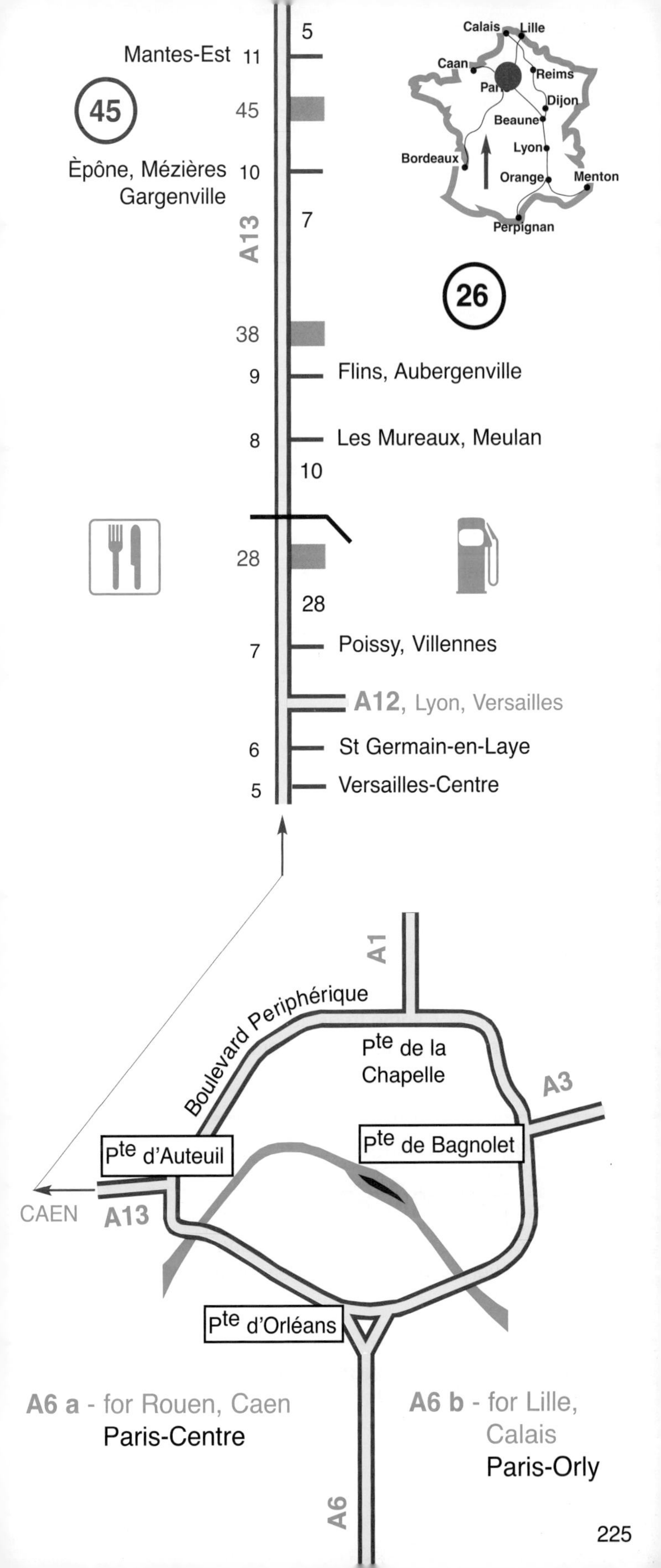

Calais
Lille
Caan
Paris
Reims
Dijon
Beaune
Lyon
Bordeaux
Orange
Menton
Perpignan
5
Mantes-Est 11
45
45
Èpône, Mézières 10
Gargenville
7
A13
26
38
9 Flins, Aubergenville
8 Les Mureaux, Meulan
10
28
28
7 Poissy, Villennes
A12, Lyon, Versailles
6 St Germain-en-Laye
5 Versailles-Centre
A1
Boulevard Periphérique
Pte de la Chapelle
A3
Pte d'Auteuil
Pte de Bagnolet
CAEN
A13
Pte d'Orléans
A6 a - for Rouen, Caen
Paris-Centre
A6 b - for Lille, Calais
Paris-Orly
A6

Aire de **Vironvay-Nord**

Spacious, mostly offering car parking facilities.
Post Office Box located by the entrance to the cafeteria.
SOS - sited in close proximity of the entry slip-road.

Aire de **Barrière de péage (Heudebouville)**

Just car parking spaces.

Aire de **Beauchêne-Nord**

There are few tables and benches in the forested part of the rest area. Parcours sportif.
SOS - located by entry slip-road on the right hand side.

Aire de **Douains-Nord**

Few benches among trees, very small.
SOS - located at the side in close proximity of the exit slip-road.

Aire Nord de la **Villeneuve-en-Chevrie (Nord)**

Open space ,grassy, some trees, tables and benches, small.
SOS - at the side, close to the exit from the rest area.

Aire de **Rosny-sur-Seine-Nord**

Spacious, open space area, mostly parking facilities.
SOS - at the very end of the rest area, by the exit slip-road.

Aire de **Barrière de péage (Buchelay)**

Two lane parking facilities.

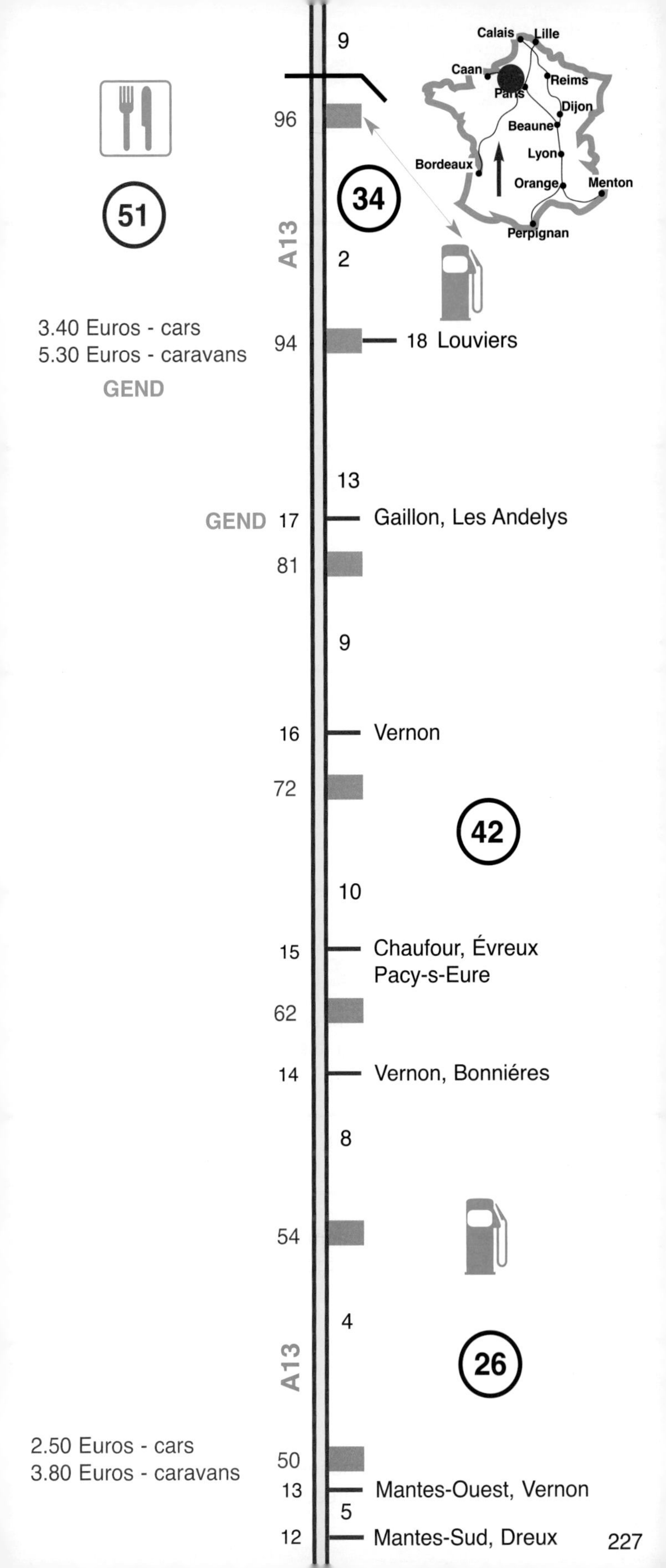

9
Calais
Lille
Caan
Paris
Reims
Dijon
Beaune
Bordeaux
Lyon
Orange
Menton
Perpignan
96
51
34
A13
2
3.40 Euros - cars
5.30 Euros - caravans
GEND
94
18 Louviers
13
GEND 17
Gaillon, Les Andelys
81
9
16
Vernon
72
42
10
15
Chaufour, Évreux
Pacy-s-Eure
62
14
Vernon, Bonniéres
8
54
4
A13
26
2.50 Euros - cars
3.80 Euros - caravans
50
13
Mantes-Ouest, Vernon
5
12
Mantes-Sud, Dreux

Aire de **Beuzeville-Nord**

Extensive parking facilities, grassy, some trees, tables and benches, spacious, attractive, offering privacy of picnicking.
SOS - at the side of the m-way, close to the exit slip-road.

Aire de **Barrière de Péage (Beuzeville)**

Just parking facilities.

Aire de **Josapha**

There are few tables and benches. Small.

SOS - 200 metres approx. from the entry to the rest area.

Not researched

Aire de **Bosquet-Nord**

Car parking spaces. Restaurant is accessed by the footbridge.
SOS - located on the rest area itself, opposite the service sta tion complex.

Aire de **Robert-le-Diable-Nord**

Open space, very small, tidy, some tables and benches.
SOS - located by the exit from the rest area on the left hand side.

Aire de **Bord-Nord**

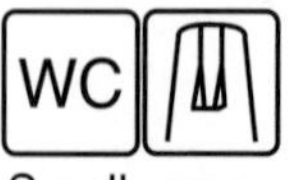

Small, grassy, tables and benches among trees.
SOS - at the side of the rest area, closer to the exit slip-road.

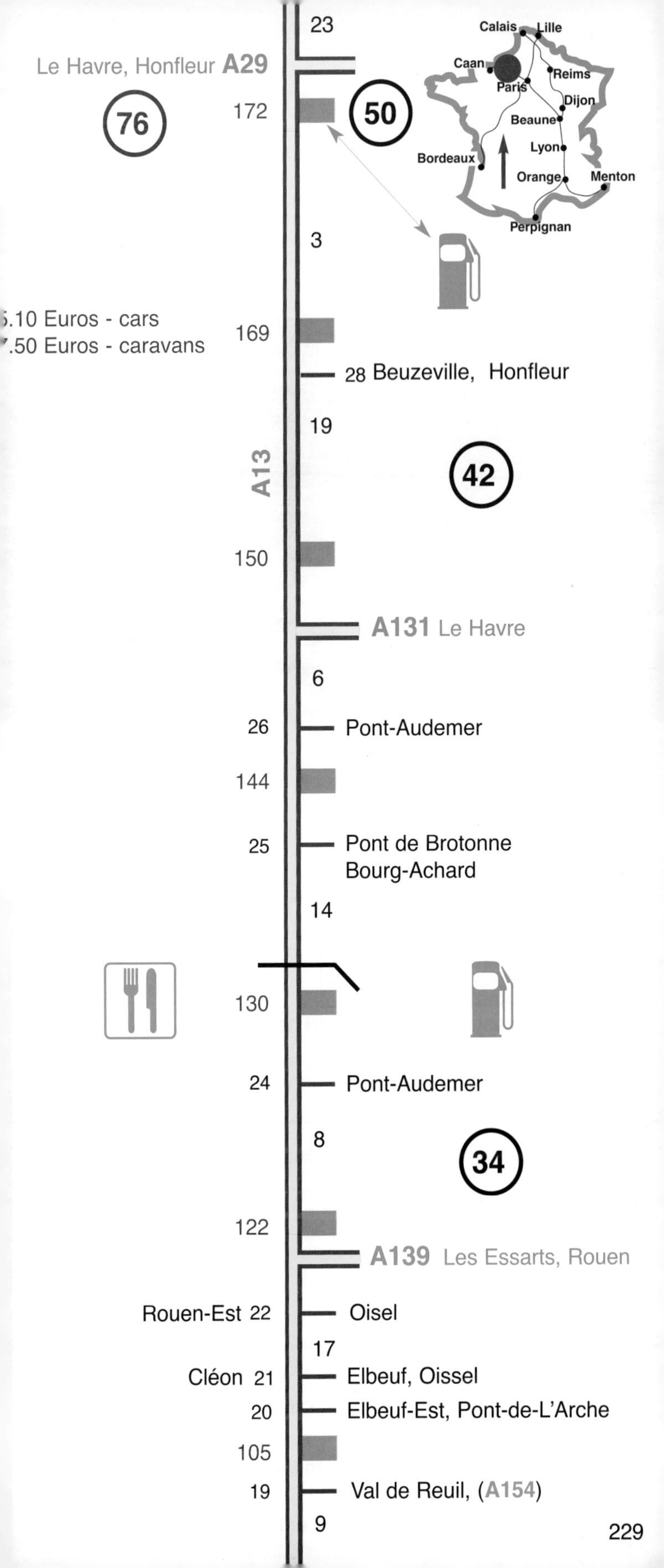
23
Le Havre, Honfleur A29
76
172
50
Calais
Lille
Caan
Reims
Paris
Dijon
Beaune
Lyon
Bordeaux
Orange
Menton
Perpignan
3
.10 Euros - cars
.50 Euros - caravans
169
28 Beuzeville, Honfleur
19
A13
42
150
A131 Le Havre
6
26
Pont-Audemer
144
25
Pont de Brotonne
Bourg-Achard
14
130
24
Pont-Audemer
8
34
122
A139 Les Essarts, Rouen
Rouen-Est 22
Oisel
17
Cléon 21
Elbeuf, Oissel
20
Elbeuf-Est, Pont-de-L'Arche
105
19
Val de Reuil, (A154)
9

Aire de **Giberville-Nord**

Spacious, grassy, some tables and benches.

SOS - at the side of the rest area.

Aire de **Barrière de péage (Dezulé)**

Just a car parking bay.

Aire d'**Annebault**

Small, open space, grassy, some trees, tables and benches. The site is screened from the motorway by a wall of trees.

SOS - located close to the entry slip-road.

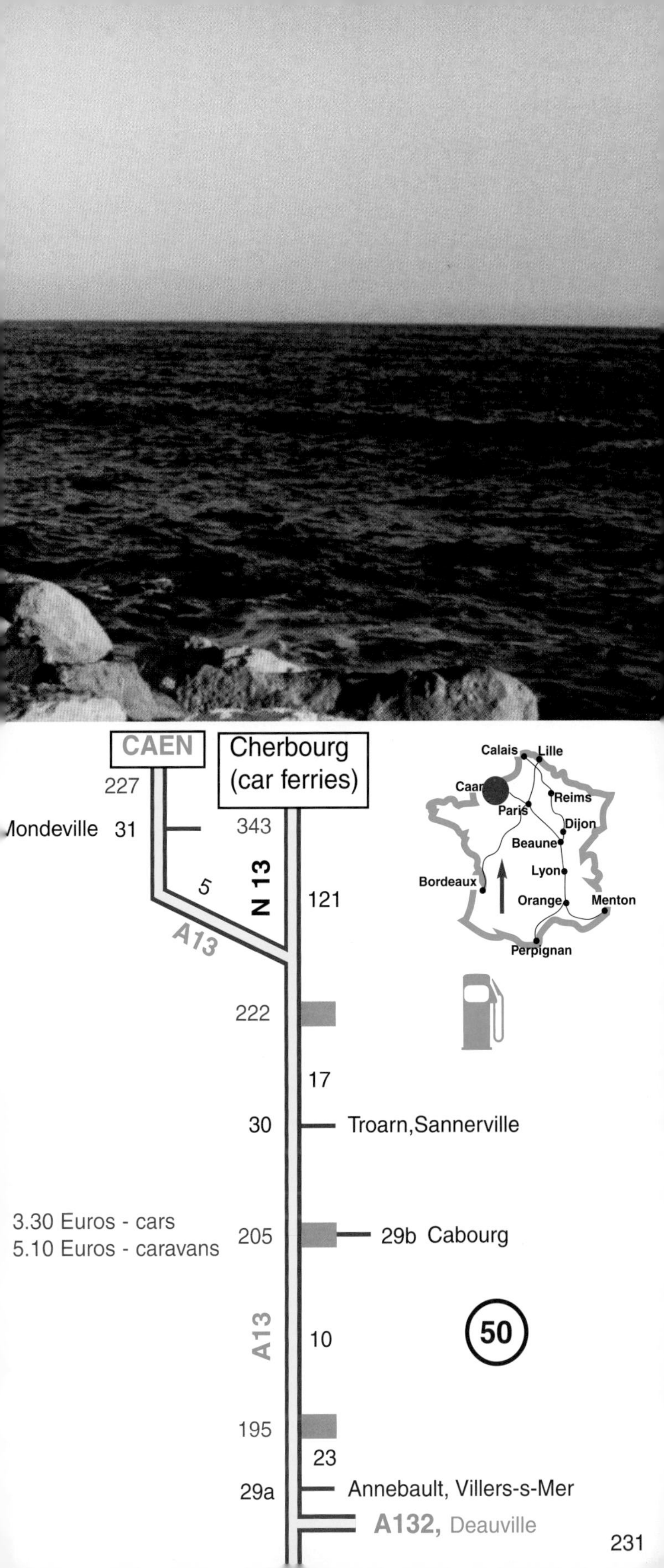

CAEN
Cherbourg
(car ferries)
227
/londeville 31
343
5
N 13
121
A13
222
17
30
Troarn,Sannerville
3.30 Euros - cars
5.10 Euros - caravans
205
29b Cabourg
A13
10
50
195
23
29a
Annebault, Villers-s-Mer
A132, Deauville
Calais
Lille
Caen
Reims
Paris
Dijon
Beaune
Lyon
Bordeaux
Orange
Menton
Perpignan

INDEX

A

Aire de:

A8

A9

A8

A9

A13

A26

A13

A26